THE UN-PAID PROSTITUTE

THE UN-PAID PROSTITUTE

S. J. COSTON

T&D Blocker Publishing

The Un-Paid Prostitute

Copyright © 2022 by S.J. Coston

Cover design by Breanna Blocker
Illustrator Mik Jimenez

First Printing, 2022

I would like to thank my entire family for every avenue of support that was so generously given in order to make my dream of publishing a book into a reality. I also want to thank two friends that took the time to encourage me and allow me to vent. You know who you are. Above all, and most importantly, I want to thank God for sending His son, Jesus, to redeem lost souls and for giving me the ability and the opportunity to tell my story. I give this book to Him to use to His glory.

Contents

From the Author

Right up front I want to say that this book is not intended to be a self-help explanation about how to deal with any particular trauma that may be manifesting in your life. It is merely the story of my life that is hopefully written in such a way that it will generate a curiosity to know more about an obsession that became an addiction. During my agonizing search for love, I never even knew there was a name for the decadent lifestyle I was trapped in. I just knew that I hated myself for who I was and what I did. When I finally heard the words love addiction, I recognized that I had exhibited multiple symptoms of that addiction for many years. I learned that it is possible that lack of nurturing as a child or childhood trauma may be a contributing factor, so that is where my story starts. There are many events I write about that happened either before I was born or before I was old enough to remember some things. Fortunately, over the years I have heard enough snippets of conversations and whisperings from relatives and family friends to be able to fill in some blanks. However, there are a few places I had to rely on artistic license to complete the story line. My life also had some unusual twists and turns apart from my addiction troubles. There were incidents that frightened me, rescued me, puzzled me, and changed me. Be sure to read the Introduction. It sets the stage for some of these strange moments in my life and may offer some insight on how I was driven to become *The Un-Paid Prostitute*.

Introduction

"Out of my way! Out of my way!" came the insolent shouts of a man-like figure as he pushed his way down a corridor lined with burning molten rock. He seemed oblivious to the fact that he was dredging through several inches of deep lava. His mission to advance to the enormous iron door at the end of the tunnel consumed his every step. As he approached the guards, he shouted with a voice that sounded as if he hadn't had a drink of water in years, "Open that door! I have an important document for the Master!" Recognizing him to be one of the workers in the communication room, the armed guards pulled the great door open to reveal an overpowering array of hideous statues lining a long, dark hallway to yet another set of doors. As the imperious messenger made his way through that gauntlet of horror his stature seemed to shrink a little more each time one of the figures on the pillars appeared to momentarily come to life. While the beings trembled in painful contortions and agonizing moans, our once demanding deliverer began to cower in fear. By the time he reached the second set of guards his demeanor had been lessened considerably. This time his plea came in a more submissive tone, "I need to see the Master, immediately, if possible." The big metal doors creaked open and the messenger walked into the Great Hall of Terror.

The ebony chamber, lit only by heaps of burning embers, beckoned the visitor toward a figure perched on a chair-like structure carved out of the molten rock. The walls and ceiling of this macabre room were lined with what appeared to be human looking creatures, although it was difficult to tell by their grotesque appearance. "Why do you bother me?" came a voice pounding out of a venomous mouth. Slimy sweat oozed out of the Master's pores with the stench of a million sewers. The messenger bowed, "Oh most noble one, I have the recent list." "Bring it to me!" snarled the Master. A trembling arm reached out to present the document to his demanding boss. The Master's eyes lit up with fire as he gazed upon this special list of newborn babies. Suddenly, a string of vulgar obscenities not yet heard on this earth spilled forth blasphemous filth. He could not control his excitement as he intently scoured the parched scroll. An evil grin gave way to a thunderous laugh that rattled the gates of Hell. "We can start to deceive these children right away. Their parents are already following me, so the doors to my kingdom are wide open. Send in my workers from the assignment section at once! There must not be any delay in starting my influence on this new group." Quickly, the list bearer departed as three larger and more powerful workers entered the chamber. The Master beckoned for them to sit at his feet. "I have new assignments for you. Gather your army and proceed with the usual plan of deception and fear. Have your field agents go in while the children are still young and plant our evil seeds early. I am confident that you three know the drill. Now get out there and give them hell on earth!"

As my thoughts continued to become words on a page, I pondered the seriousness of my undertaking. Because, you see, my name was on that list. Those three big evil workers assigned to everyone on the list were named Condemnation, Fear, and Rejection. Fear worked slowly and meticulously, so at first you never saw it coming while Condemnation started boldly as soon as it received the list. That spirit called Rejection would eventually assault me repeatedly without mercy. Those fiendish beings worked hand in hand to make sure I grew up manipulated by fear and loneliness, culminating in a distorted perspective on life and love. I don't know how many names were on that list or what happened to the others, but this is my story.

One

In the Beginning

The announcement of my life came on a hot summer day in a west Texas border town. I was born on the longest day of the year and from then on whenever that was mentioned my mother would say, "And boy was it!" That comment was always followed by, "I have heard women say that after the labor and delivery you forget about the pain when you see your baby; well, I never have!" Then there was usually a complete rundown on how much she suffered in childbirth, more than twenty-four hours of hard labor as she told it. That story was repeated multiple times during my pre-school years. My mother's *poor me* rendition of my birth did not exactly make me feel like she was glad I was around. Every time I heard about her grueling ordeal, I shrank a little further into my already forming shell of low self-esteem. Later in life I would come to realize that whenever she had to suffer with something, like her asthma, she made it much harder on herself than it had to be. So, I always wondered if that was why she had such a hard time birthing me. I was not even a big baby, only 5 lbs. 5 oz., and I was a week late. As an adult I was told that smokers usually had small babies. My mom was always so proud of the fact that she did not drink alcohol while she was pregnant, but she did smoke. Anyway, my mother always gave me the impression that she did not like me, and I wondered if it was because

I was the reason for all that pain she admitted was never forgotten. Or, maybe she just was not really into being a mother. Actually, she probably thought she would never have to deal with children because doctors told her she would never get pregnant because of some female issues. I'm sure I was an unwelcomed surprise to her perfect world of self-absorbed behaviors. You might say her emotional attachment to me was more like someone raising a show animal. As a matter of fact, my mother actually did put me in a contest. At nine months old I was in a Baby Show and selected to be a Duchess in the Queen's court. Obviously, she fed me well and made sure I was clean and groomed and had all my shots. Whenever we went somewhere everyone could see what a good mother she was by how cute I looked in my pretty clothes. It was all a facade just for the sake of appearance. I would think most show animals were at least petted sometimes or even nurtured in a way that they recognized affection. My mom never hugged me or kissed me or said, "I love you." She didn't breast feed me which was not surprising because that would have taken emotional attachment and cuddling. I have often wondered if my mother ever held me at all. I don't remember any if she did, but you would think there had to be a few times when I was a baby. I only remember my daddy holding me. Sometimes, I felt as if she was jealous of his attention towards me. My daddy was twenty-two years older than my mom, so whenever he was caring and nice to me, she would accuse him of treating me like a grandchild. So, it was not long before all of her complaining put a stop to any signs of affection in our family. My final show of emotion that appeared as if I cared about my mother was when she left me with my first grade teacher. I remember standing at the door of the classroom crying my eyes out for what seemed like forever. I was traumatized because I had never been away from my mother before. I had not gone to kindergarten like the other kids. In fact, I had never even heard of kindergarten. But somewhere between that awful morning and the end of that school day, I must have had an epiphany. Because when I realized how much better life was at school than at home, I was very anxious to go back the next day. At six years old I had no concept of what love was. However, if I could have put a name on what I felt that first day of school, it would have been called love. From then on, I was practically obsessed with everything about school. Year after year school became my sanctuary, my place of happiness where I felt important and teachers encouraged me. In other words, I was finally experiencing a loving atmosphere.

But prior to starting first grade, I had a very lonely childhood. I was an only child with no children my age to play with in our neighborhood. Since there wasn't much to do, I usually slept until noon to help make the day seem shorter and spend less time with my mother. I don't remember playing outside very much at all. The only time I do recall being outside was when I would play with my kid-size kitchen. Daddy had set it up on a shelf at the back of our house. I would make mudpies on a tiny metal stove. My doll would eat fake food from the tiny refrigerator, and I would wash small metal dishes in the tiny sink. I acquired an active imagination. I never played any childhood games like Hide and Seek and really did not have much physical activity at all. My mom would not let me have a bicycle because she was afraid I would get hit by a car. I never understood her reasoning about that because we lived on a one block street with hardly any traffic. There were many things I did not understand about my mom. I was very young when that spirit called Condemnation began taking aggressive actions against me. I can recall crying from its criticisms as early as three years old. The person that spirit used to carry out the onslaughts was my mother. Her undiscovered obsessive-compulsive tendencies had made her useful as a perfect human battering ram. Once that condemning spirit started belittling me, it never went away. My mother became my greatest enemy. I was constantly confused as to why she acted the way she did. I thought she was just a mean and hateful person who enjoyed treating me ugly. Even at a very young age I tried to distance myself from her and the words she said. Eventually, I spent most of my days in my room enjoying my coloring books and my dolls. Soon, I graduated to paper dolls and would design and color new clothes for them. I folded pages from the Sears catalog to form furniture for my paper dolls to sit on. My mom would get mad at me for spending so much time in my room and make me leave my happy place. She complained, "Why do you stay in your room all the time? You are never going to learn anything just sitting in there. No wonder you don't have any friends!" With that, my thoughts would be, "Really? Does she not realize I don't have friends because I never go anywhere to meet other children?" Usually during the weekdays, the only time I saw or talked to any other people was on laundry day and grocery day. And that was always adults. Day after day she would never just leave me alone no matter what I was doing. Sometimes to try and stop her nagging, I would look for things to do around the house. When I was old enough, I liked ironing the pillow cases and Daddy's handkerchiefs. There was something unusually satisfying about watching the iron take the wrinkles out of the fabric. However, I could never do anything to please her. She would complain, "Why are you folding them like that? I told you to do it this way. You can never do anything right!" Many times, when I was forced out of my room, I would often sit by the radio and listen to shows like the Lone Ranger or George Burns and Gracie Allen. I could almost see the scenes in my mind. It was a great escape from reality. Often, my mother would interrupt that, too by revisiting one of my prior offenses. Finally, to escape the condemnation, I would either end up back in my room or back outside with my kitchen. I preferred to be outside because she seemed to not bother me as much out there. Out of sight, out of mind, I guess. That routine was pretty much my daily emotional seesaw for years until I escaped to start school. On the weekends I would have to spend every Friday and Saturday night in smoke-filled barrooms. Their favorite hangouts were by Daddy's work place or in Mexico. I had been a regular at the bars in Mexico since I was a baby. My mom said she used to change my diaper on top of the counter. That must have been some sight to see. I never thought to ask her how old I was when she finally stopped exposing me to the bar crowd. And, where was I the whole time they were drinking? Was I still lying on the bar, or did she have a baby carriage to put me in? I wished I had asked more questions when I was older. She said she would have the bartenders warm my bottle in their kitchen. Did she hold me to feed me in order to make a good impression? Weekend after weekend, year after year, I was always in a bar. There was not much for a preschooler to do in a place like that. My parents would buy me lots of food and sodas to pass some of the time. I remember one night when I was around five years old, I sang a song into a microphone in a Mexican club. My parents always stayed until the bars closed, so I would usually put two chairs together and lie down and sleep until they were ready to leave. So, you can imagine, with the kind of lifestyle I was used to what a dramatic difference it was when I finally experienced school. That's why school would become the most important part of my existence. All my younger years I was locked in an invisible cage with loneliness, sadness, condemnation, and drunks. Thankfully I would eventually find a whole new world with normal people, kids my age, and the joy of learning.

For all I say negative about my mother, because there will be much more, she was a hard worker. I will give her that. In my early years, most families did not have many luxuries in their homes. People were recovering from the end of WWII and were working hard to eke out a better life for themselves. We lived in the center apartment of a triplex house that my parents were fortunate enough to own. Two units were rented out, one on each side of us. None of the three units were very big. My parents worked hard to maintain those apartments, and don't you know my mom was a tough landlady. My home town housed a very large Army base and a smaller Air Force base, so our tenants were always in the military. If the renters got on Mom's bad side there would be hell to pay. But if the tenants were favorable, they became fast friends and usually drinking buddies. My mom was obsessive about cleaning, especially the bathroom. She would scrub our bathtub and sink every day. And to clean the toilet, she would get down on her hands and knees and work on it for at least ten minutes. There was no way the toilet was that dirty all the time. For years my mom did not have a washing machine, and until I was fourteen, we only had one car which Daddy drove to work. Therefore, when I was young, she had to pull a red wagon full of dirty clothes and walk about eight blocks to a do-it-yourself laundry run by a sweet Chinese couple. The machines were not automatic washers either. You had to put the clothes in large open tubs with soap and bluing, and a center post would slosh them around for a while. But then, you had to take them all out of those tubs, wring the water out, and put them into different tubs of clean water. Then you repeated the process again before moving them to the final rinse tubs. After you wrung them all out from those tubs, you had to run all of the wet clothes through a machine with these really tight rollers that squeezed all of the excess water out of the clean clothes. One time a little boy got his hand caught in the rollers. Boy, did he scream! It taught me to respect those rollers. Now even though the water was squeezed out of the stack of clothes, they were still damp and heavy. The laundry only had washers, no dryers. So now, my mother would have to pull the wagon full of damp clothes back home the eight blocks. And then, she had to spend almost an hour out in the backyard hanging those clothes up to dry on the clothesline. Finally, if that was not enough, the clothes that needed ironing were put in a basket to go back in the house where they were immediately ironed that day before they dried too much. There were no steam irons back then. Those were the days when women set aside a *washday* because it actually took the entire day to get it all done. My mom repeated that routine weekly for years before they were finally able to afford a washing machine. She still had to hang the clothes out to dry, but at least she did not have to haul them back and forth in the wagon for eight blocks.

Then there was my daddy. My sweet, sweet Daddy. My father was my hero. He could do no wrong. As I grew older, I realized I loved him very much, and I somehow knew he loved me. It wasn't because he was particularly affectionate or outwardly caring like some fathers, but he had an inward tenderness. I hated the way my mother treated him. She was always nagging him about something. I never saw them be affectionate to each other, even when they were drunk. My mom was constantly telling my daddy what to do. She would complain, "I told you to do that or I told you to fix whatever." Always, I told you, I told you, I told you. He used to say to her, "You're always tolding me." I often wondered why he divorced his first wife to marry my mother. I thought, "Boy, the first one must have really been bad." Daddy had a son by that marriage who was the same age as my mom. His son's wife used to say her mother-in-law was crazy, but for some reason she liked my mom. I could not figure out why she liked her because I thought my mother was crazy. Sometimes when Mom was really on a tangent, I would imagine calling a mental hospital and men in white jackets would come and take her away wearing a straitjacket. Daddy never smiled in pictures and not really any other time. Occasionally when he was partying, he would laugh or smile at a joke. However, he was usually the life of the party. He liked to dance and tell funny stories. He would let me dance with him sometimes, and then I got to that age where it was embarrassing. It is sad we get to that age. When he was drinking, his favorite funny story was about when he was a baby crawling around naked on their old wood floor. There was a knot hole in one of the planks and his little penis got stuck in the hole. In those days, the late 1800s, families kept chickens under the house. He said one of those old hens thought she saw a worm and bit him, and he had been henpecked ever since. I am sure it was not true, but everybody thought it was a very funny story. Like any little girl, I loved being with my daddy. When Mom would leave us alone, Daddy and I had a lot of fun together. When I was school-age he would play ball with me and help me make projects for class. One time I got a doll house for Christmas, and he had gone through and wired every room with a tiny light bulb, so I could play with it after dark. That made me really happy. Daddy had a soft heart even though he hid it with his stoic exterior. The Christmas I found out there was no Santa Clause made me extremely sad. So, my sweet, generous Daddy took me to the Western Auto Store. It was like an Auto Zone that had a Toyland every Christmas complete with a highly anticipated Christmas catalog. He handed me their small shopping cart and said I could have anything I could fit in the cart. What an amazing gift for any child! I forgot all about Santa. When we finally got television, Daddy and I would watch baseball, football, and basketball. We even watched boxing and would score each round separately to see who picked the winner. We had such a good time. I was glad my mom only liked baseball so Daddy and I could have all that quality time together. We also watched wrestling matches. They were not like today's violent matches; they were for show and entertaining. Daddy took me to the local Coliseum to see Gorgeous George, a famous wrestler in the 1950s. Mr. G.G. had wavy platinum blond hair and gave out platinum bobby pins to every fan. If Daddy had not already had a boy, I would have thought he probably wished I was one. But that was not the reason, we just enjoyed each other. He worked really hard, too. He was a shipping clerk and was on his feet all day on a cement floor. And then, he would work every weekend at home taking care of the apartments, the car, and the yard. Even with all he had to do, he would always help a friend in need, often working on their cars, too. Everyone loved my daddy. Sometimes at his job truck drivers would leave promotional gifts, mostly stuffed animals. Daddy would always bring them home to me. One day he totally surprised me with a huge teddy bear! I immediately fell in love with it and named it Soapy from a TV character. I still have him today, and Soapy is over sixty-five years old. Even though Daddy and I shared no hugging or kissing or saying, "I love you," I knew without a doubt that he loved me and I loved him. Those few moments of closeness were so important to me, but gradually, my mom's dominance took over, and my special times with Daddy faded away.

Before I started first grade, I thought everybody lived as we did. We were probably considered lower middle class. We were not starving, we had nice clothes from Sears and Roebuck, but we lived on a one block long street by a railroad track. There were well kept little houses, and there were some not so well kept. Fortunately, those were at the other end of the block. Our end of the street was a bit nicer. Being in a border town, most of our neighbors were Hispanic, which was not a word back then, they were all Mexicans. Nobody cared about being *Politically Correct*, and everyone was happy together. We were particularly close to two families on the street. The Avila's had four daughters, all older than I. On a very rare occasion when I was in grade school, they were allowed to babysit me. Their grandfather, old man Joe as he was called, lived with them. The Escobar's lived next door and had two daughters and a son, also all older than I. As it turned out, there were still no children my age in the neighborhood. Most of my days alone were pretty boring and depressing. From the time I was born, my life in general was never very happy. Even when something happened that gave me a feeling of joy or happiness it would always be shot down by someone, usually my mom. It seemed as if I could never wallow in being happy long enough to make it a memory. As far back as I can remember, I never seemed to think like a child. I acted like a child, but my inside person was different from my outside person. I always watched people's actions and listened to their words as it all went deep into my soul. I wondered about life and why everything happened the way it did, always thinking about something. For a few years I tried to convince myself that surely my life was not that different from other families. But, a voice deep inside me kept asking, "Do you see other children in the bars?" Most people we knew thought we were an okay family, but most of those people were not even okay themselves. The majority of my parent's acquaintances were barroom friends. The life I thought was normal was already filled with misery and void of any form of love or peace.

Every day was basically the same uneventful passing of time except for two incredible weeks in July. That was when Daddy got his vacation and our family would go on a two-week road trip. Since Mom was busy with different people and the fact that Daddy was around all the time, she kind of toned down her usual barrage of condemnations. It would normally be a nice two weeks. We would spend the first week with my grandparents in central Texas and the next week visiting other relatives along the way. Eventually, my parent's finances allowed us to travel to someplace exciting like California, Arizona or Las Vegas during the second week. Unfortunately, the money also enabled my parents to drink that whole week. They could not drink the week we were at my grandparent's house which was a wonderful reprieve. Thank goodness their little town was *dry* which meant no alcohol at all was sold there. Sometimes for the second week my friend Margaret would travel with us, and we would have a fun time. Margaret was the only person I would ask to come along because she was used to being around heavy drinkers. Our parents met in a bar, but Margaret's mom and dad never brought her with them. She and I were told that we first met when we were babies, so we considered ourselves like sisters. She was an only child, too. However, it was not until we were in grade school that Margaret's parents started coming to our house to have beers. Margaret would come to play with me which made for a great day. Looking back, it is hard to believe all the vacation miles my parents drove under the influence and sometimes down right drunk. And, they never had an accident or got a ticket. Over the course of several years my family and I saw all the sights while driving to California from Texas, with them drinking all the way. We also covered all of southern California from San Diego to Los Angeles and on up to Las Vegas and other parts of Arizona. All of those trips were in the middle of summer with no air conditioner in the car. One year a very amazing thing happened in Arizona. My mom had been drinking beer all day on the way to the Grand Canyon. By the time we got there she was her usual belligerent self. Now if I had not seen this with my own eyes, I probably would not have believed it. When Mom got out of the car and walked to the canyon viewpoint, she was totally drunk. With one breathtaking look at the majestic Grand Canyon, she was completely sober. What a testament to the grandeur of one of the most beautiful sights in America! I know it sounds impossible, but it's entirely true that the Canyon shocked her sober.

The absolutely best part of our vacation time was going to see my grandparents. I loved their house and the small town where they lived. It was a totally different world. I wallowed in contentment the whole week we were there and wished it would never end. The atmosphere was so peaceful and quiet you were able to hear the hoot owls early in the morning and the frogs and crickets at night. There were trees and flowers and green grass. Nothing like the dry, drab desert where I lived. People went to church and sat on the front porch and visited, and no one was drinking. I even developed a great friendship with a local girl named Charlotte. In our early teens she would drive us around in her dad's truck way before she was old enough for a license. That was one of the perks of living in an extremely small town. Because of its size, there was a local joke that traveling salesmen called the place a graveyard with electric lights. I positively loved my grandparents; they were my mom's parents. Daddy's parents had already passed away long before I was born. Grandma always made my favorite dish, her homemade peach cobbler. I enjoyed helping her pick vegetables from the garden and snapping green beans to cook for supper. They got their drinking water from a cistern. It was kind of like a well. I would help Grandma pull the bucket up to the top and use a ladle to taste the fresh cold water. Sometimes in the afternoon she and I would walk the short distance to town for ice cream, and along the way we would feed mesquite beans to some horses. In the evening Grandma would let down her very long hair, down to her bottom, and I would help her brush it. She braided her graying red hair every morning into Princess Leia type buns on each side of her head, and when she combed them out her hair was beautiful and wavy. I was proud to be a redhead like her. My grandpa was an absolute character with a mischievous smile and a great sense of humor. I would love it when he took me for a ride in his old Model T Ford. I liked honking the horn. I remember he always had little holes in his shirts because he rolled his own cigarettes, and when they burned tiny pieces of tobacco or paper would drop on his shirt. I liked the aroma of Prince Albert tobacco in the can because it smelled like Grandpa. Cap, as they called him down at the domino hall, was known as the Domino King of their small town. He loved the game and taught me how to play as soon as I could learn. We played dominos on the front porch every summer night we were there. Grandpa could tell everyone playing exactly what they had in their hand. If you took too long to put down a domino he might say, "Play your 6-2; it's the only play you have." That was such fun. When it was time for bed, I was ready because I loved where I slept. They had a long room with side-by-side windows on two walls that they called the sleeping porch. The bed was so comfy, and I could lie there and see millions of stars and listen to the night sounds. And for that incredible week, I did not sleep until noon. There was a picture that always hung on the sleeping porch of a young girl asleep in a field with her faithful dog watching over her. When I was at my grandparent's home, I always felt safe and peaceful like the girl in the picture. The summers with my grandparents are the only truly happy times I remember from my childhood. And, that picture of the little girl and her dog has hung in my bedroom for the past fifty plus years.

At this point, I suppose it would be a good idea to take a look at my parent's backgrounds in order to capture the real picture. To start we will go back to the early 1900s and to that very small town in central Texas. There on a cold winter day, December 23rd, was born an adorable baby girl named Lorraine. The parents of the newborn both had older children from previous marriages. So, Lorraine, my mother, just happened along to a couple approaching late middle age and without a lot of money to raise a child. World War I had just ended, and everyone had felt the economic strain caused by the war. And to make matters worse, the Spanish Flu had been raging for several months prior to her birth. The end of the pandemic would not come until Lorraine was around two years old. Her parents had to work very hard to try to make ends meet which left Lorraine without much supervision or discipline. On top of that, she was a very self-willed child aggravated by an extreme need for glasses. Her inability to see properly would remain unknown to her parents until Lorraine's second year in school. So, this lack of attention, made worse by not being able to see anything in focus, caused Lorraine to become a very self-centered, selfish, and immature brat. Needless to say, all of those factors shaped my mom's personality, values, and character. Finally, some structure came into her life when she started school. But since Lorraine could not see well, she was made fun of for being stupid and failed the first grade. The next year when she was repeating the grade, her teacher finally realized how much Lorraine was struggling to read the blackboard and sent a note to her parents to have her eyes checked. When she was evaluated, Lorraine was found to have an extreme astigmatism and in dire need of glasses. Getting those glasses gave her a whole new confidence in life, but many bad patterns had already been established in her as a person. Then when Lorraine was around eleven, The Great Depression began. My grandparents lived in survival mode as did multitudes of people during that time in history. They were more fortunate than some because Joseph, my grandpa, was able to keep his job at the local cotton gin. But because he had to take a reduction in pay, they had to take on boarders. So, Lucille, my grandma, was in charge of renting out beds in their house to traveling salesmen and such. That was when they built the sleeping porch. Grandma spent the whole day, every day, cooking three meals for several people and doing laundry and cleaning all the time. Therefore, Lorraine was left to play on her own and to do whatever she wanted, whenever she wanted.

The older Lorraine got the more rebellious she became and totally disrespected her parents. Well, her actions completely opened the door to some evil spirits that were lurking around. Late one night when she was fifteen years old, something life changing happened to Lorraine when one of those spirits crept into her room. The person it used was the last salesman who had rented a place to sleep. Her parents were doing better financially, so they no longer needed to take in boarders and wanted to lessen their workload. Lorraine's parents worked very hard, and they slept equally hard, so they did not hear any noises. The salesman tiptoed quietly into Lorraine's room and whispered her name. She was barely dozing off and sat up startled and at first scared. When she realized who was there, she asked, "What are you doing up?" He put his finger to his lips and shushed her. She knew him well because he had lived there for two months and was due to leave the next day. The salesman came over and sat on the side of her bed and whispered, "I am leaving early in the morning, and I wanted to say goodbye in case you were still asleep." Lorraine said, "I wish you didn't have to leave." She really liked him because he joked with her and brought her candy. He said, "I am going to miss you, too. May I give you a little kiss?" Lorraine was surprised and excited! This was her first kiss, and she could tell her friends! She said, "Sure!" He scooted closer, put his arm around her waist and softly kissed her lips. She felt feelings in her body she had never felt before, and she loved it. He backed off and she said, "Kiss me again!" He pressed his lips on hers as he began to lie her back on to her pillow. She was in ecstasy! She kissed him back. Lorraine had never had anyone show her so much affection. He began to reach under her gown and slowly caress her youthful body. As he crawled on to her bed, he left his pajama bottoms on the floor. Lorraine thought this must be what love feels like. But when he entered into her, the euphoria came to a screeching halt. She yelled, "Stop! That hurts!" He whispered, "Shhh, I will be slow and gentle, just relax." She tried to relax, but Lorraine thought this part was not as much fun as the kissing and the petting. The salesman got as far as he could with a fifteen year old virgin, and when it was over Lorraine was officially hooked on the opposite sex. As he got up, she whispered, "Let's do it again! I will do better this time." She was too young to even know that could take a while. Besides, he had obtained his satisfaction and was ready for bed and sleep. After he said goodbye, she was left with a mess to clean up. Lorraine could not let her parents see the sheet, so she changed the bed and sneaked outside to stuff it under some rubbish in the burn pile. Her mother had dozens of sheets because of boarders; she would never miss one. In the morning when Lorraine woke up the salesman was gone, but the damage had been done. She could not wait to tell her closest friend and to figure out a way to make it happen again.

By high school Lorraine had started smoking and drinking with her friends from school. Being in a small town everyone knew what everybody else was doing, except the parents who were clueless. As word got out about Lorraine, she became quite popular with the boys. On weekends almost all of the teenagers in her town would pile into available cars. There was no driver's license needed in those days. Then they would all drive to a somewhat larger nearby town where they went to dance and drink and flirt. Although Lorraine was hell to live with at home, she was well liked by her peers because she was a lot of fun to party with. She was a good dancer, loved her beer and could be sweet at times, especially with her drinking buddies. As long as everything was going her way, she was a joy to be around. After high school graduation Lorraine moved to her party town to go to the local Beauty College. There she immediately found new drinking pals as most of her friends from high school were settling down and getting married. By now she was living in the Big Band era, and dancing was the thing to do. So, every spare evening was spent at the Rooftop Dance Hall. This hot spot was destined to be an important place in my life because it was where my mother and my father first met. The Rooftop was the *in* place to meet the ladies, so naturally when Lawrence, my dad, was in town he would make a beeline for the dance hall. He was a traveling salesman and loved to drink and dance and party as much as Lorraine. He was also quite the ladies' man, but there was one little problem. Lawrence was married, for over twenty years, and he had a son the same age as Lorraine. But she thought Lawrence was fun and a good dancer, and he made her laugh. Being with him caused her to think back to her first encounter with a man, who was also much older than she was and made her laugh. Lorraine was very comfortable with Lawrence and felt a sense of security when she was with him. If you think about it, Lawrence's maturity and attentiveness filled a big void in her life. Lorraine, in her fragile younger years, was unable to get the attention she needed from her father because he was always working to put food on the table. Lawrence became almost a father figure to Lorraine, and she would often call him "Daddy."

Now as for Lawrence, he was born into an entirely different era. On Christmas Day in the late 1800s he became one of three sons born to poor farmers in south central Texas. His parents would go on to also have a baby girl. My father was never sure of the exact year he was born because his birth records were destroyed in a fire. I will not forget one year when I was in my late teens, Daddy received a letter from the Social Security Office telling him they were going to start sending him his Social Security check. Well, you would think that was good news, except my dad thought he was several years younger than retirement age. And now, he felt like an old man. Evidently there must have been some records somewhere. Daddy was never quite the same after that day. It kind of took the wind out of his sail. Not to mention, expectations were different back then, and he was forced to retire from the job he loved and ended up working part time at a convenience store near the house. Anyway, back to Lawrence's childhood. I wish he had shared more stories about how he grew up. I am sure there were some tales to tell having lived during that time period, but he was not much of a true life story teller. He would rather tell jokes and humorous quips. I do vaguely remember my daddy talking about working out on the range and eating beans off the fender of an old truck. I have a picture of him and one of his brothers in a car they built from scratch in the 1920s. I do know his mother died fairly young of an illness, and his father died much older in a hotel fire. It appeared my late grandfather had accumulated some wealth by then because he owned the hotel. I also know my dad was completely bald in his twenties. All of that information was the extent of my knowledge about his upbringing. Except for Daddy's baby sister who was my Aunt Gertrude, his niece Loretta, and my half-brother Lawrence junior, I never got to know any of my daddy's family. I'm sure that was probably because they were all so much older than I was.

Two

So Many Changes

Now when Lawrence and Lorraine met, they were both in a place of transition. Lorraine had graduated from Beauty School and was working in a local salon, but not really liking her job. Lawrence was very unhappy in his marriage to a woman who was supposedly psycho. That was why he stayed on the road as much as possible as a traveling salesman. I guess Lorraine was a whole lot better than what he had at home, plus she was young and a lot of fun. What followed after they met was a one-year love affair which brought Lawrence back to Lorraine's town every chance he got. Finally growing tired of the arrangement, Lawrence filed for divorce and married Lorraine on the same day his divorce was final, Friday the 13th. To get a new start in life, Lawrence and Lorraine remained in the big city of Houston, Texas where they had gone to get married. Lorraine was now twenty-four and Lawrence was forty-six. They had been there just a few months and were settling into jobs and meeting new partying friends when a big surprise came in the mail. Lawrence had been drafted into the Army! At the age of forty-six! They could not believe it. World War II was nearing the end, but the military was still drafting. The draft age kept going up as they ran out of younger men to call up. Lawrence had never served; therefore, his name was chosen. Age did not matter; they just needed warm bodies for their quota. So, two weeks later, Lorraine and Lawrence had packed all their belongings and were driving west across the big state of Texas. They were headed for a godforsaken desert city in far west Texas. That was where one of the largest Army boot camps was located. After driving for most of the day, they began to understand just how big Texas was when they realized they were only halfway there. They were forced to find a cheap motel to get some sleep. The next day was really hot and the road became more desolate as the landscape changed into nothing but desert. The couple drove for what seemed like forever down long straight highways before reaching the next small town. The roads were like an illusion. They appeared as if when you looked down the highway you thought you could see the end of it, but it took hours to get there. Finally, they reached their destination to find a relatively large city with no trees and small cinder block houses with dirt filled yards covered with weeds and rocks. The place was so different from the grass, trees, and flowers of central and east Texas. However, the area was interesting because there was a huge mountain range that the whole city was built around. Being a border town with Mexico, the Spanish influence was noticeable in the architecture and in the restaurants. As Lawrence and Lorraine drove through the city, the uniqueness of the place was quite appealing. After stopping to eat some of the best Mexican food they had ever consumed, they got directions to the local Army base. They knew their time there would be short, but they really liked what they saw of the city and hoped the war would end so they could stay there. Nevertheless, eight weeks later Lawrence completed his basic training, and Uncle Sam moved them to an Army base in Oklahoma. The winter cold began not long after they moved there, followed by freezing cold snow for the holidays. That really made them hate being there. But their discontent was soon eased as they both quickly made new friends and new drinking buddies. Most of the people they hung around with were much younger than Lawrence or even Lorraine. All the young guys really liked Lawrence and helped him fit right in. As for Lorraine, she absolutely loved being around so many men. And in most of the pictures I have of their Army days, she was hanging on to the arm of a young GI while Lawrence stood off to the side. In fact, I have several pictures throughout their marriage that were taken when partying with other couples that showed Lorraine locked arm in arm with the husband of the other woman and Lawrence rather detached.

The plus side of being drafted was Lawrence worked in the base warehouse where all the parts and equipment were shipped out to other bases. It was good training and would become useful later on. In less than a year the Army decided they did not need him anymore, and Lawrence was honorably discharged. About the same time that news rolled in, Lorraine had some news of her own; she was pregnant. She was not exactly overjoyed about having a baby. She and Lawrence were having too much fun, plus she was never supposed to be able to get pregnant. Then when the doctor told her she could not drink alcohol while she was expecting, Lorraine really disliked the idea of a baby even more. Unfortunately for me, she was allowed to continue to smoke. Here she was with a husband with no job, a baby on the way, and she could not even drown her sorrows with a stiff drink. With her world turned upside down, Lorraine was not a happy camper. Lawrence, being much older, took a more mature approach to the current events. He made the decision to move back to the border town where he had done his basic training. They both liked the weather there and especially liked going to the clubs across the border in Mexico. So, with severance pay from the Army, Lawrence and Lorraine began the long trip back to west Texas. There was nothing pleasant about the ride this time. Lorraine kept having Lawrence stop the car so she could throw up. And the more she stopped, the more aggravated she became and the more she threw up. Most of the trip she was complaining, and he was not talking. Needless to say, by the time they arrived at the city that would be their new home, their relationship was definitely strained. But Lawrence, being the smart guy he was, did not just roll into town without a plan. Before leaving Oklahoma, he had contacted some of the friends he had made when they lived there before. They all really liked Lawrence. So, they were more than willing to help him scout around for job possibilities, and they already had some lined up for him when he arrived. The experience he had in the Army warehouse landed him a job in a battery and car parts store as their only shipping clerk. That actually meant he was in charge of the entire shipping department. Lawrence and Lorraine found a small house to rent in an older part of town and tried to get settled in before the birth of the baby, ME! Even though Lorraine could not drink, on the weekends they still went to the smoke-filled bars with their friends. After all, they could still dance for a while yet. Then several months later, into the world came a tiny innocent child shackled from the womb with generational hand-me-downs of divorce, adultery, bitterness, selfishness, rebellion, disobedience, and the list goes on. How could that happen? It's a question that would be answered decades later.

That was not exactly the joyful scenario you expected to describe the birth of a baby, was it? Well, there was nothing pleasant about my birth. My mother screamed with the agony of labor for hours. She hated everybody in sight and she especially hated me for causing her so much pain. Maybe I took longer to come out because I heard all the screaming. I never have liked conflict. As soon as I was born, my mother was exhausted and went to sleep. She did not even hold me until the next day when the nurses insisted. That could have possibly been one of the few times I was held by her. In those days women who had babies stayed in the hospital almost a week. So, while my daddy proudly handed out cigars because he had a girl, my mom let the nurses take care of me whenever she could. Finally, the day arrived to go home. Lawrence actually smiled as he held his little redheaded baby girl for the first time. Lorraine was impatient and ready to leave, "Come on, let's go. You can hold her all you want when we get home." And when they got home, Lawrence found out she was not kidding. My mom figured since Daddy had already raised a child, he should be the one to change me, feed me, and hold me because he already knew how. My crying irritated her and kept her awake. She would make him pick me up, so she could go back to sleep. When Daddy finally had to go back to work, my mom panicked. She had never been around babies, never babysat and did not really like being around little kids. But yet, there she was standing by the crib looking at this hungry, wet, and crying infant. Lorraine thought, "I have got to do something to shut this kid up." So, after lowering the side of the crib, she nervously removed my sleeper and my wet diaper. After putting a fresh diaper and sleeper on me, she raised the rail back up. Lorraine went to the kitchen to prepare a bottle while I laid there in the cold and lonely crib crying at the top of my lungs. When she returned with the bottle, she again lowered the side, stuck the bottle in my mouth and stood there while I drank my breakfast. After the bottle was empty, she raised the side back up and left me lying in the crib, never burped, never cuddled and never loved. Fortunately, Lawrence decided to come home for lunch to check on us. He went straight to my crib, picked me up onto his shoulder, and I let out an enormous burp. By now my diaper was poopy, so he told Lorraine to change it while he ate lunch. She said, "You change it. The smell makes me sick." Lawrence was furious. He laid me in my crib, went back to the kitchen and tightly grabbed Lorraine's arm and shoulder and forcibly escorted her to me. He angrily pushed her onto the rail of the crib and said, "Get your baby's diaper changed right now! If you throw up, it better not be on the baby. Don't you ever let me hear you refuse to take care of your child again!" My daddy left the room, ate his lunch and went back to work. My mom changed the poopy diaper, did not get sick, but still did not bother to pick me up.

Later that day a woman came by to see the new baby girl. Kathleen and her husband had a small neighborhood grocery store just down the hill, and she and my mom had become friends. She was a good Christian woman and a most unlikely candidate to become Lorraine's best friend. But somehow, I guess it was a match made in heaven, and they would continue to have a lifelong friendship. Kathleen carefully picked me up from my crib and lovingly cuddled me in her arms, "She is adorable. I love that beautiful red hair." Lorraine just stared and finally asked, "How did you do that?" "Do what?" Kathleen replied. "Hold her like that. I don't know how," Lorraine lamented. Kathleen was so sweet, "Oh Lorraine, you can learn how. Sit down in that chair over there, and I will show you how to hold her. Now, put your hand under her head and neck and cradle her in your arm. See, you are doing fine." But I started crying because I did not feel secure. My mother held me stiff and not close to her body. "See, she doesn't like me," Lorraine whined. Kathleen could never be anything but sweet and encouraging, "Of course she likes you. You are her mother. Just keep practicing, keep her close to you and rock her. She will get used to you, and you will get used to her. A mother and her child have a special bond." Sorry, sweet Kathleen, nothing could have been further from the truth. There would never be a special bond between us. But my mother did finally learn how to care for me best she could, I guess. Although, I never in my entire life ever felt as if she liked me, let alone loved me. I don't remember her ever saying, "I love you." Somehow, I have learned to live with that. But the hurt I always felt deep down inside was because I really wished she had liked me. Decades later I had a very strange dream. Most of my dreams were usually vague and all over the place, but this one was surprisingly vivid. I felt as if I was looking at where I was from inside the person of a baby. I was inside a baby looking out, and I was scared. I could not find my mother anywhere I looked around. I felt as if she had been gone a long time. I thought, "Where is she? I want my mommy!" I was not crying. I just felt very alone and frightened, almost a feeling of being abandoned. Suddenly, I woke up very shaken and curious. I could not help but wonder if my mother had left me and my daddy at some point when I was a baby. Unfortunately, or maybe fortunately, that would be an unanswered question forever. Anyone I could have asked about that time period was no longer living, including my parents. Maybe it was better that way because I had overcome enough bad memories without adding abandonment to the list. Nevertheless, the continual lack of a mother's love was just the beginning of a long life of rejection and loneliness.

Apparently, Lorraine finally got the hang of raising a baby because I never heard of any life-threatening occurrences in my infancy. Although, there was one instance I do have a slight memory of. It was the day I was in my crib playing with a pocket flashlight. Mom never believed that I had a vague recollection of the incident because I was less than two years old. I had managed to take the flashlight apart and had swallowed the little spring that pushed on the bulb. I remember my mom sticking her finger down my throat and pulling the spring out. What I do not have any memory of was being picked up or consoled in any way. But instead, I remember standing in the crib crying my eyes out after the traumatic removal. Recalling events that happened in my life during the years before starting first grade are few and far between. Incredibly though, there was one amazing and unforgettable incident that happened one night when I was around three. I had been sick and was sleeping restlessly on my side facing the wall that was right against the bed. I turned to roll over to my other side when I saw an angel kneeling in prayer beside my bed. However, at that time of my life I did not know she was praying because I didn't know what prayer was. She had a soft glow as I saw her hands together and her head bowed. She had big wings, but no halo. I was not dreaming. She was as real as seeing my parents. She was not a ghost. I could not see through her. She had on a flowing gown, and she was beautiful. But since I was so young, it really scared me. I could not move for a moment then I quickly rolled back over, practically plastered to the wall, and screamed for my daddy. He came running to my bed, "What's wrong? Did you have a bad dream?" I turned back around for Daddy, and she was gone. I excitedly explained to my daddy, "I saw an angel by my bed, and I was scared! I know she was an angel because she looked like a picture Miss Kathleen showed me. She had her hands like this, and she was looking down like this. Did you see her Daddy?" He rationalized that she was not real, but probably just a reaction to the medicine I was taking. Daddy stayed with me until I went back to sleep. But, as I laid there with him and thought about what he had said, I was not convinced. Even in my three year old mind, I knew what I saw, and I never forgot how real that angel was.

Even though my preschool days were long and lonely, I was not a mischievous child. I just spent a lot of time in the house playing by myself. My mom would usually find fault with something I was doing and get mad at me. There was one day though that she had every right to be mad when I did a stupid little kid thing and almost started a fire. I was around four and Mom was in the bathtub, and I was playing with dolls in the living room. We had a large upright gas heater that had little windows on the door you would open to light the burners. I knew to never touch the door because it was very hot. I was cold, so I pushed an upholstered ottoman against the heater door and sat there briefly. Then I left the room but did not move the ottoman away from the heater. Pretty soon my mom smelled smoke. She leaped out of the tub and ran, stark naked and dripping wet, to the living room to find the ottoman smoldering and almost on fire. She picked it up, ran to the bathroom and threw the ottoman in the tub. Her screaming at me could probably be heard for blocks away. Maybe recalling preschool memories was difficult because most of them were not good ones. My mother's verbal condemnations were a constant reminder that I had to be the worse person on earth. She would say things I did not always understand. All I knew was she was being mean and made me cry. Even at that young age and totally clueless about what was happening, I could feel myself changing. I was not happy. By now, I had already been across the border to Mexico hundreds of times. That was definitely not the best environment for any young child. But Mom never wanted to leave me with a babysitter, which was surprising considering her attitude towards me. The one and only memory I have of a mother's somewhat tender touch was every time we got back home from Mexico, she would stand behind me at the kitchen sink and repeatedly wash my hands. I loved the intimacy of that moment with her and the smell of the soap. Unfortunately, all those trips across the border were just the beginning of many years of weekends spent around people getting drunk and all the excessiveness that went along with that.

I began to change the way I felt about my mother. I did not like her. I think I still loved her, but I did not like her, especially when she was drinking. And right now, I am still talking about before I started first grade. She did not exactly help the situation with some of her actions. One time I was really sick with what was called the Croup, which caused a constant deep barking cough. This one particular night I was in bad shape, so Daddy got me out of bed and took me to the rocking chair in their room. He cuddled me in a blanket and began to rock me, so I could maybe fall asleep. He had, of course, turned on the light to check on me, which also shone in their room. Our house was very small. I was so happy to be in his arms and sitting up a little so I could breathe. The rocking motion was very soothing, and I was about to finally doze off when Mom yelled, "Turn off that light! I can't sleep with it on!" I may have only been four, but I knew she was being so selfish. I think that was the day I started hating the sound of my mother's voice. Not long after that incident, there was another time that impacted the way I felt about her. It happened one evening when we were sitting in the living room listening to the radio; we did not have a TV yet. Like most little girls around four, I loved getting up on my daddy's lap and would do so every chance I got. I was snuggled in, hugging his neck, when my mom whined in a voice I was learning to hate, "Why don't you ever sit on my lap and hug my neck?" It is so sad, but I plainly remember as a four year old, hearing that question, pondering it in my mind and making the decision to climb down off of Daddy's lap. I had decided that if I had to sit on her lap to get to sit on my daddy's lap, I would give up ever snuggling with him again and enjoying him in that way. Sadly, I never sat on Daddy's lap again, and he never knew the reason why. It is even difficult for me to believe a child that age could make such a deeply emotional sacrifice, and I am the one who did it! But somehow, I survived my sad life, and eventually there came the biggest change ever . . . School!

Three

My Sanctuary

Even with all the emotional changes I experienced prior to first grade, I believed that deep down inside of me somewhere I still had a love for my mother. However, I was constantly conflicted on a daily basis about how I should feel about her. It was an emotional roller coaster that any young child should not have to bear. Yet, after spending six years of my life with her always there twenty-four hours a day, seven days a week, I must have felt some sense of security in having her around. Because when she left me in the classroom on the first day of school, it was a horrifying event for me. After my mother walked away, I am not sure how long I stood at the door to the first grade room crying uncontrollably. As I recall I think I was the only child that cried. Thankfully, I had a very kind and understanding teacher, so eventually I began to enjoy the day. It was nice to actually have other children to play with for a change. At outside recess I learned to play games like *Duck Duck Goose, Tag* and *Keep Away*. At first, I had a difficult time running very fast and would often turn my ankle. My lack of prior physical activity put me at a real disadvantage. But I was determined to play the games and be good at them. That was a trait I did not know I had, but would ultimately conclude that I always wanted to excel in anything I did. Then in the classroom we did finger painting and used modeling clay. I didn't know those things existed. The teacher was so caring. She read us a story as we rested. No one had ever read me a story. I didn't even have any children's books at home. I quickly realized how great it had been not hearing my mother's voice all day. It only took that first day, and I was hooked. I loved school! From then on, every morning I could hardly wait to get back there.

I discovered that I loved learning and reading. I found out that I could be proud of myself, and I worked hard to earn gold stars in every subject. Going home was just an interruption. I could have lived at school. By the end of first grade, I did not want summer vacation. Back then school ended right before Memorial Day and did not start again until after Labor Day. That meant three long months of no fun except for the two weeks' vacation in July. Plus, I had to spend all that time with my mom again. I did have one unusual surprise that summer. Mom had signed me up for a very special moment in my life. However, when good things happened to me, I always figured Daddy was really the one that caused them to materialize. There was this local radio show called *Uncle Roy*. He would interview several children in the studio and give the parents a vinyl record of their child talking to him. Mom really dressed me up cute in a white dress with big green polka dots, matching green socks with white patent leather shoes and a green bow in my red hair. Too bad it wasn't color TV. On the show there was always a color of the day, and if you said that color during your interview you would win a special prize. Well, guess what I said when Uncle Roy asked me my favorite color as I sat there all dressed in green. Of course, I said, "Gold." And what was the secret color of the day? You guessed it. It was green. Even so, I wasn't bothered by that and had a fun time. I was very happy when we left the radio station. But after the program, we went straight to the local bar where all my parent's friends had listened to the radio show. When I walked in all dressed in green everybody started laughing about me saying gold when the color was green. One man said, "Isn't that just like a female to always be thinking about money!" I did not understand why my saying gold was so funny. I thought I had done something stupid. My happiness was gone and deep sadness took its place. That emotional flip flop became a recurring pattern for my life. Happiness never seemed to last very long, and sadness became my constant companion. I still have the Uncle Roy record.

With summer finally over, I could not wait to get back to school. My first year of school had somewhat changed my parent's drinking schedule to only one weekend night. I was sure hoping that would continue on through second grade, so I did not have to spend so much time in the bars. On a rare occasion Mom would allow the teenage daughters of their friends down the street to come over and stay with me when they went out. That was so great! They would brush my hair, scratch my back, and tell funny stories. They taught me the words to popular songs and how to make flowers with tissues. I was very happy whenever they babysat me. Well, that was fun while it lasted, but soon I was back in the bars. I was older now so I would spend my time feeding the jukebox and playing shuffleboard, which made the hours a little less miserable. I got so good at shuffleboard sometimes I could beat the adults. It was the type played on a long table top alley and you would slide metal pucks with your hand to try and get them as close to the other end as you could without them falling off the edge. On weekends I could never spend time with any of my school friends because my friends in school did not have parents that were *bar flies*. I basically led two lives. The excellent student with perfect attendance and the other person that had seen more than her young years should have ever been exposed to. School became a sanctuary for me and homework an excuse to stay away from my mom. It was important to me to do well and be a good student. It gave me not only a sense of belonging, but also self-worth. It did not bode well with me if my sanctuary time was threatened. One night during the week my parents had out-of-town company, so they went drinking across the border. I had a sitter since it was a school night. The next morning, I woke up suddenly and wondered why my mother had not come in to wake me. I got dressed for school, but things were unusual because there was no breakfast, and then I noticed the kitchen clock. It was ten o'clock in the morning! I had no alarm clock of my own at that time. I panicked! I never missed school! I always got perfect attendance ribbons, and I did not want to ruin my chance for another one. Daddy had gone to work, and Mom was still in bed asleep. I pushed on her and said, "Get up! I need to go to school!" If I had been older, I could have walked to school by myself. But I was only seven, and I had to cross a busy street with no traffic light. She moaned, "Leave me alone and go back to bed." I got mad and pushed even harder. You could still smell alcohol on her breath. I yelled, "Get up now!" I was furious. I pulled the covers off and screamed at her. She got mad at me and said her head hurt, and she could not walk me to school. I said, "Well, I am going by myself then," and headed for the door. Finally, she staggered out of bed and mumbled something about my daddy would be upset with her and said, "Stop making my head hurt worse. I will walk you to school." I made her write an excuse for being late, so I would not lose my perfect attendance. I finally got to school in time for lunch. Fortunately, she never pulled that stunt again.

For some reason I was always able to be a normal person at school. The students in my classes, and the teachers, had no idea what was taking place in my homelife. When I was in my sanctuary the real me was allowed to show up. I was able to flourish in an atmosphere that was not always critical or uncaring. I discovered that I was actually smart. I found out that I had a love for people and developed many friendships, only at school. Those few hours of reprieve from 8:00 a.m. until 3:00 p.m. were the happiest times of my young life. But when I recall some of the worst incidents that a small child had to witness, even I am amazed how that child had the ability to separate her two worlds. For instance, at the still tender age of seven, there were times when my parents would drink so much, they would get in big fights that would scare me. One night there was a really bad argument in the kitchen. Mom was yelling at Daddy, so he grabbed her by the hair and hurled her through the doorway to the living room. I was screaming at the top of my lungs for them to quit fighting! Then Daddy picked up a dinette chair and threw it at her. I was crying frantically and felt as if I should do something to stop them. I ran over to the kitchen counter, opened a drawer and pulled out a butcher knife. I turned to Daddy and pointed it at him and screamed, "Stop it!" As he reached out to grab my hand and the knife, I quickly pulled it back and accidentally sliced his hand with the blade! When the blood poured out, I dropped the knife and started crying and screaming even more! It was horrible! I had hurt my precious daddy! Without a word, he put the knife in the sink, wrapped his hand in a towel and left the house. I ran to my room shaking and gushing with tears. Daddy was gone! And he was bleeding! And it was all my fault! Mom did not even come to check on me. I cried and cried and cried until I finally cried myself to sleep. The next morning Daddy was back home. Nothing at all was said about the night before. But after that awful night, my parents never had another fight. My mom still complained and nagged, they still got drunk on the weekends, but Daddy would hardly ever say a word about much of anything from then on.

About a year later Daddy had to go to Mexico for a business dinner with his co-workers. It was the only time I had ever seen either one of my parents go out without the other one. When I got up the next morning Daddy had not come home. It scared me! Where was he? Mom didn't know either. I was freaking out, "Where is my daddy?!" I was in a panic and I could not stop crying. Fortunately, it was a Saturday, so I did not have to think about trying to go to school in the midst of my hysteria. Finally, later that day we got a phone call. Daddy was in a Mexican jail across the border. A friend took Mom to pick him up while I stayed with the neighbors. What Daddy said had happened was he had left the meeting and was walking down the street to head home when a fight broke out blocking the sidewalk. He was standing with a small crowd that had gathered to watch when the police arrived. The Mexican police were notorious for finding any way they could to make a dollar. Daddy said the police started shoving anybody in sight into the paddy wagons, including him. So, he spent the night in a dirty jail and had to pay to get out. It was a horrible feeling to have my daddy missing, so I ran and hugged him when he got home. Sadly, it had been years since I had hugged him. Our family environment was not conducive to hugs. But I believed Daddy would have loved for it to be different. I say that because one day a year or so later something unusual happened when he came home from work. Mom was cooking and I was doing my homework at the dinette table. None of us ever talked about our feelings or expressed our emotional needs, so I am not sure where this came from that day as he walked into the kitchen. Daddy said, "Why don't I ever get a welcome home or even a hug when I get home from work?" Mom just basically ignored the unusual request, and I was so shocked I think my mouth must have dropped open. Daddy never ever talked like that! I was so surprised I could not move and did not respond. Since neither one of us said anything, he just turned and walked off. It was a moment in time that would never happen again. I have always regretted that I did not immediately jump up and hug him that day. Some kind of response might have changed our future.

I certainly realize there are people who have experienced a lot worse childhood than I did, but for me, my life at home was hell. For years I spent many nights crying in my room asking, "Why me?" I was an emotional wreck by sixth grade. Nobody knew that, but me and my stuffed animals. That was because my life at school was heaven. I was the perfect student. I was intelligent, friendly, respectful and happy. All of my teachers liked me because I made high tests scores and good conduct marks. I was really shy though except with a couple of real close girlfriends. I enjoyed a completely different environment when I was at school. The elementary school I attended was really fun. For every special holiday all the grades, first through sixth, would make decorations, hats and noise makers, and we would parade around the whole school, marching in the street, laughing and singing. It was amazing! In May we always looked forward to May Day. For the event everyone had to wear all white, so every year I got a new white dress, white socks and white shoes. We would put on an outdoor program for the parents which included a big dance around the May Pole as we wrapped big white ribbons around it. I felt so special that day. Those happy times really helped me get through the early school years. In fifth and sixth grade I loved that every day during lunch a bunch of us girls would line the entire sidewalk in front of the school, sitting in groups on the concrete, playing Jacks. We did not play the usual novice games of Jacks like *Pigs in a Pen* or *Onesie, Twosie*. We played really challenging games like *Over the Moon and Back Again, Criss Cross Swat the Fly*, and *Picking Cherries*, just to mention a few. There were about eight different skills we learned. I really have no idea where our difficult Jack games came from, but we all practiced hard to perfect them. We even had Jack tournaments to make it more competitive. Each of us girls had our own set of heavy-duty Jacks in a pouch with our own golf ball. We all used golf balls instead of those little rubber balls because golf balls would bounce higher. Boy, those were the days of pure fun and competition! If only the fun could have lasted and I did not have to go home. The daily internal back and forth was starting to affect my sense of security. I felt as if I were two people waging war against each other. It was not noticeable on the outside, but inside I was withdrawn, confused, and vulnerable.

The summer before fifth grade started out extremely boring. Three weeks into the monotonous daily routine, I even began reading our encyclopedias just to have something to do. Now that was boredom to the max. I really missed being at school. Then I received a five-year diary for my birthday. They were all the fad at the time. When I found it some years later and read through it, I wondered why I had even bothered writing a diary. It was full of pages of doing the ironing, cleaning the house or washing my hair. It got a little better at the beginning of high school, but still not much excitement. By the time my life finally started getting somewhat interesting, the diary was already completely full of mundane information. Then something very unusual happened. My mom starting acting nicer to me. Her condemnations were considerably less, except when she was drinking. I didn't know what was going on. I was afraid to let my guard down. She decided to teach me some card games she knew. We played Double Solitaire and 500 Rummy almost every day. I could see the reflection of her cards in her glasses, but I would never cheat. I just had fun telling her what she was holding in her hand. We actually had a good time. And sometimes, we would sit on her bed and eat saltine crackers and drink a big glass of milk. Then

Mom decided to buy a badminton set and we played all summer. We all still went to the bars on the weekends, but the other days were basically enjoyable. But just as I expected, those times were short lived and overshadowed by many darker memories. That old spirit of Condemnation was not about to let me get away that easy. Out of the nineteen years I eventually spent in my mother's house, I would say that those brief encounters were the extent of any resemblance to a mother-daughter relationship. I remained puzzled as to why my mom had tried to be so nice. I thought maybe her Christian friend, Kathleen, had been talking to her about our relationship. Whatever the reason was, my mom's hot and cold actions actually made matters worse. I had been able to have a glimpse of what normalcy could look like in our home, so when it disappeared, I was even more despondent. The night all the fun went away was when my mom took me to the local amusement park. We had been riding several thrilling rides when she decided we should go on the Ferris wheel. We went around a couple of times, and I was not particularly nervous about being up that high. Then the Ferris wheel operator began the process of unloading the riders. When it was our turn to be stopped at the top of the wheel, Mom started rocking our car back and forth and would not quit. I was terrified and became horribly scared! I screamed for her to stop, but she just laughed, "Don't be such a sissy." By the time our car moved down some I was crying in fear, and she was still making it rock. She thought it was so funny that I was that scared. Then her ugliness came back in full force and our fun days were over forever. But thank goodness school was on the horizon, and I was anxious to see what my fifth grade adventures would be.

As my mother returned to her onslaught of condemnations aimed at me, school became even more important because it always gave my life meaning and purpose. There were so many opportunities to feel as if I mattered, like when I was in the Spelling Bee or working as a Patrol Girl during lunch. I continued to feel a sense of accomplishment as I still received gold stars on all of my report cards. The sad thing was my parents never acknowledged my hard work or ever said they were proud of me. My grade school would have a Parent's Night every year and each class would make special projects to show off and the teachers would go through each student's folder with the parents. I remember each year when my parents would just stand there as my teacher told them how smart I was and what an asset I was to the class; they would not have any reaction or comment. I guess I should have just been thankful they went even though I wondered why they bothered. When I was at school, I was very happy, but when I went home, I was miserable, especially on Fridays. That had become the day we always went straight to the bar as soon as Daddy got off work. I never understood how people could enjoy just sitting on a barstool drinking beer for hours at a time. Mom usually got a head start with a few beers at home. I could always tell she had been drinking when I saw her after school. She would get this different look on her face that would tell me to tread lightly or be in for a verbal brow beating. She could never have just one beer and stop. She had to consume at least a dozen and close down the bar. It was like a chemical reaction or an alcoholic spirit that took hold of her. It is no coincidence that the signs on the liquor stores say *Spirits*. I considered her a weekend alcoholic because she did not drink during the week unless on a rare occasion when they might entertain out-of-town company. Daddy also only drank on weekends now, but he never appeared to be drunk and could stop at any point. He just got talkative and funny and seemed happier.

Believe me, I heard and saw more than any young child should ever experience. My innocence was always in jeopardy. And you must understand, that this was a totally different era when children were still completely sheltered to the things of the world. In my personal environment I never even saw my dad with his shirt off or my mom in her underwear. The only time I witnessed any PDA was in bars when men would be slobbering drunk kisses on some woman. Shows on TV were highly monitored for language and moral conduct. Actual married television couples were not allowed to even share a blanket, let alone sleep in the same bed. When a popular TV comedienne wrote her pregnancy into the script, it shook industry standards and required approval from the clergy to be aired on television. They were not even allowed to say she was pregnant; they were required to say *expecting*. So, my exposure to lewd and crude situations were not the norm in the 1950s. One weekend when I was about ten, those sensual spirits on assignment were working overtime. My parents decided to take some of their out-of-town friends to a floor show across the border in Mexico and, of course, I had to go with them. Some of the night clubs had good entertainment with acts you might see on television, but not this particular night. The show ended up being a striptease act. This place had a hydraulic dance floor that rose up high so you would not miss a thing. The floor show was called *Beauty and the Beast*. The music started and this woman came out who looked too old to be stripping at all. She had on a ton of makeup and wore an evening gown, very high heels, and long evening gloves. She pranced around on stage to the beat of the music for a while, and then she began peeling off one of the long gloves and threw it to the band amidst the clatter of symbols. Then slowly, off came the other glove. Men and women were hollering, "Take it off. Take it all off." The stripper pranced around some more, then turned her back to the audience and began to slowly unzip her gown from the back. She got about halfway down and stopped with a teasing grin and walked around again to the beat of the music. The crowd was whistling and yelling as she turned back around and slowly unzipped the gown all the way down. Still with her back to the onlookers, she wiggled out of the gown and held it in front of her body. Her figure was not bad, but her less than firm skin showed her age. She had on what would be equivalent to a thong today and obviously no bra. She turned around while holding the gown to cover her front side and pranced around again. When the audience reached a frenzied state, she threw the gown aside to reveal her G-string and her semi-sagging breasts with pasty tassels flopping around on her nipples. The spotlight went out and she went offstage. Now if that was not bad enough for a child to see, it gets worse. My mind and my senses were overloaded, and I just was not too sure what to make of all that. As I was looking around trying to process the whole scene, I saw the stripper standing behind part of the curtain. She had a relatively large bottle of a clear alcohol, like Tequila or Vodka, and she was chug-a-lugging that thing as fast as she could. Even as a child in grade school, my heart went out to her. I thought, "How drunk does she have to get to do that awful act on stage?" I felt so sorry for her. I have never forgotten that sense of discernment and compassion I felt when I saw her in the wings. Then the music started up again and all of a sudden, this big hairy ape, not real of course, began leaping around the stage and making gorilla noises. Soon the stripper came back out, still half-naked, and acted out a chase scene with the ape. He finally caught her and laid her on the stage. Then he got on top of her and pretended to have sex with her. Now at the time, I had no idea what he was acting out. As I watched, I had a strong feeling inside that this was something I should not be seeing. My parents would not have allowed me to look at a dirty magazine, yet they had no problem with me watching an obscene strip show. All the other adults in the audience thought it was a great performance and apparently no one considered it inappropriate for a little girl to be watching all that. I never told my friends at school. Not only because I did not understand what I had seen, but because I was too ashamed that I had been to a strip show.

In fact, I never would let anyone know how much of my time was spent in bars. If I ever complained to my parents about being there all the time my mother would say, "You ought to be ashamed of yourself for talking like that!" Those few words had become her new mantra, and I would hear them on repeat for years to come. Eventually, I would be full of shame. My mom continued, "You should be ashamed for being ugly to us. We work hard all week and we deserve to have some fun. You are so selfish. We give you everything, and you are complaining about us relaxing a little bit!" I was not only in the bars every weekend, but there was never a Thanksgiving, Christmas or Easter that went by without eating in Mexico. I loved the delicious bacon wrapped filet mignons at our favorite restaurant, but the marathon drinking always came after the eating. Mom never ever cooked a holiday meal, except for New Year's Eve, she did make us menudo. It was a Mexican tradition for that time of year. The one and only thing I loved about my mom in those days was that her cooking was amazing! I always overate and was chunky until high school. On New Year's Eve I would stay with a sitter because things got pretty wild across the border on that night. My parents would still be drinking the next morning when we went to the New Year's Day Parade. Daddy would make funny comments to the people on the floats and get them laughing. Afterwards we came home and ate the homemade menudo and watched football. My parents usually fell asleep during the game, so I would start taking the tinsel and ornaments off the Christmas tree. I always decorated the tree by myself around Thanksgiving and took it down by myself on New Year's Day. Our holiday season was not traditional by any stretch of the imagination. And as for me, it was actually the saddest and loneliest time of the year. No one ever knew that. I could pretend very well.

Sadly, I was pretty well known at many places in that town in Mexico. After all, I was practically raised there. I called myself a *wetback*. That was a term the Mexicans frequently used. The bartenders had known me forever and would always make me a Shirley Temple, a non-alcoholic strawberry drink. One of them, Armando, would take a lime and make it look like a little pig. Using the lime peel, he fashioned ears and a corkscrew tail and used wooden matches for eyes and legs. The lime was the body. I felt special when he did that for me. In fact, I kept the last little pig he made for me when I was a teenager. I still have the dried-up memento with my keepsakes. There was another nice man in Mexico who really made me feel special, Mr. Diego. He sold leather goods from bar to bar, and that was how he made a living for his family. He always called me *The Baby* because he had known me since I was one. Even when I was in my twenties he would ask my parents, "How's the Baby?" Ever since I was small, he would give me little leather purses or zippered coin pouches. I still have one of those, too. It's the one I kept my Jacks and golf ball in. You would always see him dressed in a suit and tie to sell his wares. He was a very decent man and a gentleman through and through. Then there were these four amazing musicians that played on a long marimba and sang Mexican songs. They were so talented they could have been famous. They knew how much I loved hearing them play. As soon as I walked into the bar, they would start playing my favorite tune. Sometimes they would let me bang on the marimba with the long sticks; there was a big soft thing on one end. The guys were a lot of fun. But even with all these nice people, I was so tired of being forced to spend every weekend in a club or a bar. I was almost a teenager by the time I really started getting adamant about not wanting to go hang out for hours in a smoke-filled place full of foul language and staggering drunks. I wanted to spend time with my friends doing the fun things they were doing. I guess some teens rebelled and tried to go to the bars. I rebelled and wanted out of the bars.

I will never forget this one Saturday night in Mexico. I had just recently turned thirteen. I was so fed up with the same routine every weekend, but they would not let me go with my friends or just stay home. I was furious! I did not understand why, but I always felt that Mom was the one who forced the decision. It was almost like even though she did not really seem to care about me, she did not want anyone else to care about me either. That particular day my parents started drinking at the local bar after Daddy got off work at noon. The place had incredible tacos and gorditas, so I would get a bunch of food and a soda to go and sit in the car and eat while listening to my transistor radio. At least I was allowed to do that. Finally, after about three hours they came out. I thought we were going home, but noooo, we were going across the border. I begged them, "Please take me home first!" Mom would be so hateful to me when she was drunk, "We bought you all that food and now you want us to drive you all the way home. And then, make us have to come all the way back downtown to cross the bridge! You are the most ungrateful person in the world! All you do is think about yourself! You ought to be ashamed!" And on and on she went about everything that was wrong with me with a list of past instances when I should have "been ashamed of myself." So, off to Mexico we went. I tagged along to all their favorite stops while getting more and more disgusted by the minute. After several hours I was really nagging, "Let's go home!" Each time my pleas were met with the same run down of how selfish I was. Daddy would never say anything. I don't know why. Finally, after midnight, I was so physically and mentally tired that

I was done with all of it. I'd had enough. I got the car keys out of my mom's purse, told her I was going to the car and walked out of the bar. I never looked back. There I was, a thirteen year old kid walking down the sidewalk, past all the strip clubs and bars at 12:30 in the morning, and no one even seemed to notice. I think I was covered by guardian angels, although I knew nothing about them at the time. I had to walk several blocks to the bridge you crossed to go back over to our city. I was so mad and tired, I walked with purpose in every step and looked straight ahead. When I came to the Border Patrol crossing point I had to stop and declare my American citizenship. Not a question was asked as to why a very young teenage girl was crossing the border all alone at that time of night. My parents had parked the car in a lot under the bridge. It was not well lit. But with key in hand, I was too upset to feel fear as I walked down the steps to the empty parking lot. I did not look to the right or the left, but made a beeline to our car and quickly opened the lock, got in and immediately relocked the door. Letting out a sigh of relief, I felt good about what I had done even if I caught hell about it later. I crawled to the back seat and laid down. Obscured in the darkness and completely exhausted, I fell asleep. It seemed like only minutes when I was awakened by a tapping on the car window. I was startled, but fortunately it was my parents. I thought, "Oh good, they came to check on me." But as I reached to pull up the door lock, I glanced at my watch. It had been over two hours since I walked out of the bar. They had stayed and finished drinking until the bar closed! Their little girl had walked the streets of Mexico, crossed the border to a dark parking lot, and they were not even concerned about my safety. I was so flabbergasted! But you know what? I did not catch hell. In fact, nothing at all was ever said. And from then on, some things began to change for the better.

Four

From Bars to Bowling

By the time seventh grade was ready to start, Mary Beth, who had now lived on my street a couple of years, had become my closest friend. Our school only went to sixth grade, so we had to change schools. Mary Beth and I never knew why the decision was made, but she and I were the only students from our elementary school who did not go to the newly built middle school which was several miles away. It was probably because neither of our moms had a vehicle to drive us, and they both did not want us to ride the bus. Instead, for one year Mary Beth and I went to another elementary school that had a seventh grade, but was somewhat farther from our houses than our old one. She and I walked the long blocks together to and from school and had to cross a very busy street. To make the trek more entertaining, Mary Beth and I would talk in Pig Latin and laugh and have such a good time. At first, it was weird not knowing anybody at school after being with the same people for six years. I was really nervous and did not like the fact that my sanctuary had been displaced. But fortunately, I was able to make friends fast because the school had so many activities to help us get to know each other. They had organized sports games during school, one class against another and dance classes with boys and girls. On weekends we had school sponsored Sock Hops or roller-skating parties. Even though I was a wall flower and did not usually dance, the Sock Hops were crazy fun. We all had to take off our shoes and throw them into a big pile. Then when the dance was over, shoes were flying everywhere as everybody tried to find their own pair. It was a wonderful time in my dysfunctional life because I had a school activity almost every weekend. That enabled me to escape the local bars and the ones across the border. One day during school, I received a surprise visit from my hormones. I started my menstrual period. Even though in health class we girls had read the book *You're a Woman Now*, I was still freaked out when I saw all the blood. I went straight to the nurses' office for help. If I had not received that brief teaching on what to expect and what to do, it would have really been bad because my mother never explained anything to me. When I got home and told her about it, she just laughed. Then we made a quick trip to the neighborhood drug store. I could not understand why she thought my harrowing experience was so funny. But all in all, the school year turned out to be great. Plus, I had made a lot of new friends that would be going with me to eighth grade at the high school annex. I was also very happy because my sanctuary had survived the transition. Everything about my seventh grade school was so special, and it just overflowed with joy. I thought maybe the happy atmosphere had something to do with the fact that the leadership seemed to like praying. Each day the principal would open with a short prayer before making the announcements over the intercom. Also at lunch, we always had a prayer over our food. That seventh grade year was my first introduction to any form of praying. Even though I was clueless, there was a possibility that the whole event of changing schools was just to teach me what prayer looked like.

During the summer between seventh and eighth grade, an amazing change happened to me and my parents. My family discovered bowling! My dad said the doctor told him it would be good for his arthritis. But I do not think it was coincidental that this change took place not long after my rebellious walk to the car in Mexico. The three of us had never done anything together except go to the bars or an occasional drive-in movie. My parents finally found something fun to do instead of just sitting on a barstool. Oh, they did not stop drinking. They just found out they could drink beer and bowl at the same time. But once my parents joined a bowling league, the only time we went across the border was to eat on holidays, with drinking after, of course. The really great thing about them bowling was I could have fun, too by bowling with the other parent's kids. Eventually, I joined a junior league that bowled on Saturdays. That was the beginning of decades of bowling for me. Amazingly, being on the league afforded me a chance to be on a local TV show called *Pin Busters*. I was chosen along with another girl because we had the highest averages in our junior league. My partner did great, but I was so nervous seeing those cameras pointed at me I did terrible. Embarrassing! There was a period of time my parents and I practically lived at the bowling alley, sometimes on more than one league at a time. I could not have been happier to have such a reprieve from the awful smoke-filled bars. Even though they still drank all the time at the lanes, the bowling years were so much better than the bar years.

I wish I could say that everything changed for the better, but this was not the case at home. Mom was still nagging and running me down with malicious verbal attacks. It seemed as if she resented the fact that I was happy because that was when she would always start some off the wall tirade. Many times, she just made up things in her head and went on and on about stuff that did not even make sense. I would come home in such a good mood after bowling because I had so much fun with my friends, and immediately I would hear all the things I had done wrong since the day I was born. I may be exaggerating a little bit, but that was the way it felt to me. Sometimes it was like she had this enormous file cabinet in her head, and at any given moment she could pull out something I had done or said. Complete condemnation would follow with details of the wrongdoings that were often incorrect or embellished. I wish I had a dollar for every time I heard, "You should be ashamed of yourself." I would be a rich person. It's difficult to describe the emotional chaos that played with my mind on a daily basis. Sometimes I would have terrible thoughts about how much I hated my mother. For instance, one day Daddy had asked me to go get him a hammer from the small storage room next to the bathroom. Mom was on her knees, bent over the toilet doing her daily obsessive cleaning. When I walked behind her with hammer in hand, I wanted to hit her in the head with it. Thank goodness something inside of me restrained me! Despite my terribly sad thoughts at home, all of my thoughts in school were normal because I was really not a bad kid. I never got into trouble in school, I still made straight A's, and all of my teachers still liked me. Probably the worst thing I actually did at home was try to ignore my mother. I really could not stand conflict, so after years of fighting, I eventually got to where I would just clam up and pretend she was not there. Daddy seemed to ignore her, too and never really had much to say. Especially, when Mom was lashing out at me with one of her ridiculous attacks. I always wondered why he never spoke up to defend me. I guess he was tired of arguing, too.

There were times that seemed as if she had spent days mulling over some terrible wrong I supposedly committed until she exploded with untrue accusations that came out of nowhere. Those kinds of attacks were particularly difficult to take and hard to ignore because they were so crazy and hurtful. With that kind of stuff going on every day, I was never able to go to bed happy. And, I was still leading a double life. Having to flip the switch from home to school and then from school to home was emotionally draining. Half the day while I was at school, I was so content, but the other half of the day at home, I was miserable. This emotional elevator of ups and downs was beginning to take a toll on my psyche. My friends never knew the life I had at home because I never talked about it. I became a very private person. I never had anyone over to my house except for Margaret because of the way my mom acted. I was afraid she would blow up about something and embarrass me. Margaret had already known for many years what she was like. One day Daddy asked me, "Why don't you ever bring any of your friends home with you?" It was another one of those rare and unusual moments for him to say anything like that or show any emotion. He was always so stoic. And since communicating or having conversations were never part of our daily family life, I didn't know what to answer. Yet again,

I felt as if I had hurt him because he thought I was ashamed of where we lived. That idea had never ever entered into my mind or my heart. But I could not tell him that the real reason was because I was afraid Mom would act out when I had someone over. I did not think he would understand. So, I just told Daddy, "No, that is not at all true. I like where we live." I am not sure he believed me, but I was so hoping he did. He worked very hard to keep our place looking nice. I was never ashamed of where we lived.

Not only did I learn about bowling before eighth grade, I also learned about the birds and the bees. And you should know by now, the information did not come from my parents. If my mom could not explain menstruation, she sure could not explain intercourse. And my daddy? Forget it. No way! I remember one time I came home and innocently asked about a word I had seen on a bathroom stall. I should have known better than to even ask, but I had no idea what the *F word* meant. Oh my gosh, you would have thought I told them I had just done that instead of spelled it. With no explanation, they both yelled at me. I could not believe it, even Daddy was condemning me. He said, "Don't you ever let us hear you say that word in this house again!" I never found out the meaning of the word from them. Later on, I had to ask one of my friends. So, the actual explanation of sex came one evening when my half-brother Larry and his wife Phyllis were visiting from out of town. Phyllis was a nurse, so I guess Mom was glad to let her do the job. I don't know if the discussion was pre-planned, but my mom, Phyllis and I were conveniently sitting outside on the glider after supper one night while Daddy and his son watched TV. Phyllis began the conversation by asking if I had started my period yet. Then she wanted to know if I knew why women had one and what the menstrual cycle had to do with babies. All I knew was what I had read in that little book in health class, which was not a whole lot. Then Phyllis asked what I knew about sex. I started blushing because to me that subject was taboo. It was a different world back then. I was very naive and shy when talking about such things, even among my girlfriends. When she began to explain some details, I was blown away and just sat there wide-eyed.

She was very gentle with the information, but very specific. I guess that came from being in the medical field. But when she was explaining how and why a boy may try to fondle me in my private area, a revelation came to me about a situation I had never really understood. Something had happened several times when I was around ten or eleven. Do you remember me mentioning our neighbor, old man Joe, who lived down the street with his son? Well, many times he would come over to visit and have a beer with my mom. In our living room we had a couch that laid flat, sort of like the modern-day futon, and most of the time it was laid open. I liked to lie on it and watch TV, and sometimes old man Joe would sit next to me. A perfect opportunity for the devil to work his evil through the heart of a sinful man. When Mom would go to the kitchen or even outside, Joe would put his fingers into the legs of my shorts and feel around under my panties. I actually liked the feeling I got from it, so I did not stop him. Well, this happened quite a few times, and he would always say, "Shhh, do not tell your mom." I had no idea what it all meant. I just knew I liked it, so I was not about to tell her because I wanted him to keep doing it. I think that was due to the fact that I rarely felt pleasure, and what he did filled a void. When Phyllis continued explaining what could happen after the fondling, plus the feelings I would have leading up to intercourse, I blurted out, "That was what old man Joe did to me on the couch! He touched me down there, and I got those feelings!" Needless to say, Phyllis was speechless. But Mom, being true to form, instead of being shocked and angry at Joe for sexually abusing her daughter, had this to say to me, "You should be ashamed of yourself accusing old man Joe of such a terrible thing! He has been nothing but nice to you. He gives you money all the time and makes your favorite green chili sauce. You should really be ashamed of making up such an awful story about him!" Mom was so mad at me, and poor Phyllis was totally confused, so she just got up and left us to our shouting match. The more I said, "It's true!" the madder Mom got until I was in tears. After another "You should be ashamed of yourself" statement, she got up and went inside. I was left alone to be attacked by every negative thought that could fit in my mind. I went to bed that night laden with guilt that the whole incident with old man Joe was somehow my fault. I condemned myself and felt ashamed because I had enjoyed the feelings he aroused in me. I was confused about sex and its purpose because Phyllis never got to finish her explanation. I cried and cried and cried until my insides hurt. I hated my life, I hated my mother, and I hated that dirty old man.

I know it's difficult to imagine that any mother would have that response to the news that her daughter had been violated several times. But for my mom, that reaction was typical. Remember, she did not like me, so it didn't matter whether the conflict was between me and her, my daddy and her, or with anyone else, she always found a way to blame me. I also believed she never told Daddy about Joe. Because, I knew Daddy would have had a completely different reaction, and Joe would have had hell to pay and would never be allowed to come into our house again. But he did come back, just as much as before, only now I stayed far away from him. What none of us had a clue about was what was going on in the spirit realm. My exposure to strip clubs, filthy conversations in the bars and now physical violation were all part of a master plan to slowly destroy me. These influences were just the beginning of events in my life that would ultimately cause great deception, deep depression, and emotional torment. Because of all the years of condemnation, I had developed a very low self-esteem and zero self-confidence, especially when it came to how I looked. I really thought I was ugly. Some of my school pictures could prove I was right, but we have all had those awful photos in our teenage years. I had no one to teach me how to wear my hair or how to wear makeup. I did not get to do the things where girls learned those skills, like sleepovers. So, since I had no sisters or a mother that would help, I had to learn on my own by trial and error. And there were some ugly errors. Just about everything I ever learned to do in my life was on my own. I never felt my mom could teach me any social graces because she did not have any. Sometimes she was so rude and crude, without tact or inhibitions and lacked normal manners. You know how people say you think you know more than your parents when you are young, and then you grow up and realize you did not. Well, I never had that happen. And, I am not being prideful. The main reason was, I cannot remember them ever trying to teach me any life lessons about anything. There seemed to be a person inside of me that just knew how to act in public. I am not saying I always made the right decisions because obviously I did not. If I had I would probably not be writing this book. I had to learn my life skills by making mistakes, sometimes big ones. And even though I was highly intelligent, I was void of wisdom in many areas. It seemed I always had to learn things the hard way. And, the hard way got even harder the older I became.

Going back to what I said about Mom being rude and crude, she would pass gas or belch loudly anywhere she was and then flash her silly grin as if that was funny. If I said a word about it not being a nice thing to do, she would promptly turn it back on me, "Nobody cares, but you. You think you know everything. You should be ashamed of the way you talk to me!" But that was not the worst of her unsocial graces. In the summer we would sometimes go to the drive-in theater. You would not believe what she would do. Mom did not want to use the public rest-room, so she would bring a large metal pot to use to go pee in the car. I was so embarrassed. I just knew the people in the cars next to us could not only see her in the back seat on the pot, but they could surely hear the pee hitting the metal container. Then she would open the door and pour it out on the ground! Thank goodness cars in those days did not have a light that came on when you opened the door. When I was little, she would make me use the pot, too. But when I got older, I refused and would try to leave and go to the snack bar before she peed. By the time I waited in line for the restroom and got some food at the snack bar, she would be finished when I returned. I was always met with the same question, "You didn't sit on the toilet, did you?"

My thirteen year old summer was definitely not as boring as they usually were. The difference was we were spending more and more time at the bowling alley. By the end of the summer my parents were bowling on two leagues each week. School would be starting soon, so as I tried to mentally prepare myself for eighth grade and another new school, I began to distance myself from my mom even more. I was determined my home life was going to be better this year. Daddy still did not say much. He just worked and watched TV except for bowling nights. Those nights were the highlight of my week. I had made many new friends at the lanes, boys and girls, and we would bowl or hang out in the restaurant while we were waiting for our parents. I was really getting interested in boys, but I still didn't know what to say to them. And being a fair complected redhead, if they talked to me, I would blush ten shades of pink. Added to my embarrassment was my Bucky Beaver front teeth. Fortunately, hope came later that year in the form of braces. I always believed Mom's friend, Kathleen, had suggested the braces because my parents would not have thought that way. And, I was still a little over weight. So, with all those factors crushing my self-esteem even more, I was convinced I was ugly, and no boy would want to ask me out. However, I was always excited to start a new school year, and this one was extra special. Not only because it was eighth grade, but because the classes would be at the high school. There was a separate section there just for eighth grade. That gave me the expectation that I would have a secure sanctuary for at least five years. We could go to all the sporting events and to the high school assemblies, plus we had access to the high school cafeteria. That made us lowly eighth graders feel like hot stuff. The students that went to the new middle school would have to wait until the next year to experience all that. Everything was going great. I joined a couple of clubs and started playing tennis. I loved tennis so much sometimes I would play at the park on Saturdays. I was losing weight and slimming down, the braces were doing their job, and there was some improvement in doing my hair and makeup. I was finally feeling somewhat better about myself. I started having a lot of homework, so I was able to stay in the sanctity of my room all evening. If Mom came around to bug me, I could just say, "You need to leave me alone. I have to study." My life was on the upswing until one night it hit a temporary road block.

I was awakened from my sleep with a horrible stomach ache. I had never had cramps or anything that hurt so bad! The pain was so intense it caused me to draw my legs up to my chest in a fetal position. I could not get out of bed. I yelled for my daddy. He came quickly to my room where he found me moaning in pain. He asked a few questions about where it hurt then promptly went to the phone and called our family doctor. Now this was in the late fifties when doctors still made house calls. That seems so unreal today that a physician would get up out of a sound sleep and a warm bed, get dressed, leave his family, and drive across town at 2:00 a.m. to take care of somebody. Soon our family doctor entered my room and placed his proverbial black bag on the bed. After poking around my abdomen, the diagnosis was an appendix attack. My parents were ordered to immediately take me to the hospital emergency room, and he would meet us there to prepare me for surgery. That was another big difference from the way things are done today. Our family doctor, basically our primary care doctor, did my appendectomy. Daddy bundled me up because it was winter, Mom packed a few things in a bag, and off we went to the hospital which was several miles away. I laid on the back seat covered with blankets and still doubled up with pain. When we got to the hospital everything went so fast. Before I knew it, I was on a gurney being rapidly pushed down the hall to a large room with bright lights. I was not sure what was happening, but strangely, I was not even scared. The nurses had already put a hospital gown on me. They were very nice and so gentle and caring as they covered me with warm blankets. But now, they were sticking needles into my arm and hand. I did not like that because it hurt, but not as bad as the pain in my belly. I just wanted that pain to stop. I began getting nervous as the nurses worked quickly to hook me up to numerous machines. I felt some of my anxiety subside when I saw our family doctor walk up to me and smile. He asked if I was doing okay. As I looked above me at a huge round light, I was not too sure what I should answer, but I nodded and said yes. Then my doctor asked me to start counting out loud backwards from 100. That was a puzzling request, but I obeyed and began with 100, 99, 98, 97, 96, 95, then I woke up in a hospital room, and the surgery was over. Wow! I thought that was amazing! I had been counting, then nothing. There were no thoughts, no dreams, no awareness of time, and no existence. I wondered if that was what it was like to be dead. I found out later the stuff they shot in my vein was called Sodium Pentothal, also known as a truth serum. Now that worried me because I wondered if I had said anything during surgery about my family life. But I never heard any concerns from my doctor or the nurses, so I guess I didn't. This event actually turned out to be a very pleasant time in my life. I was allowed to stay in the hospital five days. It was so peaceful and quiet. The nurses took such good care of me. They helped me to the bathroom, would give me sponge baths, and helped me walk down the hall. Everything they did was very tender and encouraging. I had never before been in an environment like that. Just like at home, I had good food and a TV to watch, but I had never experienced real nurturing. I felt as if I was being truly loved, and I was wallowing in it. Even with the sting of the stitches, I was genuinely happy. But sadly, the day came to go home. One of the nurses came and helped me shower and dress before my parents came to get me. She said, "I'll bet you are anxious to get back home." I didn't know if I could really tell her the truth, however I shyly answered, "No, not really. I wish I could stay here." She paused for a moment as she pondered my unusual reply, then continued her work as she said, "Oh, don't be silly, of course you want to go home." Probably in today's world if a child said that to a nurse, she would be calling the Child Protective Services to question the parents. But in the fifties, the nurse was not quite sure what to do with that kind of statement, so she did nothing. I was so sad to leave such a loving place and go back to my meager existence. And even worse, I could not go to school, play tennis or bowl. I was stuck at home with my mom for four weeks. In a way my reality became even more depressing because now I had a true picture of what nurturing looked like and just how unloving my family really was. The next month took forever to pass by. Mom brought school work home, so at least I had that to do. My friend Margaret would come over and try to make me laugh because I told her not to because it hurt. However, that was really okay. I enjoyed her company. But as far as having any loving care at home, it was like night and day compared to the hospital. I mostly stayed in my room and played my records and slept a lot. Daddy always looked in on me when he got home from work, so I would get up to eat and watch TV with him. Finally, the day came when I could go back to school, but I could not play tennis for another month. The first day back I was so nervous that my incision would accidentally get hit in the crowded halls during class changes. Fortunately, the days flew by without a hitch or a stitch, and soon I was back on the tennis courts and back on the bowling league. Also, I was so relieved when report cards came out that I had been able to maintain my straight A average throughout the whole ordeal. Grades had always been important to me ever since all the gold stars I earned in elementary school. Even though my parents never acknowledged my successes, I wanted to excel for my own self-satisfaction. It was the only part of me I felt proud of. As long as I made all A's I could pat myself on the back and feel good that I was finally doing something right.

Then one day, as eighth grade was coming to an end, a revelation happened that would make good grades an even more important necessity throughout my high school years. I was walking to class when all the graduating Seniors came through our building to exit the doors to the lower ball field. They were all dressed in their navy-blue graduation gowns to practice for the ceremony. Then at the end of the long line of graduates came a group of students wearing beautiful off-white gowns and caps. They looked so outstanding compared to the normal navy color. Something leaped inside of me as I was totally absorbed in how amazing those white gowns were. I had no idea why some were different, so I asked a nearby teacher. She said they were the top ten percent of the graduating class. I thought, "Top 10%? I want to do that. I want to graduate in a white gown." I do not think my monumental decision was based so much on achieving the goal of being in the top of the class as it was on wearing that beautiful white gown. But whichever the reason was, that day set the stage for my entire next four years of high school. Making the highest grades possible and reaching that crowning achievement became my first official obsession.

Five

High Times Ahead

School was out and another uneventful summer was about to start, or so I thought. Mom and Dad were just starting to discuss plans for our usual trip to see Grandma and Grandpa and then where to go for the second week of Daddy's vacation. We had only been out of school about a week when the phone call came. My precious Grandpa had died suddenly of a heart attack! Mom was hysterical. I was in shock. I had not yet known anyone who had died. I went to my room and started crying. Immediately, I started thinking of all the joy I would not have anymore. I could no longer help Grandpa work in the garden, there would be no more fun domino games on the front porch, and I would never again see his cute smile when he would humorously tease me. Then I really started sobbing. Mom frantically called Daddy at work. As soon as he got home plans were quickly made, and the following morning we were on our way to be with Grandma and attend Grandpa's funeral. On the long drive over there, nobody felt like talking. My mind was racing. I was so nervous thinking, "What do I say to Grandma? What is a funeral like? Is it okay to be crying all the time?" And the worse thought of all, "Would I have to look at Grandpa in the casket?" When we got to Grandma's house, we found her sitting on her kitchen stool snapping a big pile of fresh green beans from the garden. My mom seemed disgusted that Grandma was doing such a normal every-day task and practically chewed her out for not caring enough to be as upset as she was. Well, now Grandma was upset, but not so much about Grandpa; she was handling that quite well. I thought Mom was really being cruel, so I went over and hugged Grandma and we both started weeping. The funeral would be in two days. When the time came, I was so glad my friend Charlotte came over and sat with me in church. Surprisingly, I was not scared at all when I walked past the casket. It didn't even really look like Grandpa. Dead people did not look real. After my friend and I sat back down, the funniest thing happened. The preacher was talking when a big fly began circling over the open casket. Charlotte and I were intently watching the fly when suddenly it landed right on Grandpa's nose. We both thought we were going to bust a gut trying to keep from screaming with laughter. The fly spent quite a long time surveying the ins and outs of Grandpa's nose before finally taking off. Charlotte and I were in tears, but not from crying, and neither of us heard a word the preacher said. Other than my mom's half-sister wailing through the entire ceremony and having to be carried out of the church, the fly was the highlight of the funeral. I was thankful for those distractions, or I would have had a rough time making it through the funeral. We stayed there about a week to help Grandma before heading home. That summer we did not go on another trip anywhere. It took a while to stop feeling sad. I was sure going to miss Grandpa and the smell of Prince Albert in a can.

Not long after returning home I turned fourteen and celebrated with my two friends, Margaret and Mary Beth. Sadly, growing up I never had an actual birthday party or a birthday cake. We all just went to a movie and came back home and played records and acted silly like teenage girls do. My friend Mary Beth was moving away, so it was also a goodbye party for her. That made the celebration both happy and sad. All three of us were excited about becoming Freshmen in high school, but also nervous. Especially Mary Beth, who was going to another state. We did not want the day to end because there was more than just the day that was ending. Before long August arrived, and it was time to go register for my first year in high school. I was jittery and excited as I walked the halls of the main school building. They seemed so wide and were lined on each side with hundreds of lockers. In the front foyer there was a life-size bronze statue of a golden cougar poised to pounce on its prey. He was our mascot voiced in our spirit chant, "We are the Cougars. The mighty, mighty Cougars." Registration tables lined part of a hallway. I was beginning to get anxious and confused when I saw my next-door neighbor, Consuela, better known as Connie. She was a Senior that year and knew exactly what to do. She led me to the appropriate places to register and helped me understand the process. Most of my teachers were already assigned because I was on the College Route taking accelerated classes. I only had to pick teachers for a few electives, arrange the schedule, get my locker number, and the combination lock. Connie helped me with all of that, and I was very grateful.

The first day of school was like having a reunion. All the kids from my old grade school that had gone to the new middle school were now back, so we were together again. It was great seeing so many familiar faces. There was also an overwhelming number of new students coming from the other schools in the area. The new Freshman class numbered around four hundred students. Even with all the people I knew, I felt alone because my good friend Mary Beth had moved, and my friend Margaret was not going to be in any of my classes. Plus, people I knew were scarce for the lunch time I had been assigned, so I did not have anyone to eat with. I was not feeling very happy and was wondering what had happened to my sanctuary. As that first day progressed, I was concerned if I would ever find a good friend again. Then that afternoon I went to my first biology class. The teacher was incredibly funny and entertaining. I knew this would be a great experience. Then she called out names and assigned each of us as lab partners for the rest of the year. Mine was a match made in heaven. I was assigned to a girl named Rosemary who had gone to my old grade school, but was never in my class. Well, that day we became lab partners and ultimately lifelong friends. We were a perfect lab pair because Rosemary did not like cutting up the specimens, so I did the dirty work and she took the notes.

We would laugh all the time during the dissections, so we would not gross out. We were also in the same tennis class where we always tried to play each other or be partners for the doubles matches. We became the top two players in the class and spent the whole year trading back and forth for first and second place on the class challenge ladder. Rosemary and I loved tennis so much we would meet up at the park almost every Saturday and play for hours. In fact, tennis was so much a part of my life that in my Sophomore year I took tennis for first period so another friend and I could come to school one hour early and play for two hours before regular classes. I used a lot of deodorant and perfume that year. I was so thankful that Rosemary and I were able to spend most of our school day together, including lunch, which was always a fun time. Believe it or not, we both loved the cafeteria food, especially on Fridays when they would have very delicious Mexican food. Rosemary and I were absolutely giddy about Friday's lunchtime.

You notice I have not had to mention much about dealing with my mother. Because now, the enormous amount of homework I had from the advanced classes allowed me to have even more solitude in my bedroom. Every night after supper I could go to my room, close the door, turn on some music, and be by myself. I could totally saturate myself with studying, particularly math. I really liked geometry, but algebra was my very favorite. And later in high school there would be trigonometry, calculus, logic, and slide rule. I thought math was amazing. I know it sounds strange, but I was actually happy challenging my brain to figure out the solutions to the problems. It was like being in a competition with myself, and when I arrived at the correct answer I won. Each year the math classes and the problems got more difficult, but I loved it all. One night when I was a Senior, I had been working on this one calculus problem for a couple of hours and just could not come up with an answer. By midnight I finally had to reluctantly give up and go to sleep. Around 2:00 a.m. I had a dream I was working on that problem, and I dreamed the answer. Honest to God I did! Suddenly, I woke up and wrote down the solution and then went back to sleep. The next morning, I quickly applied what I had dreamed and it worked! That was very strange, but incredible.

My high school years were probably some of the best times I had, and that's saying a lot considering there would also be some extremely low moments. Daddy enjoyed taking me to our football games on Friday night. He did not even mind if I sometimes left him to go sit with my friends for a while. The games were always exciting because football was an extremely competitive sport in our city. There were several high schools at that time and my school and one of the others had been arch rivals for years. Whenever we played each other, the whole city took sides and came out for the game. It was also always our Homecoming, which added to the frenzy. I previously mentioned we were the Cougars, well, the other high school was the Leopards. Whoever won the game would possess the coveted Claw statuette to display in the school's trophy case for one year. The Claw was a large gold front paw with claws and part of about twelve inches of a leg of a wild cat. The encased piece of bronze was highly esteemed by the two schools. The football game between our two high schools was so huge for the city that every year on the day of the game our whole school met in our very large gym and would participate in a pep rally which was broadcast over a local radio station. Each school would have a sound system set up, so we could hear each other cheering for our respective teams. Our cheer leaders would lead us in resounding football songs, chants and cheers. The other school could hear us at their assembly. Then we would stop and they would do their yells back at us and we could hear them. Each time the cheers would get louder and louder as this back and forth school spirit went on about an hour. Most of the city would tune in to the radio station where they could hear both schools cheering. It was a very exciting day!

There were many fun moments in high school that became welcomed diversions from my homelife. In fact, high school was so great it made being at home even worse. My highs were higher and my lows were lower. Whenever I had to be around my mom for any length of time, she would always start an argument about something, and I would end up in my room crying and hugging my stuffed animals and still asking, "Why me?" It mostly happened on weekends because during the week I could usually get her to leave me alone so I could do homework. Whenever I brought my straight A report cards home there was still no, "I'm proud of you" or "Good work." Instead, Mom hardly ever missed an opportunity to tell me my faults or what I could never be able to do, and Daddy never intervened to help me out. The lifelong condemnations were still affecting my self-esteem around boys; even though getting braces made me not so ugly. I never had a boyfriend or even a date until my Junior year. Since I was still one kind of person at school and another kind of person at home, I had many insecurities. I was told my zodiac sign was Gemini, the twins. I thought maybe that was why I felt like I was two people. During the day I could be myself and act and react in ways that came from my heart. I loved being friendly and relished my relationships with my girlfriends. That made me happy. At · home the evil twin came out, and I reacted from my emotions because I was so unhappy there. That made me very sad and depressed. Although the devil had not pulled a blatant attack on me since the old man Joe episode, he was wearing me down by engaging in daily covert missions to make me miserable. It was not until the last two years of high school that he began to accelerate his plan. It began with a gradual onslaught that would slowly intensify and subtly overtake me. Have you ever heard the story of how to boil a frog in a pot of water? Do you bring the water to a boil and toss the frog into the boiling water? Of course not. The frog would immediately jump out of the pot. What you do is put cool water in a large pot and place the frog into that water. The frog thinks, "Oh, this feels great like a cool pond." After he is all comfy in the pot, you turn the burner on very low. You wait awhile making sure the frog still likes where he's at. Then gradually, a little at a time, you begin to turn up the heat. The frog does not notice the change in temperature because it's not obvious. As the water gets warmer, the frog gets more and more lethargic until he eventually slips into a state of unconsciousness. Now the water is allowed to come to a boil, and within a few seconds the frog is dead, and he never even knew what hit him. Well, that is the way the devil moves in our lives. If he jumped out and said, "Gotcha!" you would run for your life. But if he can make you feel comfy as he turns up the heat, he will gradually step up the attacks until he kills you and takes your soul to hell. Just like the frog in the pot, you will not even know what happened until it is too late. By now, I had been sitting in that pot of water for several years. The fire had been extremely low, but a slight increase was on its way. I am now a seasoned high schooler about to enter my Junior year and my confidence level had increased significantly. I was proud that I had made it through two years with a straight A average, still focused on that top ten percent. I had an English teacher who loved the way I wrote my essays and quite often would give me an A double plus (A++) on my papers. I really enjoyed writing and was excited that I could finally take journalism in my Junior year. That meant I could write for the school newspaper. I was now active in many clubs and enjoyed going to their meetings and parties. I felt more satisfied with my looks since my braces were off and my teeth were beautiful. With all that tennis I played my formerly chunky body had slimmed down even more, and I had perfected the way I did my hair and makeup, so I felt like I looked good. Boys were beginning to talk to me more, and I did better talking to them. Best of all, I had turned sixteen during the summer and now possessed the coveted driver's license. Unbelievably, my parents allowed me to take our two year old new car to pick up Rosemary and our new friend Shirley. I guess they thought I was a good enough driver to be trusted with their first ever new car. On the weekend my friends and I would go buzz the local drive-in restaurant looking for something to gossip about. The very popular hangout was built in a circle where cars could park all around it. We would join all the teens who would slowly drive around and around the circle to see who was there and who they were with. Then we would park and order sodas and giggle about everyone we had seen. My parents would have absolutely had a hissy fit if they had known that we did a Chinese Fire Drill at the red lights. That was when we were stopped at a red light all three of us would get out of the car and run around it trying to get back in before the light changed. I especially had to hurry because I was the driver. Rosemary, Shirley and I were together just about every weekend. We had many good times and are all still friends in our old age.

My Junior year did have some high points. My parent's drinking had almost dwindled to holidays and bowling nights. But when Mom did drink, things were still never pleasant. Life was great though because I had a boyfriend, Timothy, and we had known each other since grade school. He was a lot taller than I was and also had red hair. He had a great sense of humor and made me laugh all the time. We would always sit together at assemblies and talk on the phone every night. Once, he actually came over to my house, and we played dreamy records on a slower speed and danced together, hardly moving. Nothing is more romantic than rocking back and forth to *Sleep Walk* played at 33 1/3 rpm. And miraculously, Mom never bothered us. At Christmas one of the clubs I was in was going caroling, so I invited Timothy. He was the life of the party. All the girls liked him and I did, too, a lot. Then one of the clubs Timothy was in was having a formal New Year's Eve party, and I was very excited when he invited me. We had so much fun dancing to a live band. The party was over before midnight, so we waited outside on the steps for his mom to pick us up. The entire evening had been one of the most incredible moments of my teenage life, and I was actually happy long enough to make it a memory. It took his mom awhile to get there, and I was getting cold. Timothy snuggled up and put his arms around me to keep me warm. I was in heaven sitting there with my head on his shoulder. Then he put his hand under my chin, tilted my head up and kissed me. My first kiss!! My head was literally spinning. What euphoria! At that point I was hoping his mother would never come. Thank goodness she did take longer to get there, so we could get in a few more smooches. It still was not midnight yet, but it was an amazing Happy New Year kiss. When school started back after the holidays we still *dated*, mostly seeing each other at school. I just knew our relationship would last forever. I was already dreaming about graduating together and maybe even more. Now that Timothy had introduced me to the joy of kissing, I could not get enough. I was obsessed with the sensation of love I felt when he kissed me. So, every chance we had, we found various places to indulge ourselves. Timothy was more than happy to satisfy my yearning. I stayed on this fairy tale high for several months with only a happy ending in sight.

My world was wonderful until one day everything suddenly changed. I knew Timothy was almost two years older than I was and had been held back a grade, but it never came up that he was soon turning eighteen. All I cared about was he made me feel wanted and needed and important. I finally felt loved. Timothy filled my days with joy and happiness, emotions I never experienced at home. But, remember the frog in the pot? Just as I was settling into a comfy, cozy relationship with Timothy that spirit on assignment named Rejection decided to turn up the heat a little more. Timothy and I always talked on the phone as much as possible, but one fateful day we had been talking for a while when he got very quiet. That was not like him, so I asked, "What's wrong?" He said, "I need to tell you something I have been dreading to say." "What?" I responded nervously. Slowly Timothy answered, "I have joined the Navy and will be leaving in two weeks." "What!" I felt like I couldn't breathe. Where did this come from? When? Why? I could not talk. I was devastated! Finally, he said, "Say something," and I started crying. My world, my life had ended! Sobbing, I asked, "When can I see you?" And then it got worse. Timothy said, "I'm not going back to school. I'm getting my GED in the Navy. These next two weeks are going to be really busy, and my mom thinks since I am leaving it would be better not to see each other again because I am not coming back." I could not believe what I was hearing! No hug, no kiss goodbye. How could his mom be so cruel? "I have to see you!" I pleaded. He said, "I will write to you when I get to boot camp." I could not stop crying. Finally, he said, "I have got to hang up now." "No!" I begged. "You cannot hang up. Please! You don't understand. I have got to see you!" Timothy kindly said, "I am sorry this hurts you so much. I will miss you and I will write to you, but I really have to go now. I am so sorry. Goodbye." My mind was racing and my heart was pounding. It was over! I cannot handle this! Someone who cared about me will be gone forever! Click, dial tone. "No!! Come back!!" I held the receiver in my hand, listening to the dial tone until the off the hook beeping started. Then I slowly hung up the phone. I felt so alone and empty. I hurt inside to the very core of my being, and I felt sick to my stomach. I was glad my parents were not home. I ran to my room and hugged my big teddy bear while crying my eyes out. I put *Sleep Walk* on the record player and played it over and over and cried and cried. I thought, "How can this be happening? Why me? Other couples in school have been together for years. It's just not fair!" I got under the covers to try and feel secure and cried myself to sleep. Little did I know that I had just experienced the initial pangs of an obsession that would someday become an addiction. Even though all Timothy and I ever did was kiss, a lot, it was enough at that stage of my life to make me feel loved, and now I was losing my first supplier!

The next day was a Saturday, and I just wanted to stay in bed all day. I was so depressed and devastated. I could not tell my mom about what had happened. She thought our *going together* was silly anyway. She would say, "How can you be going together when you don't ever go anywhere together?" Then she would laugh at me. That day I just told her I did not feel good and wanted to stay under the covers. If it had not been for school, I would have stayed in bed forever. Again, the importance of making good grades and having perfect attendance was my saving grace. It was extremely difficult functioning for the first few days. I was used to seeing Timothy every day at school. We would hold hands as he walked me to my classes. By the end of that week the tests and homework had managed to help me keep my mind from feeling in a panic most of the time. The weekend was the hardest. To try and ease the pain, I constantly talked about Timothy to my friend Rosemary. Another week passed, and I was still hoping to hear from him before he left, but nothing. For some reason I really did not believe he would write me, so I never ran to the mailbox in hopes of seeing a letter. It had now been over a month since that fateful phone call when Mom picked me up at school and said with a smirky smile, "You have a letter in the glove box." I never got letters, could it be? It was! Timothy really wrote to me! Excitedly, I tore open the envelope and read how grueling boot camp was. He said even though it was difficult, he liked it, and he missed me. It was a wonderful letter. When I got home, I read it over and over again. He had asked me to write him back, so I immediately grabbed some notebook paper and began to tell him about school and how much I missed him. We exchanged several letters throughout boot camp. Then he graduated and was assigned to go out to sea. He wrote several times after he was on the ship, and I was beginning to think this relationship still might be a lasting one. But then one day, I received the last letter I would ever get from him. Timothy said our lives were so different now, and he wanted to be honest with me because I meant a lot to him. He would never want to just string me along because he really cared about me. He said when the ship went to port there was always lots of women wanting to go out with the sailors, and he would like to be able to go along with his buddies without feeling bad. He did not see any possibility of him ever coming back to our town, so he thought it was better to stop writing to each other. It was bad enough to be rejected once, but to be rejected twice by the same person was unbearable. Again, I cried for days, feeling so unwanted. Timothy's rejection of me put a real dent in my self-confidence. So, I just continued feeling sorry for myself and again asked, "Why me?" I missed the Junior Prom because no one asked me to go which made me even more despondent. With about a month left until the end of that school year, I was still extremely depressed and did not see much hope for the future. I was wishing I could go to summer school to stay away from home. But I had above a 4.0 average, so I was not exactly a candidate for summer classes. I was going to turn seventeen soon, and I thought, "What for? Nobody cares if I live or die. Is my life ever going to get better?" Well, little did I know better was just around the corner.

My friend Shirley saw that I was still moping around and wanted to help me snap out of it. So, she planned a blind double date with her and her boyfriend. I went over to her house to wait for the fellows to arrive, and I was so nervous! Finally, they drove up, and I was peering through the curtains to get a look at him. As they came up the sidewalk, and I saw how cute he was, I became even more nervous. I thought he was too cute for me, and he would not like me. But when we were introduced, he was very nice and friendly. We all went to a drive-in movie which was a little scary for a blind date. The coziness of the back seat was intimidating at first, but my date made me feel very comfortable. We got food and drinks at the concession stand and made wisecracks about the movie and laughed a lot. On the drive home I was completely at ease, so he began to kiss me. I was all into it because he kissed even better than Timothy! He wanted to see me again, but I found out there was just one problem; he was two years younger than I was. He did not have a car or a license, and his parents would not stand for him to be picked up by a girl. So, Shirley and I just planned more double dates. It was awesome, and I really liked him, and he never seemed two years younger. One exciting day I was actually invited to go with him and his parents to the local lake for a picnic. I thought that was great because they seemed to like me, so maybe they would rethink their rule about him being picked up by a girl. When it got dark, he and I walked around until we found a secluded spot to make out. We were lying on the grass, looking at the stars, when he rolled over beside me and we kissed and kissed and kissed. It was all very innocent kissing without a hint of petting or sex, which really made it more enjoyable. I was extremely hooked on him, but I did not realize that was literal. However, as my life would have it, after three months of double dating his parents decided we were seeing too much of each other, and I was too old for him. Not again! When he told me that over the phone I was, of course, devastated, but it was a different type of feeling this time. When Timothy broke up with me, I was unbearably crushed, but he was far away in the middle of the ocean, totally unreachable. But this guy was still in town. The impact was much more horrific because I felt I could somehow control the situation and find a way to see him. The panic I felt turned into trying to manipulate my way out of this rejection because I was again losing my supplier of attention that made me feel loved. One day I went over to Shirley's house, so I could call him and talk freely without my mom's interference. Glued to the phone, I sat secluded on her bathroom floor begging him for two hours to change his parent's mind. I just knew if I talked enough, with the right words, I could make it happen! But it did not happen, and I was falling apart. I didn't know at the time that I was trying so unreasonably hard to fix things because I needed a *fix* of sorts. Although not aware of it, I had begun to associate the feeling of being loved and accepted with the physical attentions of the opposite sex. I was like a dry sponge soaking up the feeling of love I experienced when a guy kissed me. I always wanted more, so when it ended, I felt as if the rug had been pulled out from under me. And not just the rug, but the floor, the earth and the air! After the two hour phone call the relationship was really over. I went right back into my depressed state, but not showing it to my friends, especially Shirley. I did not want her to feel bad about having introduced us. These early bouts with loss of what I so desperately needed were just the tip of an iceberg that later in life would become full-fledged love addiction. Now my Junior year was over, and as far as I was concerned so was my life. After another uneventful birthday, the only thing that was pushing me to go on each day was my dream of graduating in that beautiful white gown. For my Senior year, I had already decided I would load up my schedule, so I would not have time to think about how miserable my life was. Barely hanging on to my sanity, I could not have known that this summer vacation was not going to be the usual boring three months I was dreading. However, considering some of what did happen, boring would have been better.

Six

Two Scary Nights

Well, here I was facing my last high school summer vacation. I had turned seventeen and then in two more months I would be registering for my Senior classes. It seemed as if it was only yesterday that Connie had helped me with my first registration when she was a Senior; now I was one. Every school year I started with such high hopes for a happy nine months, but so far that had not happened. So, I felt like that summer should be special, different somehow. I thought something should happen, so I would never forget that particular summer vacation. My thoughts, of course, were for good to happen, not something terrible. But really, why would I think that anything could get better? My life was still never completely happy. Other people seemed to be happy all the time. I talked about my dilemma with my friend Shirley, and she invited me to go to church with her. I had not been to a church since I was eight, when for a while my mom would drop me off for Sunday School only. Neither she or Daddy ever went to church themselves. I remembered I liked Sunday School and my teacher because she always read us interesting stories. However, all I recalled about observing the church itself was the ladies in their fancy hats and dresses always talking about what they or someone else was wearing. I thought they were all hypocrites, a term I had picked up from my daddy. He did not go to church because of something that had happened when he was young which caused him to believe church goers were *all a bunch of hypocrites.* Since I believed everything Daddy said, I thought so, too. But now my life was so depressing, maybe church was what I needed. Besides, Shirley went to a different church, and I had met her pastor at her house one time. He was a good friend of Shirley's parents, and when he was there, they were all having a mixed drink. Now as much as I hated my parent's drinking, I thought he was a cool preacher because he was drinking alcohol. Somewhere in my warped mind I did not think he was a hypocrite because he had a mixed drink. So, I decided to start going to Shirley's church every Sunday. Now I could drive myself, so I was sure to get there. I really felt good being in church because everyone made me feel welcomed, and the people seemed happy. And while I was there for that hour or so, I felt happy, too. But I must have made the devil mad by going to church because my mom became absolutely intolerable. She went on at me even more than usual, and she was upset at every little thing. I tried hard to ignore her, but she would not have it and pushed every one of my buttons she could find. We had constant arguments. Since I was older now, I would stand up for myself more, and she did not like that one bit.

One Saturday afternoon we were having a huge fight when I realized I did not have to stay there and listen to her verbal abuse. I was seventeen now, and I did not have to put up with her rantings; I could leave. I told her that, and she grabbed the car keys, so I could not drive off. I was not even thinking about using the car, but when she did that, I got more determined to get out of the house. So, I grabbed my wallet and walked out the back door and did not look back. It was in the middle of the afternoon, and I thought I might need money to get food because I was planning to stay gone for the rest of the day. I just kept on walking out of the neighborhood down to a main road that was well traveled. I was still fuming as I continued walking on the sidewalk along the busy street. I was wearing a cute short set and was looking pretty good. But I was so mad, how I looked was not on my mind when a car pulled up beside me with two GIs from the local Army base. They seemed nice, but how could I have known that evil spirits were on assignment in both of them. They asked, "Do you need a ride somewhere?" I said, "No, not really." The driver said they were just cruising around looking for some fun and would I like to go with them. Well, I hadn't had a guy pay attention to me in quite a while, so I was reeled in. This was great, I could go on a date with two guys. I was SO naive. I got in the backseat, sitting by myself. We rode around awhile trying to decide what to do, then they stopped at some girl's house to see if she could go with us. Her mother would not let her so we left. Only now, the bigger guy got in the backseat with me. After we were on the main road, he pulled me over to him and started kissing me. The one thing I did not initially realize was that he was not like my other two boyfriends I had enjoyed kisses with. Whenever we made out, they had been complete gentlemen, but this guy was no gentleman. He pushed me down on to the seat and was trying to feel under my shirt. I pushed him off best I could, and he got upset, and I got a little scared. He was a really big guy. He sat up, but forcibly made me put my head on his leg, so he could continue groping me. He said to be still, that was all he wanted. I had never experienced a boy putting his hands all over me, so I was getting sensations I had never felt before, but I did not let him know that. The sun was beginning to go down, and the shorter guy kept driving, but I could not see where we were going because I was still lying on the seat. After quite some time the car stopped. They both opened their doors and got out of the car, so I was finally able to sit up and see where we were. He had driven us to the other side of the mountain and up high on a street where some new homes were under construction. It was completely dark, and we were way in the back of the new subdivision, totally alone. I had the feeling they had been here before. They had walked a short distance from the car and were talking. I was trying to look around to see if I could get out of the car and run. But the terrain was very rocky, and there was a lot of construction equipment on the unfinished road. I could not see any safe way to escape. Pretty soon the shorter guy, who had been driving, came back to the car and got in the backseat with me while the bigger one stayed up on the hill. They must have flipped a coin for first shot at me. I was still a virgin, so my mind was racing, "What was I going to do?" He unzipped his jeans and pushed me down on the seat with no interest in kissing, but proceeded to try and pull my shorts off. I was pulling on his hands trying to keep my shorts on when he grabbed my hands and forced them over my head as he plunged his body on mine and started kissing me really rough. I was horribly scared! With one hand holding my arms over my head, he was trying desperately to get my clothes off of me, but I kept struggling best I could. When he almost had my shorts and underwear down, I just knew I was about to be raped! Then all of a sudden, from out of nowhere, I heard myself saying, "What would your mother say if she knew what you were doing?" Immediately, he stopped cold, leaned up off of me and haughtily said, "You're probably too tight anyway." He zipped up his pants, called his friend over and said, "We're leaving!" He was obviously the boss. So, with no questions asked, the big guy got in the back seat again, so he could continue to put his hands all over me on the way back to town. I had no idea why I had said those words to that guy. I had not even thought of them in my mind. I didn't know anything about him or his background, but somehow, I was protected from being raped by those words that I blurted out of my mouth. I had always promised myself I would be a virgin when I got married because my mother wasn't, and I did not want to be like her. At that time in my life, I had no idea where protection like that came from. I just thought I was sure lucky that the guy had decided to stop when I asked about his mom. They drove me back to the area where they had picked me up and insisted they take me to my house. I did not want them to know where I lived, so I had them drop me off at a random house in a neighborhood near mine. I walked up the steps to the front door and pretended to look for a key in my wallet, hoping they would leave, but they didn't. I pulled on the screen door; thank goodness it was unlocked! Then I acted like I was unlocking the door. Finally, they drove off. Fortunately, it was late enough that the people in the house I picked were asleep, so they never knew I was on their front porch. When I was sure the guys were gone, I left that house and walked cautiously to my own home.

My parents were also sound asleep when I went to my room. Again, I just figured they didn't care enough about me to stay awake and be worried, even though I had been gone for hours. I thought to myself, "If I ever had children there would be no way I could go to sleep before I knew they were home safe." Anyway, when I got to my room, I grabbed clean underwear and my pajamas and went to the bathroom. I felt so dirty all over. I wanted to take a bath, but my parents might have heard the water running. Their heads were at the wall by the tub, and the walls were thin, and bathing that time of night would be unusual. So not to raise questions, I cleaned all my body with a wash cloth. I was exhausted, and my bed felt so clean and safe. As I dozed off, I was thinking, "I guess going to church works. That probably saved me from being raped tonight." The next day my parents never asked where I went or what time I got home, and I certainly was not going to bring it up.

That summer, life at home was getting worse and worse. The more independent I became, the more agitated my mom seemed to get. Since I was going to be a Senior when school started, that meant graduation and getting on with my life. You would think as little as my mother seemed to care about me, she would be excited to get rid of me, but NO! Whenever I would mention what I might do after graduation she would pound me down with all her remarks of, "You cannot do this, you don't know how to do that, you will never be able to," and so on and so on. We would usually end up in a big argument, so I finally just stopped talking about my future all together. I should have known better than to even try since we never had communication about anything else. Then one night during one of those arguments a very strange occurrence happened. Mom and I had been in a heated verbal exchange for quite a while when she claimed to be having an asthma attack. Of course, she blamed me for the attack. I felt she brought it on herself by the way she carried on, and I told her so. Plus, you never knew for sure how much was real and how much was drama. I was sitting in the kitchen which was next to their bedroom, and Mom was lying on the bed moaning and groaning, saying it was all my fault that she could not breathe. Even I had enough sense to know if she would just relax and calm down it would help her breathe easier. But she went on and on about how I was the cause of all her problems. Then she went off on this tangent I had never heard before. She started mumbling about how I was driving her insane and started talking really crazy about how she was feeling so weird, and I was just evil and wanted her to be a mental case. While she was saying all that really strange stuff, her eyes got really big and she acted like she was staring off into space in a trance or something. She was freaking me out! I had no idea her eerie antics were opening the door for more evil spirits to come into our house. I didn't know a thing about the reality of tormenting spirits such as fear, who wait for the perfect moment to move in and affect your whole life. Most of the time they sneak into your life without you even knowing, and their influences begin to change you ever so slowly. It could take years before you realize the impact. But this particular night, the manifestation was not gradual, it was invasive. As Mom continued her strange babblings, I was still sitting at the kitchen table when all of a sudden one of those spirits jumped on me. The only way I can describe what happened is to say it was as if someone or something had its hand inside my head and snapped their fingers. I felt a strong pop inside my head that made my body jump and my skin crawl. Immediately, like a wave, a spirit of fear came over me that I had not ever known before. Up until that moment I was only shy, lacked self-confidence and trembled when I had to give an oral report, but I was not particularly fearful about most things. But that night, I became afraid of everything. I was suddenly afraid of the dark, afraid to be alone, afraid to die, and afraid to live. Fear is a very powerful tool the devil uses to maneuver us like puppets in order to wreak havoc. We spend our lives blaming our parents, our spouses, or anybody else we can zero in on. Many times, we even blame God for all our troubles. It took me half my life to come to a place where I learned the truth. Meanwhile, my journey from that freaky night on continued to be filled with intimidation, condemnation, persecution, insecurity, and unnatural fear. In one split second of time, I had changed forever.

After all the weird stuff that had been happening to me, I definitely made sure I went to church every Sunday. But my fears were still out of control. The scary TV shows I used to watch without blinking an eye were now popping up in my mind and my dreams with frightening images. Before, on weekends, I would normally stay up late and loved to watch Twilight Zone and all the monster movies, but I could no longer do that. I had to stop watching them. I had absolutely no peace of mind. I could not wait for school to start in hopes that my sanctuary would chase away all the strangeness that was embedded in every waking moment. For my Senior year I registered for a fully loaded schedule of accelerated classes. That way I could stay busy and maybe not feel the fear. My final school year started off too normal. I wanted it to be different and memorable. Then the assignments started rolling in and I was up to my neck in weekly tests. That was what I wanted, no time to think. I would stay up later and later doing homework because I did not want to go to sleep and have the terrible nightmares. By now, I was in more clubs with lots of meetings, social events, and service projects. The busier I could stay the less I would think about my fears. I was promoted to Feature Editor of the school paper, which I loved! That kept me real busy gathering articles for my page. I was still playing tennis as often as I could, bowling on a Saturday league, and I had been selected as one of the coveted ROTC Sponsors. That was an elite group of Senior girls attached to the boy's ROTC. We had to try out by marching and be voted on by the boy's with only around forty positions available. I could not believe I made it, and Rosemary did, too! But anyone who knew me could not tell that on the inside I was not the same person. It used to be that even though I had no peace, I could get alone in my room with my stuffed animals and somehow escape the turmoil. Only now, there was never any peace anywhere. I felt detached from reality like I was an actor on a stage going through the motions of everyday life. I began having frequent Deja vu experiences. There were so many I started playing a game with myself. When I felt one of those moments coming on, I would try to see if I could think fast enough to know what was going to happen before it actually did. Now of course, all of that took place in less than a split second. Amazingly though, one day I was able to grab my thoughts fast enough to really make it work. I was sitting in class doing my lesson when some word with some action set the Deja vu process in motion. That made me feel as if I had lived that exact same moment before. I looked up and with lightning speed I thought, "Benjamin, who was sitting in the back of the class, is going to get up, walk to the front, and sharpen his pencil." I had no sooner finished the scenario in my mind when Benjamin got up, walked to the front, and sharpened his pencil. I thought, "Wow! I just guessed the future!" I was amazed at my ability to make it work! All those mind games I was playing were just one of the devil's tricks to eventually lure me into ESP or clairvoyance. Fortunately, I did not take the bait. For me it was all just a challenge and not a curiosity. So, that one time of knowing what would happen seemed to satisfy me, and I stopped trying to guess. Eventually, the Deja vu moments subsided. But that did not stop my interest in the unknown. Instead, I chose the route of horoscopes, Ouija boards, and Tarot card readings. These new interests would open the door to a whole new set of evil spirits.

At the same time all this craziness was happening I was somehow still able to focus on what was important to me in school. I continued to strive for the top ten percent, enjoyed journalism and preparing my feature page each week, and reveled in the crowning achievement of being an ROTC Sponsor. In my school being a Sponsor was really a big deal for selected Senior girls. I finally felt like a big cheese on campus. There was plenty of work involved in being an ROTC Sponsor. I was part of a girl's precision marching drill team, and we practiced silent formation drills for one hour every day during school. I absolutely could not wait to march and learn new routines. Plus, with all that exercise I slimmed down to a size seven. I had never been that small before, and I knew I was looking good; especially when I was in my uniform. We wore Army green Eisenhower jackets with gold buttons and gold braiding on one shoulder and a matching A-line skirt. We had to wear hose with our brown penny loafers along with white gloves and topped off with one of those flat type caps with our rank on it. Most of us in the unit were 1st or 2nd Lieutenants. Only the popular girls were Captains or Majors. I think rank had to do with how many votes you received. But I didn't care at all about what rank I was. I was just happy being in the squad and that Rosemary was in it with me. We wore our uniform to school every Monday, so each weekend I had to polish the brass, iron out the wrinkles in my skirt and polish my shoes. I thought it looked amazing, and I was very proud of myself. I really felt important walking around school with that uniform on, especially when the underclass girls would stare in anticipation of one day being an ROTC Sponsor, too. That was by far one of my best high school memories.

Not long after school started, one Sunday after church some of our members planned an outing to a picturesque part of the desert that had huge sand dunes. We rode in several cars for the hour or so drive out there. I was with my friend Shirley and some of the youth group. After we ate our sack lunches, we spent the rest of the afternoon sliding down the dunes on pieces of cardboard. We were having a really good time. I had not realized that one of the new guys at church had been watching me with an interested eye. Well, while we were sitting around resting, he came over and sat down beside me. His name was Russell. He inquired if I was having a good time and we made small talk. He was very nice to me and cute, too. But I could tell he was several years older than I was. As we talked more, I discovered that he was from up East and had already gone to college for a couple of years. He was now in the Army and was twenty-four years old. I was only seventeen, but I was very impressed with him, and he really seemed to like me. We spent the rest of the afternoon together having fun playing in the sand dunes. It was getting dark, so we all went to the cars we had come in. He asked if he could ride home with me, so my friend Shirley switched with him. It had been a long time since I had felt that much excitement. He put his arm around me and held me close, and I felt safe. We rode in the backseat, hardly talking, just enjoying the moment. When we were about halfway to town, he turned my face to his and kissed me. I was ecstatic! It was so wonderful to feel emotions of happiness again instead of the usual feelings of depression and darkness. When we arrived back at the church Shirley's parents were there to pick us up.

Russell wrote down my phone number and said he would call. I was on cloud nine! On the way back to my house, I was telling Shirley all about what happened in the car with him. She was excited for me because she was already dating one of the Army guys from church. I could hardly sleep that night thinking about the glorious day I had. When I finally dozed off, I did not have any bad dreams. The next day I could not wait to get to school to tell Rosemary all about Russell. We giggled about it all day. I felt so alive again, but negative thoughts kept bombarding my mind, trying to drag me down and burst my bubble. I would hear, "He won't call you. Do you really think he cares anything about a high school kid? He has a girlfriend back home, or he's already engaged or even married!" I was at war with my thoughts, and by the end of that day they were winning. Needless to say, when I got home from school, I was in a totally different state of mind than I had been that morning. Then an hour later the phone rang, and it was Russell! Joy flooded over me like an ocean wave. He said he had thought about me all day. When he asked if I had thought about him, I could not tell him about all of my crazy ones, I just answered, "Of course!" He wanted to go out the next night, but I guess he forgot about school nights, so I couldn't. Instead, he made plans for a movie Friday night. He was so in charge and mature. I loved it! This was actually the first time I had a boyfriend with a car and money for a real date. I so hoped this was the beginning of a long-lasting relationship, so I could be happy forever. He called me every day that week until the night of our date finally arrived. Russell was such a gentleman, opening my car door and other doors. He bought us popcorn and a drink at the movie, plus he enjoyed having his arm around me. After the movie we walked around downtown just holding hands and talking. The night was beautiful, and I was incredibly happy. It had been such a long, long time since I had felt so much peace of mind. We stopped and sat on a park bench and he kissed me tenderly. Then again in the car and again when he saw me to my door at home. I loved kissing him and could not wait to do it again. Amazingly, he said he wanted to go out again the next night if I wanted to. "He likes me! He really likes me!" I thought. I was so excited! That night was the beginning of many more wonderful times together with someone who made me feel important and loved. I had a new supplier.

My relationship with Russell was an incredible time in my life. He deeply cared for me and wanted to be with me whenever possible. Because of school our time was usually limited to the weekends, so we were together Friday, Saturday, and Sunday. Whether we were bowling, skating, going to movies or meeting his friends from base, we were always having fun. On Sunday, he would pick me up for church and sometimes we would go out to lunch afterwards. Occasionally, he would have lunch at my house, but he really didn't like to because he did not care for my mom. She was not particularly crazy about him either. She felt he was too old for me, and she did not like the fact that she could not push him around. I absolutely loved being with someone more mature, who knew how to plan things to do, and I always felt safe with him. But along with that maturity, came an experienced man in the area of sex. But nothing had changed in me. I was still determined to be a virgin when I got married. Fortunately, Russell respected that. However, that did not stop us from getting as close to the actual act as we could. Until my relationship with Russell, except for that horrible event in the summer, my physical experience with a guy had only been kissing. Now I had entered the erotic world of maximum petting, and I could not get enough. The emotional high I felt was like a love drug. Russell was glad I was always ready for more, but he never forced himself on me; he was very patient and gentle. Our initial trysts started off with some heated making out sessions at the drive-in movie. Then after dating a while, we would find secluded places to park where we could go further. I could not wait to get that amazing feeling I had when Russell would gently caress my body, taking me to heights of ecstasy I never knew existed. I don't know how he survived all those make out sessions without pressing me to go all the way. He must have taken a lot of cold showers when he got back to the base. But in actuality, Russell's desire was to make me happy in all we did. So, our intimate encounters were always more about satisfying me than for him. I had never had anybody give me such unselfish attention in any area of my life. I was floating on air! My needing-to-feel-loved meter was overflowing! I had absolutely no thoughts or concerns that this relationship would ever end.

We had dated for a few months, and other than an occasional football game we never attended any of my school functions. But now, I was to be a part of the ROTC Military Ball where we had to wear formal gowns and long white evening gloves. We would be introduced individually as we were escorted into the ballroom by one of the ROTC Cadets who would be decked out in his dress uniform. It was a big deal! Fortunately, the Cadet did not have to be my date, so Russell was excited to go with me to such a gala. My family did not have a lot of money, so we borrowed a pretty fuchsia colored formal from my mom's friend Kathleen. Her daughter had only worn it once. We still had to buy the long white gloves and new shoes. Russell had bought a new suit for the occasion, and when he picked me up, he had another surprise. He handed me a beautiful velvet covered box, and when I opened it there was a gorgeous rhinestone necklace and bracelet set. After fastening the necklace for me, he pinned a beautiful corsage on my dress, and the surprises were not over. I was shocked to the max when Mom and Dad pulled out a big box with a big bow on top and said it was an early Christmas present. I could not believe my eyes when I opened the box to find a fur mouton jacket! They were all the rage. Everybody had one, and I had wanted one forever. That was so unlike my parents. They were always reasonably generous at Christmas, but they had never showed such an act of planned kindness and surprise. I felt like Cinderella going to the ball. The moment was incredible when I walked out to be introduced along with my Cadet. Across the ballroom, I could see Russell proudly smiling at me. We had a sit-down dinner then dancing to a live orchestra. The evening was all so high class. Russell was a big hit with all my friends. They had never really got to know him before because we usually hung out with his Army buddies or our church friends. We had amazing fun at the Military Ball. After leaving, we parked at a scenic spot that overlooked the city in order to enjoy the night view and submerge ourselves in the happiness of the evening. Russell's kisses were so gentle, but we did not even go beyond kissing. It would have ruined a wonderful moment. Then he reached into his pocket and pulled out a small envelope. "What's that?" I curiously asked. "Patience, you'll see." He grinned as he opened the envelope and pulled out a little pin of some kind. He pulled back my jacket and proceeded to anchor the little pin to my dress. "What are you doing?" I laughed. Then Russell began to explain, "You already know I spent two years in college. Well, I was also in a fraternity. And whenever we had a special girl in our life, she would be *pinned*. So, if you would accept this, I would like you to wear my fraternity pin. "Oh, my gosh!" I thought. "I had never heard of such a thing. And, he considered me his special girl!" I was speechless. I gave him the biggest kiss ever. I felt incredible! He put both arms around me and held me tight. Then he held my face in his hands and kissed me ever so softly. "It's getting late. I had better get you home." I wished we could have frozen that moment in time and never left there. It was certainly one of only a few happy occasions that I was able to wallow in long enough to make it a memory. When I got home Mom was asleep, so she could not start something that would ruin the evening. I actually got to go to bed completely happy. My life was finally worth living, and I could see nothing but a bright future ahead. I was going to have a lasting relationship and never be alone again.

The following Monday at school I proudly wore Russell's fraternity pin on my sweater, close to my heart. I would wait until I was at school to pin it on, so I wouldn't have to answer a gambit of questions from my mom, which would inevitably lead to an argument. I felt like something special for a change, dating a college man. No one else had a fraternity pin, not even the popular girls. Life was really good. We continued dating through the holidays and into the spring and unbelievably, I was still a virgin. I was very content and comfortable being with Russell. Then one night when he picked me up, he seemed more serious, like something was bothering him. We went to eat and then to a drive-in movie, but he was quieter than normal. I figured he was just real tired or maybe did not feel good. When the lights went out and the movie started, he reached over and pulled me close. I thought it was for our usual kissing session, but he just held me tight without saying anything. Starting to feel uneasy I asked, "Is there something wrong?" His hesitation to speak was an eternity. I was worried about him. Finally, he said, "I have orders to go to Vietnam." I cried, "No, no, no, that cannot happen! Everything is so perfect! We are committed to each other! I am wearing your pin!" I was hysterical! Shock and panic filled my entire being. Going to Vietnam was like signing your death certificate. I started crying and crying. Thoughts raced through my head, "This cannot be true, not again, and Russell's news is a hundred times worse. I will not make it without him! I must have our intimate moments together! If I don't have his loving tender touch, I will not survive!" As Russell held me tight, I lamented, "We are so happy, and we have been together almost the whole school year. Why do terrible things always happen to me? They don't happen to anyone else I know. And we have plans for the Senior Prom and graduation parties. It is just not fair!" I could not stop crying as Russell lovingly squeezed me tighter and tighter. Why am I always losing guys I really care about? And with Russell I was losing so much more than I ever had before. It was a horrible night! At the movie we had hardly kissed. We had just hugged each other tight and talked. When he took me back home, we were both so upset that neither of us thought about being careful where he parked the car. We usually parked a few houses down from my house, so we could have our intimate goodnight kisses without accidentally being seen. But that night, Russell unconsciously parked right in front of my house. It was late, and I could see that all the lights were out inside. Russell lovingly told me to keep his pin close to my heart. Then he told me he had to leave in one week. My life was shattered into little pieces. He said he was going back home for one week to be with his family and then on to Vietnam. This was possibly our last night together. I wished I had never been born. Why was God punishing me? So there in front of my house, we began to passionately kiss. Then, lost in our heartbreak, we continued our usual intimacy. As he laid me down on the seat, we were both a million miles away from reality, just loving on each other. I had no idea how long we were in the car. Neither one of us wanted to stop, or worse, have to leave each other. Finally, his maturity and common sense took over and sadly, we had to get out of the car. As we slowly walked up to the front porch, we longingly held on to each other. We were about to step on to the porch when all of a sudden, my mom came storming out of the front door and screaming at the top of her voice. She was cussing at me and calling me a slut and calling Russell a SOB. I thought, "What in the world? She had to have been sitting there watching us and waiting for us to finish! There was no other explanation for her angry words and as to the timing of how fast she came out that door! Why didn't she come out to the car and make a scene? Was she getting a thrill watching us?" She yelled at me, "I always knew you were no good, staying out to all hours of the night!" She grabbed my arm and screamed, "Get in the house!" When she jerked my arm to drag me into the house Russell was furious and pulled me back and stepped between us. Wow! I had never had anyone, not even my dad, defend me before, especially against my mom. He yelled, "If you do anything to hurt her, I will take her back home with me!" My mom screamed at him, "I will kill her before I will let you take her away from here!" Confused, I thought, "She would kill me and not him?" That did not even make good sense, but was so like her to go after me first. If she would kill me, why would she care if I left with him? So crazy! By now Mom was screaming in his face, "Get off my porch before I call the police!" I was trembling as I pulled on his arm and said it will be okay, I'll go in. I managed to give him a quick kiss and ran into the house. I stormed to my room and was shutting the door when my mom violently pushed it open. She was still going on and on running me down and condemning Russell. Then she finished with, "And, I never want you to see him again!" I screamed back at her with tears flooding my eyes, "Well, I am sure you will be very happy because he is leaving for Vietnam, and he will probably die! Now get out of my room!" Incredibly, she turned around and left and shut the door. I imagined that she was on the other side of the door grinning and basking in her victory. I hated her so much! In the days that followed Russell was able to call and check on me a few times, but we were never able to see each other again before he left. Then he called me from his parent's house before he was to leave for Vietnam. He promised he would write. I thought to myself, "Here we go again. How long would it be before I get a Dear Jane letter." But this time, there was something different about our impending separation. I had Russell's fraternity pin to hang on to, and that gave me hope for our future. Somehow, having that pin gave me a much needed sense of security and kept me from having my usual withdrawal panics. All Russell had to do now was stay alive.

Seven

It's Over

I had no idea how I was going to get through the last couple of months of school and then graduation. It was not supposed to be like this. These last days of high school should have been joyfully exciting and full of fun memories as this chapter of my life came to a close. Considering the way my life usually digressed, I guess I should have expected it. After all, my entire existence was just one big disappointment after another. It seemed as if everyone around me was bubbling with anticipation and plans for the future. I had no future. I was an emotional wreck and the heavy load of the accelerated classes was wearing me down. There were so many term papers due and a lot more tests, plus extra practice time with the ROTC Drill Team in preparation for a competition. I was very stressed and depressed. I felt like I was on the verge of a nervous breakdown. Even the letters I began to receive from Russell did not help. I was still so tired and alone. Then as if my life could not get any worse, about six weeks before the end of school my world was rocked again. It all started when my chemistry teacher had to have an operation. He was a very hard teacher, but a good one. I always made an A in his class. We ended up with a lenient substitute teacher for two weeks. I had not even noticed that I wasn't studying chemistry as much as usual because our substitute was not as demanding as our regular teacher. I just enjoyed having a little less stress in my life. Well, our teacher came back near the end of our next to the last report card period. He returned as tough as ever, but for some reason I had a difficult time readjusting to his aggressive teaching style. He piled on homework and tests, and when the report cards came out, I had made a C in Chemistry! I was beyond devastated. I had never ever made a C in all my school years! Even in high school with four years of accelerated classes the majority of my grades were all A's. I anguished in thought, "All these years of hard work down the drain. Now I will never make the top ten percent of the class!" Why was it that everything in my life always had an unhappy ending? Russell was gone, top ten was gone, we lost our drill team competition, and I was extremely despondent.

I started to take solace in some movies that were popular at that time. The plots were about teens who were wild, smoking and drinking and running with gangs. They were so opposite of me I found them enticing. I began to live vicariously through those films to escape my reality. At night, in my bed, I would imagine myself as one of the gang member's girlfriends. I felt freedom in pretending I was a bad girl. I would make up all kinds of stories in my head about being a juvenile delinquent like the kids in the movies. The love scenes back then were rated G compared to today's R ratings, but they had enough influence that caused me to act out sexual fantasies on myself. I would pretend I was with a really rebellious boy, and we were doing what Russell and I used to do. Oh, how I missed Russell. My imagination was so vivid that I could arouse the same feelings I had with him and took myself to the same sexual highs. I felt relaxed afterwards, so I did it often, like taking a drug. In essence, I was living with an alter ego because I was still a good girl by day and a wild teen rebel by night. Then one night something happened that utterly terrified me. That day had been very stressful at school, Mom had been on my back all night, and I had finished a load of homework. My mind and body were exhausted, and my heart was still broken. When I finally went to bed I began to drift off into my imaginary world, but something was very different in my room. There was an eerie presence that made my skin crawl. It was nothing you could see, but I was extremely nervous and fearful. I tried to stay in my pretend world of rebellion, but I could not concentrate. Then all of a sudden, and I was not dreaming or asleep, the walls of my room literally began moving and were closing in on me. I was plastered to my mattress in terror! I could not scream or move. I just stared in horror as the walls slowly moved closer and closer! My heart was pounding with unimaginable fear and panic when suddenly, I was jerked from my bed, and I found myself running to the bathroom. No one was there with me. I was breathing heavy and sweating. "What just happened?" I gasped. Amazingly though, I immediately no longer felt afraid. I was completely puzzled as to how, or who removed me from my bed. The best I could come up with was it must have been one of those angels I had heard about in church. I was soon calm enough to return to my room where the walls had moved back into place. I still had many questions in my head when I crawled back into bed, but I was able to go to sleep without anxiety or fear and without my usual sex fantasies. That night brought an end to my alter ego, the imagined stories, and my self-satisfying activities. And, the walls of my room never moved again. I was totally ignorant of the evil plan to destroy me and take my soul to hell and was equally unaware of another power that plucked me out of my room just in the nick of time. The old saying "What you don't know won't hurt you" is completely untrue. What you don't know can kill you!

I never shared that experience with anyone because it was all so bizarre. Who in the world would believe such a thing? If I had told that story to anyone, they would have probably locked me up in the looney ward for sure. At school my Senior year was racing toward an unwanted ending. I worked harder than I ever had for the last six weeks of chemistry. Even though I finished all my finals with flying colors and garnered straight A's on all my last report cards, that awful C was still looming over my dream of top ten percent. Nothing in my life resembled what I had pictured for my graduation, plus I had no idea what I wanted to do after high school. Even though I was on the College Route, I had no idea how to get there. College was never mentioned by my parents and school counselors just assumed anyone on that Route was going to college. In one way I was sick and tired of studying, then in another way I wished the year would never end. Time was running out, and my life was piling on top of me. I was deeply depressed over probably ruining my chance at the top ten percent and over not having anyone to take me to the Senior Prom or the after-graduation party. But I had become friends with one of the couples renting from my parents. He was in the Army and neither of them were much older than I was. They said there was this guy they knew from the base that would for sure go to the Prom with me if they asked him to. I was desperate, so why not. They had us both over for dinner so we could meet. He was very cute, a little shy, and short like me. He looked just like an actor of that era named Audie Murphy. He would make a perfect prom date, so we made our plans for that night. I began to feel somewhat better about the end of my Senior year. I was very relieved that I was going to the Prom, and I was able to buy my own formal this time. The one I picked out was a beautiful pale aqua blue color. The big night turned out to be major fun even though my date was the quiet type. Afterwards, we made plans to go to the much-anticipated graduation party to be held after the ceremony. I was still sad that Russell was not with me for the parties, but at least I was getting to go. Every day was busy with either trying on graduation gowns, getting our Senior pictures made, going to yearbook signing parties, or practicing for the graduation ceremony. During this time, for some reason, Rosemary and Shirley and I started hanging out with a new friend, Brenda. We began spending most of our limited spare time at her house playing with her Ouija board. It was my first exposure to its mystic manipulations. We would spend hours asking the board silly questions about our love life, our future, or about other people. When we first started using it the answers were short and silly, and we spent a lot of the time laughing. But as time went on, the board seemed to get more serious. One day we kept asking it, "Is (girl's name) going to marry (boy's name)?" We continued asking the same question with probably twenty or more different combinations of names. The board repeatedly answered, "No, No, No." Then a very strange thing happened that brought our bantering to an eerie halt. The board spelled, "Stop fooling around with me." We all just froze and stared at each other. Then Brenda laughed and said, "Ask it something different." So, we all laughed nervously and continued playing. Then one time it told me if I married Russell, I would have a miscarriage. It also told me I would meet my husband at the bowling alley. I figured that was a lucky guess since I practically lived at the lanes. All of us got really good at letting the disk move easily from letter to letter. However, Brenda had an unusual deeper connection to the board, almost a supernatural bond at times. She was not Hispanic, but she could speak Spanish fluently, and most of the words the board spelled out for her were in Spanish. Now Rosemary was Hispanic, but it never spoke to her in Spanish, only Brenda. Then our sessions with the Ouija board became even more scary when Brenda asked it questions, and the disk would move without her touching it. All she had to do was hold her hand over the disk, and it would begin to move and spell out words. That completely freaked us out! After the board's disk moved on its own and spelled out letters in Spanish that called Brenda a witch, we all decided enough was enough. Brenda took a hammer to the board and the disk and beat it into little pieces and threw it in the outside garbage can. Unfortunately, that would not be the last time in my life that I would seek answers to my problems through wrong avenues.

Finally, the end of school arrived. I had been inducted into the Senior National Honor Society, but I was still worried about the top ten. Condemning thoughts in my head kept telling me, "There is no way you made it." Then the day came when the morning announcements were to include naming the Top Ten Percent. I could not sit still at my desk. I kept thinking, "I had never worked so hard for so long or wanted anything so bad." I knew that I would suffer complete devastation if all those years were swept away at the last moment. I prayed, "God, if you are up there, please let me have this." I heard my heart pounding in my chest. Since the names were called alphabetically, I knew who would probably be called before me because she was very smart. Closer and closer they got to her name. I thought, "Please. Please!" As I expected I heard them call her name. I squeezed my desk so tight and waited an eternity. Then I heard my name! I did it! I did it! I finally accomplished a desire in my life and this was huge! Best of all, I would be wearing that beautiful white cap and gown when I received my diploma. I was the happiest person on earth and very proud of myself. Even my parent's mild reaction to the news did not burst my bubble that day. I had worked unbelievably hard for four long years and finally had achieved success. Several days later I woke up to a bright blue morning sky and perfect weather for Graduation Day. We had to go to the school that morning for one more run through the ceremony. Rosemary, Shirley and I were absolutely reeling with anticipation. I had bought new shoes and a real cute party dress to wear under my graduation gown. As I looked into the mirror in my room I felt pretty and so overjoyed. Months before, I thought this day would be a disaster, but everything seemed to be working out. The guy I went to the prom with and my friends from our apartments were all dressed up and ready to follow my parents to the school stadium. My date actually had his own car, so I rode with him. We were both looking forward to the after-graduation party. It was all so exciting! When we marched on to the football field to the sounds of Pomp and Circumstance, I spotted them all sitting in the stands. Even though I never heard my parents say they were proud of me, I was proud of me. There I sat on the front row with the Top Ten Percent students and wearing my beautiful white gown. I was on cloud nine! We had a pretty large class of almost four hundred students, so needless to say it was a very long ceremony. Finally, all the regular students were finished and the principal made a short speech about the accomplishments of being in the Top Ten. Now it was our turn to walk the stairs to receive our diplomas and switch our gold tassels. That moment was so amazing!

After the ceremony was over, we had to go turn in our caps and gowns. Everyone was extremely excited, hugging everybody and anxious to get to the party. I told my friends I would see them later. Then I went to the stadium to find my parents, the other couple, and my date for the party. Even my parents seemed a little excited; they were smiling. My apartment friends hugged me and handed me a present, and then I didn't see their friend, my date. I asked, "Where is he?" I knew he had been sitting in the stands with them. She said, "I am so sorry. He left when you all stood up right after the speech about the Top Ten Percent." "What! Why?" It was as if I had my legs knocked out from under me. I asked in shock, "Why did he leave?" She answered, "I do not want to tell you." "Please tell me," I begged. "He said you are too smart for him. He said he doesn't want to see you anymore because he is not smart enough to be with someone like you." Confused I cried, "How can anyone even think like that?" Isn't that just like the devil to knock you down when you feel the best about yourself. At a time when I had just accomplished my first dream come true. I was speechless as tears began to roll down my cheeks announcing another heart-breaking moment in my life. I was beyond incredibly fractured inside, but the whole thing was so ridiculous there was nothing I could say. I was in such mental shock that it never even occurred to me to just go on to the celebration by myself. All my friends would be there. So instead of being on my way to the party with my date, I was silently riding home with my parents. Here I was in my beautiful party dress and thinking, "What is this with me and being happy? It never lasts very long. All the other graduates are doing great, ready to party and have fun. Why me? Did I have a sign that's always on my back that says 'Kick Me'? Would my misery ever end?" Of all the desires I'd ever had since the day I was born, the only one that had ever resulted in an actual completed happy ending was achieving the Top Ten Percent. But now, that joyous moment was even destroyed by losing my date because I was too smart. You just cannot imagine how tired I was getting of always having my happy times crushed or broken like a piece of glass. When we got home, I quietly went to my room. I was so very, very sad. I stood looking in the mirror at myself in my pretty dress, big tears flooding my eyes. I was completely numb. Just hours ago, I was so happy. Now it is all over, no retakes. I just stood there for what seemed an eternity. Then a most unimaginable moment happened that I had never experienced before. My mom came to my door, stood there a second, and with a never before seen look of compassion on her face and empathy in her voice she asked, "Would you like for us to take you bowling?" I was so touched that she was actually displaying care and concern for me and obviously felt sorry for me, I said yes. That was the first and last time she ever did that, but God knew I really needed it that night. I changed my clothes and all three of us went bowling. Daddy bought me supper at the lanes, we bowled several games and had a reasonably good time. But the whole evening, I could not help thinking about all the fun my classmates were having at the graduation party. I went to bed realizing a huge chapter in my life had just closed with a bang and a thud. And I was tired, so unbelievably tired. At that moment the only plan I had for myself was to sleep late every day from then on. As I drifted off, I found solitude in thinking that maybe somewhere deep down inside of her, my mother really did love me.

The day after graduation felt very empty. I slept until two o'clock in the afternoon. There was really no reason to get up. My secure world of being in school was gone, Russell was gone, and the new guy was gone. I figured I might as well stay in bed and pull the covers up over my head. I had no plans for the future which still puzzles me to this day. I had just graduated in the top ten percent of my class, and not one person had ever mentioned anything to me about going to college. I knew that was not anywhere on my parent's radar because they did not grow up in a culture that promoted college. And, the people they hung around with were not products of higher education, to put it nicely. But you would have thought a school counselor or teacher or somebody would have made sure I had applied for scholarships and was ultimately enrolled in a college. I don't know if the reason they did not check on me was because they assumed I was focused on college since I was in the College Route classes. I guess they thought a person in the National Honor Society and Top Ten Percent would certainly have college plans. In hind sight, I felt as if I had fallen through the cracks. So, with no guidance or encouragement, college was not something I even considered. Isn't that strange? In high school I took the difficult courses because I loved the work, the challenge, the learning, and the solitude it brought me at home. And of course, the white cap and gown. I had poured myself into school so much that by the time I graduated I was completely burned out. I did not want to see another book or take another test. However, even though I was in that state of mind, I cannot help but think how different my life might have been if a guidance counselor had taken the time to help me. I might have realized that after a summer rest period going to college would be so much different than high school. But of course, that did not happen. So, I guess I really had no one to blame but myself.

Anyway, Rosemary called me the day after graduation and wanted to know why I was not at the party. The only words I could say was, "Don't ask." My mom's compassion did not last long. Within a few days she was back to constantly nagging me about something. The next month I turned eighteen, and I needed to find something to do to get out of the house. I had to find another sanctuary. Rosemary was not going to college either, so we talked a lot about finding a job. Mom overheard me on the phone one day as Rosemary and I made plans to go downtown together and apply at several different places. When I hung up, she could not miss an opportunity to put me down, "You will never be able to work, you can't get up in the morning. On top of that, what would you do? You don't know how to do anything. You will never be able to hold down a job." By now, I was really good at ignoring her, and besides that, I had gained tremendous confidence in myself through all my accomplishments in school. So even though her insults still hurt me deep down inside, I did not let them stop me. In a few days Rosemary and I got dressed up and ventured out into the world of business. In those days it took foot work to find a job. We went from place to place and filled out applications at the phone company, the gas and electric companies, and a few other large businesses. We were exhausted and our feet hurt. A couple of weeks went by and no word from anybody for either one of us. Then Rosemary called to tell me about her neighbor who worked at a large bank downtown, and they were hiring. The next day she and I went back downtown to apply at that bank. Lo and behold, they called us both the next day! Rosemary and I figured her neighbor had put in a good word for us. We went for our interviews the following day, and we were both hired on the spot! We could not believe they actually wanted people with no prior experience. The man I talked to kept asking me if I was sure I was not going to college in the fall. He believed that with my impressive school record I was just looking for a summer job. He was another person that could have steered me toward a different path and influenced me to go to college. But of course, he was looking for a good candidate for the job and I was one. So, I kept assuring him that I was not going to college, and he gave me the job. Rosemary and I were so excited that not only were we hired, but we would still be together at the bank and in the same department. When I told my mom I was hired by a bank, she looked majorly surprised because she did not think anyone would want me, especially that quick. It had only been a month since graduation. She said, "Well, I don't know how you are going to get up in time to get there, you barely could get up for school. And, I am not driving you downtown every day, and your daddy cannot take you. So, you will have to catch the bus which means you will never make it to work on time." Even though I always tried my best to just let her typical condemnations go in one ear and out the other, I could not help but be deeply scarred from years of negative brow beatings. Now I hoped to leave those scars hidden, tucked away in the annals of my past. On the horizon, I could already see my freedom from my mother's critical spirit. And it felt awesome! What Mom did not know was that Rosemary and I already had the bus schedule and planned to ride together. She lived a few blocks up the hill from me, so she would get on first, then the bus would come to my stop. Since I was not doing homework anymore, I could go to bed earlier and getting up in the morning would be no problem. I was so excited to start my new job and earn my own money and to declare my independence!

A week later Rosemary and I began our daily commute to our new adventure. We soon began our training for the check processing department of the bank. They preferred you being a novice, so they could teach you from scratch the way they wanted things to be done. I began learning the ten key adding machine and would spend almost the entire day keying in long lists of numbers hoping the end total would be right. I had to learn it without looking at the numbered keys. Also, part of the day I would help out in the mailroom. My boss in the checks department was an older man who chain smoked and was rumored to be a heavy drinker. I was not quite sure how to take him because sometimes he was so serious and gruff, but other times he could be really funny. However, as time went on, I realized he was just a lonely old man who had been divorced several times with no children. The girls in his department were like his kids. Every morning though when he walked in the door you would have to wait and see what his mood would be for the day and act accordingly. But his bark was worse than his bite. He was really just a big Papa Bear. His main objective each day was to balance the work as early as possible so he could get to the local bar. That was great for us though because we left early, too. We hardly ever worked the full eight hours, but got paid for the whole day. On a rare occasion we were out of balance and we had to stay until we found the mistake, no matter how long it took. And there was no overtime. That was the tradeoff for all the early days.

After perfecting the ten key adding machine, I graduated to the big check processing machine which would be my job for several years. We sorted thousands of checks from banks all over Texas and the surrounding states. Every day each of us would enter hundreds of checks and amounts and rubber band them into batches. The machine printed an endorsement date on the back of the checks showing they had been processed by our bank. The longer I worked the machine the faster I got and the more checks I could process in a day. We had several check processing machines and all the batches had to balance to a grand total. I felt a sense of accomplishment every day after everything balanced and was sent off to the mailroom. When I received my first paycheck for $95.00 for two weeks, I thought I was rich. This was the early sixties, and that was good pay for a bank. I opened a checking account, a savings account, and a Christmas Club account and had money left over to spend. I even offered to pay Mom some money each month, but she was totally offended. I also told her I wanted to start doing my own laundry and learn how to cook. You would have thought by her reaction that I had just slapped her in the face. Since none of my requests were accepted, I just thought, "Oh well, I tried." I always seemed to have plenty of money. The bank had a subsidized cafeteria with amazing food at a very low price. Sometimes Rosemary and I would go out for lunch and then window shop. We had a favorite seafood place and an incredible Italian restaurant we frequented. Even though she and I were still thin, we could each down a medium pepperoni pizza, three or four pieces of mouthwatering garlic bread, and several glasses of Pepsi. We must have had enormous metabolisms because we did not feel stuffed and never gained weight. I loved every minute of working at the bank. We actually had fun there and all the employees were like one big happy family. Many of us would get together after work or on weekends for either a backyard party, a picnic, someone's birthday, or a wedding. The bank also sponsored get togethers throughout the year like bingo parties, costume parties, Christmas office parties and a big formal Christmas dance and banquet at a fancy hotel. In all my dreams I could not have asked for a better place to work. The bank became my new source of solitude and happiness. My new sanctuary.

After we were at the bank for a few months, Rosemary started dating one of the guys from work. He began picking her up in the morning which meant I had to ride the bus to town and back by myself. When she and I rode together we talked the whole trip, so all the stops and the almost one hour it took did not seem so long. By car you could get to town in twenty minutes depending on traffic. I was getting tired of the boring commute, so I decided it was time to buy my own car. I had plenty of money in savings and had received a raise after the six-week probation period. One evening I approached Daddy with the idea, and he said he would ask around and see what he could find. He knew a lot about cars, so I trusted him to find a good one for me. Mom, on the other hand, started in again about how I would never be able to make payments or pay for gas and insurance and upkeep. I had finally perfected how Daddy stayed sane all those years by tuning her out. A couple of weeks later he told me he had found a used car in great condition that he wanted me to look at. So, the following Saturday, Daddy drove me to a car lot and led me to an adorable two-tone blue Nash Rambler. It was love at first sight. I could not help myself; I was jumping up and down and hugging him. He actually smiled. I was squealing, "I love it. I love it!" The salesman was laughing. Then Daddy said, "The only problem we might have is that this car is a standard, and you are only used to driving an automatic transmission." I exclaimed, "No, there is no problem! I will learn how to drive it. You can teach me, right?" That car was so cute and so perfect nothing was going to stop me from getting it. Daddy helped me sign the papers for the title and the payments and the car was mine! I kept thanking him over and over. He had never seen me that expressive or excited. Of course, he had to drive my car home while I drove the family car back. Mom came out to see the car, but did not have much to say about it. Right away the driving lesson started. Daddy was so patient with me. I must have killed the motor a hundred times, but he just kept having me stop and start, change the gears and learn the timing of the clutch and the gas. I was stopping and starting, going forwards and backwards for a couple of hours at least. Finally, he felt like I could try driving off our one block street and go around the neighborhood. I was not perfect, but there was slow improvement. After many more hours of driving into the night, I felt confident enough to drive myself to church the next morning. There was not much traffic on Sunday, so it was a good test run before venturing out into Monday's madness. Fortunately, Daddy was a great teacher, and I was a quick learner, so I never had a problem in the traffic. That incredible day I spent with my daddy was so special to me. I could just sense how proud he was that I was working and being productive and responsible. And since we never got to enjoy being close because of my mom's jealousy, all those hours alone together in the car, just he and I, were priceless. I believed our love for each other grew deeper that weekend. I just wished we had been able to say the words, "I love you."

Eight

A New Love

Amazingly, it seemed as if my life was finally making sense again and going in the right direction. My mom had become less of an issue for me because I was gone all the time. Oh, she still tried her condemning zingers, but my newly found independence formed a shield around my usually vulnerable nature. My fears would periodically raise their ugly heads, but all in all I was in a better place emotionally. I had a great job, a good car and money to go out with my friends from work. Mostly we would go out to eat, to movies or bowling. Back then no one I knew went to clubs that much. If they wanted to have drinks or dance, we would just have a party at someone's house. I did not care much for drinking because I had been around drunks all my life. I mostly enjoyed dancing and the backyard parties always had awesome food. One night a few of us decided to go bowling. Rosemary's new boyfriend was in the Air Force, and he and some of his friends were going to meet us there. We got a couple of lanes side by side, and the competition was on. We all laughed a lot and picked on each other in fun and had a wonderful time. During the evening I noticed there was one of the Airmen paying extra attention to me. His name was William and he was twenty-two. When we finished bowling, he asked me for my phone number. I said I would give it to him with the understanding that I already had a boyfriend that was in the Army and stationed in Vietnam. William would tell me later on that when I told him I was basically unavailable I became a challenge to him. There was so much fun to be had with the freedom of being a working girl I had decided I would date guys, if asked. But, nothing serious at all because I was still wearing Russell's fraternity pin. Well, it was not long before William called and asked me to go downtown to dinner and a movie. I said okay with thoughts no different than going out with a girlfriend; it was just something to do. At dinner we talked a lot. He told me all about his family in Central Texas. That was the first plus on his side, he was a Texan. He was jovial, and I felt comfortable with him. William was just a down to earth good old country boy who liked hunting and fishing. A complete opposite of Russell who was a somewhat polished college man and a serious type from a successful farming family on the east coast. Poor William never even finished high school because he had to go to work to help his widowed mother. Russell intended to finish college, get a high paying job and live the good life. I found William curiously interesting. After our date, when he took me to the door, he gave me a peck on the cheek and said he had fun and would call me soon. I said okay and bye. Again, I thought he was nice and might be a friend to have fun with.

I was still writing letters to Russell, but of course, I did not say anything about dating. He had enough on his mind in that dangerous place. I did not want him worrying about me. If he survived Vietnam, Russell would be back in the states in a little over a year. His letters never spoke of any future plans for us, just mostly how much he missed me and how important my letters were to him. I was about to sit down to write Russell when the phone rang, it was William. He sounded so cheerful as he told me about his week at the base. Russell never talked about his work or what went on at his base. Our dates were just about enjoying that moment in time and having fun being with each other. Not that there was anything bad about that, but compared to the conversations with William, Russell's verbal interaction with me seemed limited. After a few more dates with William, I found myself actually looking forward to the next one. So, we began to see each other more and more.

Another attribute on the plus side for William was he did not mind hanging around the house with my parents. He was not exactly fond of my mom, but he tried to treat her with respect. His mama raised him right. William just adored my dad and loved to spend time with him. He would come over and help Daddy with the yard work or help him work on the cars. William was so much like my dad in as much as he knew how to fix anything. He would help Daddy cookout, and he really liked my mom's cooking. Our neighbors teased my parents, "You had better watch out. You know what is next when the boy hangs around your house helping you out." I assured them that was not the case. They didn't know I was still writing to Russell and wearing his pin. Besides, there was a couple of negative traits where William was not like Russell. William was not at all romantic, and he could not dance a lick, although he tried his best. Whenever we went to a party with my friends from the bank, usually dancing was involved. That was one characteristic passed down from my parents that I really enjoyed, so I was wishing he was better at it. But William did enjoy being with my friends which was also different from Russell. Of course, my life was not the same now since I was not a high school kid anymore, but a working girl. So, in all fairness, Russell would have probably enjoyed hanging out with my bank friends, too. In the intimacy department, William was very different from Russell. When William and I went to a drive-in movie, we watched the show more than we made out. I thought he was just being nice because afterwards we would usually go park and kiss some more. But even then, he was not as passionate as Russell. This one night our kissing did get hot and heavy for a change when suddenly William said, "I guess you're as ready as you'll ever be." Talk about throwing cold water on a hot fire, that turned me off completely. I was not mad, but that was the most unromantic statement I had ever heard. From then on, our making out sessions seemed to decrease, but I thought that was William's way of dealing with helping me stay a virgin. Anyway, we kept on dating because we always had fun and my parents liked him.

Then one day, like always in my life, bad news barged in. William informed me that the Air Force was sending him to Vietnam. What was this? Deja vu? We had been dating a few months, but this time I did not go off the deep end. Maybe because I still had Russell on deck or maybe because the physical attention was not that passionate. Anyway, I don't know why my reaction was not the usual panic, but I still did not want to lose my source of emotional stability. I had experienced so much unhappiness and rejection in my life that sometimes in order to survive I would just withdraw from the situation, put up a wall of protection, and try to find a way to get through another unhappy ending. Even though I was shutting down on the inside, that did not keep my flesh from reacting on the outside. I was losing another supplier for my physical needs, and I was extremely upset. But then, in the midst of my tragedy, something out of the ordinary transpired. William said he had an idea he was going to implement which could keep him from going. Really? That had never happened before. Someone was actually going to try to stay in my life! I grabbed him and hugged him and excitedly wanted to know what he was thinking. He informed me that there was something called a Hardship Discharge, and he was pretty sure he could get it because of his mother's situation. She had been a widow for twenty years and had very little money. Plus, he had a sister who was mentally challenged due to a childhood accident and a brother who was married with four small children and also struggling financially. So, William was basically his mother's sole support and therefore ineligible to be sent to a war zone. In that situation he could actually leave the military with an honorable discharge. I could not believe my ears! Maybe my luck had finally changed. I did not tell him, but I began to remember what the Ouija board had said about me meeting my husband in a bowling alley. I really liked William a lot, and he was not leaving! Could he be the one?

The next day William put in for the Hardship Discharge, and it was approved within a couple of weeks. Life was finally smiling on me! Only now, William had to find a job. I encouraged him to get his GED, so he did. With that he was able to apply at several utility companies, and in a short while he was hired by the telephone company. It was amazing that everything was going so right for a change. William had been staying with a buddy from the Air Force that was now being transferred, so he had to find a new place to live. Incredibly, my parents let him rent one of their apartments that had just come available. I would get to see him all the time! It was like a miracle had happened! Everything was falling into place. I was not used to my life working out like this. It had to be fate for us to be together. By now, I had stopped wearing Russell's fraternity pin, but was still writing short letters occasionally. William and I saw each other every day since he lived right next door. We were almost like a married couple, just not living together. During the week he would come over to eat and watch TV with us. Lots of times we would go for walks to a nearby park just to be alone together. One beautiful night William and I were walking through the park holding hands, just enjoying the peace and quiet, when I realized I had actually been able to be happy for several months now. But I was always fearful that something would happen to ruin my happiness like it always had in the past. I held William's arm tightly as we walked toward some benches where we stopped to rest. We snuggled up close and kissed a little. Then out of the blue William said, "I love you." I didn't know what to say back. I had not really thought about being in love. Love was not something I was familiar with. There was no expression of love in my family. We never said, "I love you." As far as I could remember no one had ever told me that before, not even Russell. I was not sure I knew what love was much less being able to say those words out loud. So, I did not say anything back to him. I just hugged him and gave him a kiss. In the days that followed I thought a lot about my relationship with William, my past commitment to Russell and what constituted love. I knew I never wanted to be without William in my life, so that must be love. When I thought about spending my whole life with him waves of warmth filled my heart and soul. That must be love. I finally determined that all my emotions, my thoughts and my dreams for the future revolved around William, so that must definitely be love. Therefore, a few dates later I looked him in the eyes and softly said, "I love you, too." He had the biggest grin when he replied, "I was beginning to wonder." After I said those words, I felt a flood of emotions I had never experienced before. There was such a feeling of freedom in being vulnerable to someone else's love. The walls I had built around myself to protect my heart were tumbling down. It was a glorious moment and a happy memory. I had finally reached the pinnacle of everlasting love, and it felt incredible.

However, there was just one small detail that cast a shadow over our excitement. I had to write Russell and tell him I was in love with William. It broke my heart to think I had to write a *Dear John* letter to a soldier in Vietnam. But it had to be done, and I had to return Russell's fraternity pin. I rationalized the situation in my mind by thinking, "Russell never mentioned any plans for our future. And, he had never talked about love or said I love you, even in his letters." As I began to write my final correspondence with Russell, I felt so guilty. I just never liked hurting people, and I certainly hated the idea of anyone being mad at me. I had always been on the receiving end of rejection, so I knew how horrible it felt. I thought rejection was one of the most awful hurts a person could ever experience. And now, I was about to administer this terrible news to a wonderful person who had no idea it was coming. Russell had done nothing wrong to deserve this. His only iniquity was he left and did not leave my heart filled with love. I felt like an absolutely awful person. All I could hope for was that my letter would convey how sad I was that this happened to him and how much I wished he would not hate me for it. With tears in my eyes, I explained how I never expected anything like this to happen and how I had worn his pin for months, but I fell in love. I tried to make the letter short, but tender. Russell always treated me wonderfully, and I attempted to let him know how much he meant to me. Then I carefully wrapped his fraternity pin in tissue and folded the letter around it. I asked William to go with me to mail it, so he drove me to the nearest mailbox. There was a slight sense of relief that part of the breakup was over. Now I wondered if I would get a response. Weeks had passed since I sent the letter to Russell, and I had just about stopped looking for an answer. Not knowing his whereabouts over there, I hoped he had received it. If he had, I figured he was probably so hurt or mad he didn't care to write back. I tried to not spend time thinking about it because I would get sad. The way I felt about hurting Russell had nothing to do with my love for William, that was strong. I just hoped Russell was okay and that I would never ever have to cause someone to feel rejected again. Then one day I was able to stop wondering when I received a four page letter from Russell. I was apprehensive about reading it, so I asked William to be with me as I read it out loud. I was so glad he was there because Russell was very upset, and I needed William's loving support. Russell went on and on about how he thought I cared for him and how we had something special. He said the fraternity pin was a pre-engagement symbol, and he was saving money to give me a ring when he got back. I was shaking. How could I know that? He had never explained it, and he still never said he loved me. It was four pages of heartbreak. Who knew if he had told me all this before he left, would things have been different? But he had not, and I loved William and more importantly, William loved me. I knew he did because he told me. By the end of the letter, I was part hurt, part sad and part mad, but mostly I was relieved that there had been closure to the relationship. William just held me. If you remember when he and I first met, William had considered me a challenge. I was sure at that moment he felt pretty good knowing he had won the prize, my heart and my love.

Now that we had confessed our love to each other we began talking about a wedding and looked at rings. I had not mentioned any of this to my parents yet, so I could enjoy some more happy times before my mom found out. The holidays passed by without drama. William went to visit his family for Christmas, but was back for New Year's Eve. I knew I should tell my parents that we were in love, but I needed to wait for the right moment. Well, that moment came one night when William and I were on a double date with Rosemary and her boyfriend. We were riding in the back seat heading downtown for a movie. I will never understand why William decided to do what he did in that way, but I said he was not romantic. He reached in his pocket and pulled out a little box and opened it. It was an engagement ring! He made a "Shhh" motion and whispered, "Will you marry me?" I quickly nodded, and he slipped the ring on my finger. Then I squealed and scared our friends. I excitedly showed it to Rosemary. She said, "So that's why you both were so quiet back there!" I guess maybe it was kind of romantic in its own unusual way. William did always like to surprise me. That made for an exciting night of celebrating. I did not want the night to end. I never dreamed I could ever feel this kind of true happiness. I was very glad my dear friend Rosemary was there to enjoy the moment with me. So now, I had to tell my parents, but I wanted to wait until the next day so Mom could not ruin my euphoria. William and I kissed goodnight on the porch. Even though he lived right by me, I never went in his apartment. That was one of the rules issued when he moved in. But since our bedrooms shared a common wall, we never went to sleep without our special tap, tap, tap to say, "Goodnight, I love you." The next day I proudly showed my engagement ring to my parents. Daddy actually silently smiled and Mom, as expected, did not waste any time getting to her remarks. "You have no business getting married. You don't even know how to cook or do laundry." I thought to myself, "And who's fault is that?" She continued, "And besides, you are too young to get married." Daddy just quietly said, "I like the boy. Ask him to eat with us tomorrow. I'm cooking out." The next day was Sunday, and I was usually first to grab the funnies, but this time I went straight to the Society section. I read all the engagement and wedding announcements to see how I should write ours. I swooned over the wedding gowns and imagined the perfect one for me. I asked Mom, "When can we go look at wedding gowns? And, we need to get with William and set a date, so I can put our announcement in the paper." I always had naive hope that one day she would become a loving Mom. I thought surely, she would be excited to look at wedding dresses because she loved clothes. She said, "You just got the ring. Don't be in such a hurry. We have plenty of time." I told her I would like to be a June bride, and that was only three months away. We would need to reserve the church first, so we could print the invitations. Even though I had stopped going to church when I met William, I figured we would still get married in the church I had attended for about two years. I was so excited to start organizing everything. She said we would start planning soon and look at dresses. By now, Daddy was out in the backyard firing up the grill. William knocked at the front door, and when Mom let him in, she was very cold and did not even acknowledge our engagement. Then William went on outside to help my dad cook the steaks. Through the window I saw Daddy extend his arm to shake hands with William in an obvious expression of congratulations. I was excited that at least my dad seemed to be happy about our good news. As was the custom of my family, we all sat in front of the TV and ate our lunch on TV trays. The only time we ever ate together at a table was when we were at a restaurant. While we watched the New York Yankees play baseball, there was no conversation about our engagement or the wedding. After the game was over, I mentioned that William and I were going for a drive. Then my mom piped up with sarcasm in her voice, "You can't leave. If you are going to get married you need to stay here and learn how to wash dishes." She had never wanted me to do the dishes before, even when I tried to. I knew she was just being a smart aleck, but to keep the peace I told William we would go after I did the dishes. I always enjoyed doing cleaning whenever Mom would let me, so if she thought she was somehow punishing me, the joke was on her because I loved every form of household chores.

At work the next day I could finally be around people who were as excited as I was about our engagement. In the days that followed all I could think about was planning our wedding. I bought bridal magazines and read them over and over as I tried to figure out exactly how a wedding should be done. The wedding gowns were gorgeous, and it seemed that buying one was the first priority. So, I kept asking my mom, "When can we go look at wedding dresses?" I was not sure where she wanted to go or how much she wanted to spend. But she would always basically give me the same answer, "I don't know. I will let you know when I decide." Occasionally, someone would ask me if I had set a date for the wedding, but I had no idea when it would be. I could not get Mom to talk about a dress let alone a date. As usual, she was doing everything she could to make what should have been a joyous experience into a disappointing drama void of any happiness. By now it was obvious I was not going to be a June bride, and I was extremely upset and frustrated. She said my grandmother needed us to go help her. That pulled at my heart strings because I loved Grandma so much and would do anything for her. Ever since Grandpa died, she had continued to live alone at her home in central Texas, and every summer we still went to see her. This time I asked Rosemary to go with us, so I would at least have someone with me who was happy about discussing the wedding. We planned the trip for one week after my birthday. Since I was not having my wedding in June, I decided to make my nineteenth birthday the happiest one I have ever had. It started out before work with a *Happy Birthday* call from William since he left much earlier than I did. Then at the bank all the girls wished me a *Happy Birthday*, Rosemary bought my lunch, and I even received a couple of presents. After work I picked up my birthday cake which I had ordered a few days earlier. I'd never had a birthday cake or a birthday party growing up, so I decided since I earned my own money it was time to enjoy a cake, even if I had to buy it myself. Mom said I was silly buying my own cake. I asked, "Oh, were you going to get me one?" That shut her up real fast. I just kept putting the candles on and thinking, "She will never understand." About then William came in, and he looked great! We had decided to dress up and go somewhere special. As he lit my candles, I brought Daddy into the kitchen. William initiated an out of tune version of *Happy Birthday to You* with minimal participation from my parents. But to me it was a Kodak moment. I excitedly blew out all of my candles and almost cried. I had always wanted to do that. As William and I left for dinner I told my parents to make sure they ate some cake. We would enjoy some after we got back home. He took me to a beautiful fancy restaurant and then to a piano bar. Even though I could not have alcohol, I enjoyed the music. It was the most romantic night William had ever planned for us. When we got back home my parents were asleep, so I grabbed the cake and took it to William's apartment where we gorged ourselves with cake and the ice cream he had bought. It was the first time I had been in his apartment, and this time I did not care about the rules. I felt like I deserved to be there, and it made my birthday all the more special. We just sat at his kitchen table and talked for a couple of hours. Then I hurried to leave before the sun came up. That was definitely the best birthday I'd ever had.

Soon after my birthday, Rosemary and I were with my parents on our way to my grandmother's house. Rosemary had never been around my mom or dad very much, especially when they were drinking. Fortunately, the beers were minimal and my mom behaved herself. I was always thankful that Grandma's town was still *dry* which meant there was no beer available to buy in that town. My longtime friend Charlotte came over to meet Rosemary. We three walked the short distance to town to grab some food at the little cafe. We all gelled right away and had a laughing fun time. Charlotte was excited about my engagement, so we talked a lot about wedding stuff. We decided to drive to the larger nearby town to continue the fun. It was four times the size of Grandma's town, and it was known as *The Heart of Texas*. We went back to the house to tell Mom that we were riding with Charlotte and would be back before dark. My mom said to me, "You do not have any business going to that town, you are engaged." I thought, "What in the world does going there have to do with being engaged?" Then I had a revelation. The only reason my mom ever went to that town was to drink and hook up with guys. As far as she was concerned, that was all the place had to offer. Then she came close to me, and with that smirky grin of hers she whispered, "You can go if I can go with y'all." Unbelievable! I frantically pondered, "I have got to get married soon and get away from all her craziness." In her dreams she was going with us! She knew she could buy beer there. Not happening! She began acting like she was going to make it a big issue, so to save my friends from turmoil I told them to just go without me. I was glad they did because I could just imagine what was coming next. She didn't think I would give up going with my friends, and she would get her way. So, she was mad. I just left her fuming on the front porch and went inside to be with my grandma. Rosemary and Charlotte had a great time, and I heard all about it as Rosemary and I enjoyed the peacefulness of the sleeping porch. She slept in the twin bed Grandpa used to be in. I still really missed him as much as ever.

When we got back to our home, I was determined to get the wedding plans solidified. After the fiasco at my grandmother's, enough was enough. I had to get out of that house and away from my mother to maintain my own sanity. I kept asking my mom day after day, and she would say, "Okay, we will go look at gowns real soon and decide on a date for the wedding." Finally, after almost two months more of her non-committal attitude, I was overwhelmingly frustrated. I knew William and I did not have enough money for all the necessities of a big wedding, but we were willing to try and help. I thought maybe the money was the reason Mom was balking at getting started, but when I asked her about it, she just acted offended and walked off. After exhausting all reason, one particular day I had heard enough of her negative remarks, her sarcasm and her constant refusals to make my dream a reality. I reran in my mind all the terrible moments of the past few months until I was so worked up, I decided to confront her again. I was very emphatic and demanded a straight answer when I asked, "When are we going to start planning this wedding?" She knew this time I meant business. Then with a very haughty demeanor she conveyed to me, "I have no intention of ever planning this wedding because you have no place even thinking about getting married. You both do not make enough money to live on and you are too young. Your daddy and I will not sign for you to get a license, so you had better just forget about it!" This was absolutely the worst thing she had ever done to me. I was beyond the realm of furious! She had led me on for months with her lies and coldhearted deception. My anger turned to rage, and all I wanted to do was hit her. I was out of my mind with hurt that went deeper than it ever had before. I felt violated and abused and cheated and so many emotions I could not explain them all. I was screaming at her at the top of my lungs. William could hear me from his apartment and rushed to check on me. Daddy came from outside to see what was going on. They had never seen me in this condition. I was screaming and crying so hard I was choking. I could not breathe. William just held me. Daddy seemed mad and wanted an explanation. I viciously yelled, "She lied to me! All along she lied! Constantly she lied! I hate her!" William kept holding me trying to calm me down and get some answers. Finally, I was able to tell him, "She never wanted us to get married. All these months she was lying!" Daddy was apparently surprised by this information. I told William, "Let's get married right away. Okay? I cannot stay here." Mom butted in, "I told you we will not sign for you to get married." She did not know how wrong she was. She thought I had to be twenty-one. I yelled back, "You cannot stop us, I am of legal age! I do not need your permission!" The shocked look on her face was priceless. Daddy was silent. I was so sorry I was hurting him because of her. I turned to my mom and said, "I will be gone from here as soon as possible. I am sure you will be more than glad to get rid of me." With tears still streaming down my face I grabbed William by the hand and said, "Let's go for a drive." Mom just had to have the last word, "You will never find a place you can afford to live, and you are not staying in William's apartment. You don't have anything." As we walked out the front door I thought, "Think what you want. You do not even know me."

William and I drove to a quiet place to talk. I was crushed inside. I, just like most young girls, had always dreamed of a beautiful wedding gown and walking down the aisle with my daddy. What I thought would be the happiest day of my life was ruined with arguments, lies, and disappointments. I was glad that at least William and I could go ahead and get married, but so sad that life had once again robbed me of complete fulfillment. I wanted to know if William really did want to get married right away without a big wedding. He said, "Of course." This awful chaos transpired on a Thursday night, and it so happened that a week from Monday was Labor Day with three days off from work. Perfect! We decided to get married on that Friday in order to have a short honeymoon. That was fine, but the more I thought about it I really wanted some resemblance to a church wedding and a small reception with close friends. So, that night we decided on a plan that ended up being executed very smoothly, to the amazement of my mom. The following day, Friday, William and I met for lunch and got our blood tests and applied for a marriage license. I called my church for a spot the next Friday, but they were not available. So, I tried the nearby church where Mom used to drop me off for Sunday School when I was little. They said yes. I asked Rosemary to be my Maid of Honor, and William got one of his friends to be Best Man. After work I went to the bakery and ordered a small wedding cake, then on to the florist to pick out two bouquets and two boutonnieres. William made a hotel reservation for our wedding night and even arranged for a friend to take pictures at the ceremony. When I got home later that evening, I informed my mom and dad of the date and time of the wedding. As expected, Mom replied, "Well, you can just forget about us being there. We are not going." I had the feeling she thought I would just buckle and plead, "Oh, please be there." But instead, I calmly said, "Well, that is up to you if you want to miss your only child's wedding." Then I walked out and went to my room and started packing.

The next day, Saturday, William and I left early to begin our search for an apartment. It was fortunate that in those days most places were furnished. We went to an area on the east side of town that was experiencing new growth and had a lot of choices. We found a cozy one bedroom and one bath with a very small kitchen. The price was right and the furniture was new, so we paid the first month's rent plus deposit. Then we had to go shopping for wedding clothes. William had to buy a suit and tie, and I found a beautiful white brocade dress with a fur trimmed short jacket to match. I also bought white high heels and a small white veil. We felt very proud of ourselves that we had accomplished so much in such a short time. When I returned home I did not even bother being excited to show Mom my dress and accessories. I just informed them of my new address. Mom was surprisingly quiet. Daddy was always quiet. William and I each spent the evening getting most of our things ready to move to our apartment the next day. So early Sunday morning, we began taking boxes and suitcases to our new home. Again, my mom was just watching in unusual silence. Daddy actually asked if we needed help with anything. I smiled, "Nope, we are doing good." By the time we went back to work on Monday just about everything that could be done so far was completed. I called some very close friends to invite them, plus just a few from work. One very important item I had to do that week was go to the doctor and get birth control pills. And yes, I was still a virgin and proud of it. So, all that was left to do now was pick up the marriage license, the cake and the flowers and, of course, buy William's wedding ring. It had been a whirlwind week, but everything was accomplished, and the next day was Friday and the wedding.

William and I decided to rest Thursday night, so we did not see each other. He had already moved all of his belongings to our apartment and had been staying there. I was packing up last minute items when I realized this was my last night to be in the house I grew up in. It was the final time I would sleep in that bedroom where years of some good, but mostly bad memories lingered. I thought of all the Katy Keene cut outs I had thumb tacked on my wall, so many holes. And the times I made my own paper dolls and designed clothes for them and made furniture for my doll house from magazine pages. I smiled as I pondered the tender moments when my old boyfriend Timothy and I would slow dance to dreamy records. I recalled the years I spent sitting on that bed doing homework and the many hours at my desk typing term papers. I thought of all the Elvis records I had played over and over and over again. Those were some of the good memories. I chose not to reminisce about the bad ones. I would leave those there and planned to never again have to go to bed crying. About then I was surprised when both of my parents walked into my room. That had never happened before. Mom said, "We have been talking, and we will be at your wedding tomorrow night." I was so shocked and happy I think I might have hugged them. I never knew they ever talked about anything. It was obvious the decision had come from Daddy. I had been hoping he would not miss his little girl's wedding. Everything was working out perfectly, or so I thought. Before I went to bed, I had an unexpected visitor that was not at all welcomed. I started my period. It could not have waited just a few more days! I should have remembered that there was always something that kept my happy times from being perfect. I fretted, "That is just not fair!" When I told William he just laughed. "It's not funny!" I retorted. He said, "Don't worry about it, we can just wait to have sex." "You really would wait? That would be great." William had made me feel much better because I had struggled so hard to remain a virgin, I wanted him to see that I was. Everything was perfect again.

Even though it was the day of our wedding, we both had to go to work. I just stayed there half a day, so I could go get my hair done. I also ran by our apartment to set up decorations for our small reception. As I opened our tiny refrigerator to put the Bride and Groom topper on the cake, I was actually singing. I was incredibly happy! I quickly took the flowers I needed and had to get going before William got home. I did not want to see him that day until I was dressed up and at the church. Since my parents were going now, I could ride to the church with them. Everything was right on schedule. Mom and Dad even seemed a little excited. William and I and our attendants were to meet in the Pastor's chambers first. When William saw me, his eyes got big, and he was grinning from ear to ear. That was the reaction I wanted. Sadly though, I did not get to walk down the aisle or be given away by my daddy. Instead, William and I followed the Pastor into the church from his office and onto the platform area. Then the Maid of Honor and the Best Man followed. My parents and a few friends filled the first pew. There was no wedding march or music of any kind. I had not thought about paying for an organist. But all was well, we were getting married. At the end of our short double ring ceremony and the pastor's, "You may kiss the bride," everyone in attendance was clapping and smiling, even my parents. After having pictures taken, we all caravanned to our apartment for a short reception. We cut the cake and stuffed pieces into each other's mouth and made a toast. Excitedly, we opened our cards and presents and took more pictures. We had almost everything a big wedding had, just much smaller. We had reservations for the wedding party to have dinner in the club at the hotel where we were staying that night. So, the celebration moved there. We all had the best time eating, laughing, and dancing. I was so happy to dance with Daddy, and thankfully Mom behaved herself even though she was drinking beers. I think she was flabbergasted that we actually pulled it off. It was also so wonderful to be able to share the moment with Rosemary, my best friend for over five years. The club had William and I dance a Spotlight Dance as the band played *The Anniversary Waltz*. "Oh, how we danced on the night we were wed . . ." It was all so magical. Everyone stayed until closing time then we had to say goodbye. I gave my parents a hug, and William and I went upstairs to our room where he carried me over the threshold. I never imagined I could feel so happy! I changed into my negligee; William was already in bed. Previously he had said we would wait to have sex because of my period, but he had drunk quite a few mixed drinks and was feeling rambunctious. He began making love to me. After he removed my gown, I was not sure what to do and was kind of concerned about the blood. When he proceeded to try and have intercourse, I really was not all that turned on due to the mess. There was not much foreplay, and the blood made me dry. He tried, but could not get very far because it hurt me. The bed was a horrible mess! The sheets were covered with blood, plus the towel I used to clean myself. We put a large bath towel over the blood stains and slept on the top sheet. The ordeal had no resemblance to the fairy tale wedding nights you see in the movies. But I was okay with all of it because we were finally married. The worse part was how sorry I felt for the poor maids who came to clean the room after we left. They probably thought some-one was murdered there.

The next morning at our apartment, William carried me over the threshold again. I had dishes to clean from our reception, and we needed to do laundry. Also, our refrigerator was void of food, so we had to go buy groceries. Basically, our one-night honeymoon was over. I was content though because I loved the idea of being a wife. I enjoyed cleaning and doing laundry. My favorite chore was ironing. When I learned how to cook, I enjoyed that, too. Funny thing though, the first meal I cooked for us was a partial disaster. I made William a homemade hamburger and French Fries. The burger was okay, but I did not get the oil hot before putting the fries into the pan. They managed to soak up plenty of grease before they browned. They were awful! But we pressed the grease out on paper towels, and managed to eat them. William never complained about anything I cooked, and over the years I got pretty good at it. Later that day we found a pay phone and called his mother to tell her we were married. I had never talked to her, so I was nervous. Immediately though, I realized she was the sweetest person. I told her all about the wedding and our apartment. She was extremely encouraging and loving. So, the first day of our married life turned out to be very good. It was wonderful to not feel alone and be genuinely happy because I had finally found everlasting love. I went to bed with a smile on my face and peace in my heart and so thankful to not be crying anymore.

Nine

The Newlyweds

After the fast paced three day weekend holiday it was back to work as usual. Many people at the bank were not aware that William and I had married on Friday. First thing that morning I went to the Human Resources Department to change my name and address, so by lunchtime the information had spread throughout the bank. It was a juicy gossip topic because a quick weekend wedding had convinced the grapevine that I was pregnant. It was really funny. They probably would not have believed that we had never had sex, and our wedding night was a disaster. The rumor was really aflame when I gained ten pounds in two months because of the birth control pills. But I was not the type to discuss my personal life, especially sex. I thought William and I held the record at the bank for the fastest time to get married until one lady told me that she got married on her lunch hour! How crazy is that? Anyway, everyone was very excited for us. It was an amazing day. I usually got off work earlier than William even though he started an hour before me. So, I would drop him off in the morning, and then drive back over there in the afternoon and wait in the car until he got off work. The whole time we dated William only had a Harley motorcycle and would borrow a car whenever we went out. After we fell in love, we would always use my car. William decided to sell the motorcycle, so we had only one vehicle. I did not mind the driving situation at all. The usually short wait gave me time to unwind and plan supper. I was completely happy and at peace. One day I was in our tiny kitchen cooking when I turned to see William in the living room watching the news on TV, and a flood of warmth flowed over me like a wave. I felt the most tremendous love for him just pouring out of my entire being. I had finally attained the utopia of love that I had sought for my whole life. Time could have stopped right there for all I cared. I spent a few seconds just basking in the moment before returning to my stove.

Before I knew it two weeks had passed, and I had finished my period a week ago. William had never brought up making love or tried to have sex since our wedding night. I figured since that had been such a mess, he wanted to make sure I was finished before even thinking about it. So, one evening, I shyly mentioned I had been through with my period for several days. Since he had waited so long, I had imagined that when I told him he would take me straight to the bed and make passionate love to me. Instead, he commented, "That's good to know." I asked, "Do you want to make love?" He said, "Later." Those answers were surprising to me, but since I really did not know anything about how often couples had sex, I just waited. I rationalized that maybe it should be his idea. Besides, I was happy enough without it for now. My obsessive need to be loved was being fulfilled just by being married. The one thing that did kind of bother me was the fact that since we hardly had sex on our wedding night, I did not feel as if we had even consummated the marriage. I was more than ready to get things going to make that dream come true. I began to understand that William was the type that liked to make you think he was not going to do something or was not going to get something because he really wanted to surprise you. So, I figured he was just waiting to bring it on when I was least expecting it. However, as the days passed by, I became disappointed that there was also no more kissing or hugging which I usually relied on to feel loved. I knew William was not very romantic, but short of holding hands the physical attention I needed was already lacking. By now, William and I had reached our one-month anniversary. I was still very happy even with the puzzling sex situation. We decided to celebrate with Rosemary and her boyfriend, so we went out to eat and to a club. William and Rosemary's boyfriend could order mixed drinks while she and I were still underage. Rosemary and I didn't care if we could not drink, we still had fun. The four of us partied until the club closed. Then we went to a popular truck stop for breakfast and coffee. By the time we got back to our apartment it was nearly 4:00 a.m. William was in an exceptionally romantic mood for him, so when we went to bed it finally happened! It had taken a month for him to surprise me, and it was a great anniversary gift. As time went on William's schedule for sex remained at around a once a month interval. I still had no idea how that compared to most couples. But as the months passed, I began to wonder about it. I desperately needed physical pleasure, so an absence of it had put me on shaky ground. When we dated William usually seemed to enjoy making out, so I always felt loved with all the kissing and petting. Now that we were married, that portion of our relationship only happened once a month. Other than a goodnight peck, there was no regular show of affection. I tried and wanted more, but since I had not been raised with any outward expressions of love, I guess I finally yielded to what was normal for me and stopped trying. And because my life was so much better than before I got married, I basically found satisfaction in just being on my own with a good husband by my side. I enjoyed having my own place to live in and to care for, and I especially loved not having to put up with verbal attacks and arguments. I was determined that my home would be a place of peace.

Thanksgiving was fast approaching, and I decided that for the first time in my life we were going to eat a real Thanksgiving dinner at home, our home. I invited my mom and dad for my special day. I think Mom was shocked because she had never cooked a turkey in her life. Fortunately, William knew something about cooking from his mother. Our oven and refrigerator were so small that thawing and then cooking the turkey was a real challenge. I had hardly any counter space, so preparing such a feast became a juggling act. But with William's help, we actually pulled it off. With four of us sitting at our tiny dinette table there was only room for plates and glasses, so I served from the stove. Even though Daddy was not one to say much, I believed I saw a look of pride on his face as I handed him a plate full of everything you would want to eat for Thanksgiving. Mom even said the food was good and gobbled it all up, but she just could not resist a negative comment about the gravy. They stayed and watched football on our little portable TV while I served pumpkin pie with whipped cream. Then I packed up some leftovers for them to take home. It was a truly amazing day with no alcohol and no arguments. My first home cooked Thanksgiving dinner had been a complete success! I was so proud of myself and William that we had accomplished our first family holiday dinner.

For the first time in many years, I was actually excited about Christmas coming. There was so much freedom and happiness in knowing that I did not have to spend it watching my parents get drunk in Mexico. I began shopping for ornaments and decorations for our little apartment. I was thankful that I would not have to decorate the tree by myself as I had for so many Christmases past. I was even excited about finding gifts for my parents. And even though I had not met them yet, I wanted to send gifts to William's mom and to his brother, his wife and four kids. It was wonderful to have a real family to give presents to! I had found the true meaning of Christmas because I had never before experienced such a joy of giving. William and I spent Christmas Eve by ourselves. It was so peaceful. We went out to eat and then drove around to look at lights. After we came back home, we just cuddled up on the couch with only the lights of the Christmas tree shining bright and listened to carols on the radio. I never knew life could be so good. Then we decided to open just one gift each and the rest on Christmas Day. Little did we know we had started a tradition that would last for decades. My parents had offered to take us out to eat on Christmas Day, it was Daddy's birthday. Yes, poor thing only got presents once a year. We were also celebrating Mom's birthday which had been on the 23rd of December. I told her we would like to spend the day with them, but not across the border. So, they took us downtown to a very nice restaurant we had never been to, and no alcohol was served. That was a great Christmas present in itself. Mom and Dad had a wonderful birthday lunch, then afterwards we went back to our apartment to open gifts. Daddy went back outside to their car and then came in with a big wrapped box. He turned and went outside again to return with another big box. He had grin on his face as he scooted the two large gifts over to the tree. Grinning was unusual for Daddy, but he had always been a giver. All my life he was a good provider even though we were not rich. He somehow always made me feel that I could have whatever the other kids had. I was sure he must have worked very hard to accomplish that. I also knew he was always helping other people whenever they needed him, but I never truly understood what an unselfish, generous man he was until that Christmas Day. It was not the size of the gifts or how much they cost, it was the joy on his face as he gave them to us. I always loved my daddy, but that day I realized even more what a caring and compassionate heart he kept hidden inside his stoic and gruff exterior. Our little Christmas tree dwarfed in size in the midst of all the presents. Daddy said to save the big ones for last, so we all began opening the other gifts first. Finally, it was time for the two large boxes. William had been assigned to one and the other for me. Daddy told me to go first. I could not believe what I saw in the box! It was our very own television set! We did not have one of our own. We had borrowed the little portable TV from a friend until we could save enough money to buy a new one. I jumped up and hugged Daddy's neck. I had never seen him smile so much. Then William opened his box. It was a TV stand to set it on! I was overwhelmed at receiving those wonderful gifts. Mom sat there smiling, but did not say much. William was grinning from ear to ear and could not wait to put the stand together. So, he and Daddy got to work on it as Mom and I cleaned up all the wrapping paper. In no time at all the stand was together, the TV was sitting on it, and a football game was ready to be watched. It was just that simple when you did not need cable TV. That evening while William and I sat watching our new television, I was amazed at the completion of another monumental holiday with no alcohol and no Mexico. I was so incredibly happy, and boy, was I ever wallowing in that moment and in that memory.

Without a way to get around it, New Year's Eve was upon us. And in our city the place to be on that night was Mexico's border town. There were free hats and horns, cheap drinks with no age restrictions, and dancing in the streets. My parents wanted us to go with them. Since Thanksgiving and Christmas had been my way, plus the generous gifts they had given us, we agreed to go. But I warned William, if my mom started in on me when she got drunk, we were leaving. I told my parents we would meet them at our favorite restaurant, so we would have our own car. When we arrived, I could tell Mom had already been drinking because of that look she always got on her face. Since the night William and I were married, I had managed to avoid being around her whenever she drank. I was not sure what to expect at this point since things were different now that I had not been under her roof for four months. Amazingly though, we had a very enjoyable dinner. I had my usual filet mignon, delicious as always, and Daddy paid for our dinners. We wanted to pay, but he insisted. I was proud to introduce William to all the people I had known since childhood, like the bartender who made the lime pigs and our friend who sold leather purses. It was a good thing I got to see the bartender because he told me he was celebrating becoming a U.S. citizen and would be moving across the border to work a new job. So far, the evening was going well, but I could never let my guard down. We all went straight to the club where the men played the marimba. They all met William, too. We got our hats and horns and noise makers and proceeded to celebrate the new year. Mom, Dad and William were really getting loaded. I never cared much for the taste of beer or tequila, so I only had a few mild mixed drinks the whole night. We all danced and sang and told jokes, and I was actually having a good time with my parents which was highly unusual. Mom was treating me and William just like any other couple they went out with. Then five, four, three, two, one, Happy New Year!! William and I kissed and sang *Auld Lang Syne*. It was a truly joyful moment. After everybody got through hugging and kissing it was time for the best part of the evening. I did not have to stay until the bars closed. What a freedom I felt! I asked William if we could please leave, so we said our thank yous and goodbyes and walked out as Mom ordered another round of drinks. I could hardly express how good that felt. The night air seemed to make William drunker, so I drove home. I was amazed that I genuinely had fun with my parents in Mexico. I had to steady William as he got out of the car and then helped get his clothes off and into bed. There was no hope for sex that night. So, in almost four months of marriage, I could count on one hand the number of times we had made love. And still, as far as I knew, that was normal and I was happy. I was relieved when the holidays were over, and at the same time extremely satisfied that a new precedent had been set for all future celebrations. I felt empowered by the way I had handled Thanksgiving, Christmas and New Year's. Now I was no longer a naive nineteen year old, but a married woman who could not be controlled or manipulated by her mother. Excited to see what the new year would bring, William and I settled into life as a young married couple, and it was great! We never had an argument or even a slight disagreement. Our days and weeks were very routine. We did our coin operated laundry on Sunday, I ironed on Monday, we bowled on league on Tuesday, we played Parcheesi with our neighbors on Wednesday and bought groceries on Thursday. On Friday night we usually went out to eat. Occasionally, on a weekend there would be a bank party or a backyard party to go to, or we would just hang out with friends. Sometimes on Sunday we would go eat at my parent's house and watch the game. We were kind of like an orderly old married couple who rarely had sex, but we were relatively happy.

Then in late spring William's brother informed us that he, his wife and four kids were coming to visit us as soon as school was out. Holy cow! How were we going to have room for six people! I had not yet officially met any of William's family, and now the whole bunch was going to converge on our tiny apartment and on me! I was very nervous about meeting them and their children, ages 2, 4, 6 and 7, plus I had cute breakable objects setting around. The day they were to arrive came too quick. I was almost in a panic. I thought, "At least they are staying at a motel," because our apartment was way too small for all of them. There was not even a place for that many people to sit! Then came a knock at the door, "Oh my gosh, they are here!" William opened the door and in walked the most adorable two year old girl with the biggest smile, then the four and seven year old girls came behind her. Following them was a bright-eyed, cheerful six year old boy. They all walked in with their hands behind their backs and immediately sat down on the floor. I was amazed! William's brother and his wife were still outside, and I could hear them arguing, or so I thought. But I was soon to find out that they really never argued. They just picked and fussed at each other a lot. In between it all they would cut up and sometimes laugh about it. At first that was incredibly unnerving for me, and it took a few more future visits before I could be around them without feeling uncomfortable. But through the years I grew to love everything about them, and they ended up being married over sixty years, fussing all the way to the end. I had never met another couple like them who exhibited total unconditional love to not only each other, but to everyone they knew. When William's brother and his wife finally came into the apartment, they were all smiles and apologizing for each other. After we all got introduced, his brother started asking me questions like, "So what do you see in this guy?" and started teasing me and giving me a hard time. His wife told him to stop, "You just met her." He fussed at her and she fussed back. The kids had not talked yet except to say hello. It was a very unusual encounter. But even with all that, their sweetness came through loud and clear, and I began to learn what wonderful people they were. The kids were so well behaved and polite and eventually very interesting to talk to. It all turned out to be a great three day visit. Also, in the midst of his joking around, I found out that William's brother was nothing like him in the sex department. His brother was telling about how fast they had four kids and said, "The only place for my shorts (underwear) was on the bedpost." His wife agreed, "No matter how much we fuss it never comes in the bedroom door. We always makeup before we go to bed." That little discussion was the first time I had heard a hint as to what another couple's sex life seemed to be compared to ours. Even though I was not sure if I ever wanted kids, I was wishing William was more like his brother.

That visit had gone so well I felt confident enough to meet William's mother, so we planned a trip for later in the summer. We were sort of concerned about driving halfway across Texas in my little car, so we started looking at new cars. Mom heard me asking Daddy about it and chimed in with her usual negative retort, "You cannot afford a new car. How do you think you can make car payments and pay your rent, too?" We all basically ignored her. So, with information from my daddy about how they bought their new car, William and I custom ordered the one we had decided on. We picked out the color of the car inside and out, plus the material for the seats and doors. Can you believe people used to do that? It was a common practice back then. In hindsight, the only big mistake we made was not keeping my car, so we could both have a vehicle. It never crossed our minds because two car families were not the norm in those days. We wanted to keep our payments low, so we traded in my precious little blue car in order to buy the new one. Our custom built four door sedan was gorgeous and much roomier than my old two door coupe. After we picked the car up from the dealership William and I immediately drove over to show my parents. Mom was speechless, and Daddy was really happy and proud for us. And, as it turned out, we were able to make a double payment each month and paid the new car off in half the time, much to my mom's surprise. Now that we had dependable transportation, William and I planned our summer trip to visit his mother. She and I had talked on the phone a few times, and she seemed very nice, but that was not as intimidating as actually meeting her. Even though I was so nervous during the whole drive there, when I finally met her, it was love at first sight for me. She was so kind and gracious; we became friends right away. Although she was poor, she was very rich in spirit and heart. She still lived in the old house William's father had built before William was born. It was pretty run down and lacking in many areas, but at least it had indoor plumbing. His mother was never able to acquire much in her life, having to raise three young children by herself after her husband died. I wanted to buy her everything. She would not let me do a lot, but over the years we were able to give her some comforts and surprises. I loved her very much as she became the caring mother I never had, and we remained really close friends until her death many years later.

With summer ending, Labor Day was coming soon and our first wedding anniversary. William and I decided to go stay one night at the hotel where we spent our wedding night. Maybe it was so we could have a better memory of the place. At least this time I was not in my period. Not that it mattered much though because our sex life was still only once a month or so. And just because it was our anniversary celebration, there was no guarantee there would be any that night either. We had a nice dinner, danced a little, and then went to our room. Fortunately, William was in the mood, and our first year together was fully consummated. Back at the apartment the next day, we enjoyed eating the top of our small wedding cake which I had left out to thaw. William's anniversary present to me was not very romantic. He gave me a sewing machine. I did not ask for one nor did I know a thing about sewing. But he did, because his mother had taught him how to sew. He was so excited about teaching me how to use it that I gave it a real try. It was difficult, but I bought some simple patterns and actually made a few dresses that were decent enough to wear out in public. I never really enjoyed sewing though because I was always having to take out stitches and redo stuff. After a few years of frustration my sewing was reduced to making curtains or table cloths.

Our second year together was basically uneventful except for the appearance of an injured kitten crying at our apartment door on a rainy night. The poor thing looked so pitiful and could hardly walk, so we had to take it in. We put some sand in a shoe box, gave it some milk and planned to find a home for it the next day. Yeah right, famous last words. We named her Stormy because of the heavy rain on the night she showed up on our doorstep. The vet said her pelvis was crushed, but should heal after some minor surgery. So, we inherited what turned out to be a beautiful long-haired calico that gave us many pleasant memories for years to come. As William and I approached the end of two years of marriage, our bedroom encounters had stretched to over a month apart, but I still had no clue it was not a normal relationship. I just knew I was not happy about it. I know I sounded stupid according to today's knowledge of everything, but in the mid-sixties sex was just beginning to be a topic considered appropriate to discuss. It was not until the late sixties or early seventies that the sexual revolution began to make itself known nationwide. I was and still am a very private person, so I never talked about any of our personal business with anyone. In fact, it has taken decades for me to come to a place where I could even be open enough to write this book!

Since our apartment lease would need to be renewed soon, William and I began discussing the possibility of purchasing a house. We began browsing around nearby neighborhoods to see what was available. We liked the part of town we were in, so once we picked our favorite neighborhood, we got serious about looking at some houses that were for sale. After seeing a few places with a realtor, it was not long before we found the perfect one with three bedrooms, two baths, formals and a den. The house was located on a large corner lot and had a big rock fenced backyard with an oversized semi-circle patio and a carport. It was a nice all brick home in a well-kept neighborhood and in immaculate condition. It was listed for $14,500. We really wanted to buy it. But even though William and I made good money and had a reasonable amount in savings, we were concerned about the big house payment. Our apartment rent was $79 a month and the house payment would be $120 a month, plus higher utilities and we had no furnishings. We decided to talk to my daddy about it. He said they had some extra things from the apartments that maybe we could temporarily borrow. I expected the usual negative reaction from my mom, "You can't afford a house, blah, blah, blah," but I was shockingly surprised. I figured after over three years of proof that I could do what I said, she finally believed me. After all, in spite of years of her "You can't", I had been at a great job for over three years, I had bought a car of my own, and we had bought a brand new one. I had got married, maintained a clean apartment and became a pretty good cook. So, when we announced that we were buying a house, BOTH of my parents said, "Congratulations." With much appreciated help from Daddy, William and I moved into our 1550 sq. ft. house with an apartment size refrigerator, a twin size roll away bed, and a card table with four chairs. We bought a stove and a washing machine right away. To have our own home was the most amazing accomplishment we had experienced in our young marriage. Slowly, every payday, we would buy something for the house. Within six months, we had purchased a new side-by-side refrigerator, a five-piece master bedroom set, a dinette set, and a four-piece guest bedroom set. By our third anniversary we had comfy den furniture and a five-piece wrought iron patio set. Our house was completely furnished by our fourth anniversary including a six-piece formal living room set and a formal dining room with matching China cabinet. For our fifth anniversary present to ourselves we purchased a color TV. Incredibly, it seemed as if money went further back then even though salaries were not that big. People paid cash for everything and if you did not have the money to buy something you saved up until you did. That was exactly how William and I filled our home with nice furnishings, and it was all paid for. No one used credit cards because at that time there were not any. Therefore, you did not waste your money on paying interest. Our lives were pretty busy now with our jobs and working on the house to get it just right. We were still doing well financially and through the years we took nice vacations to California and Las Vegas. One year we even bought an almost brand new car from Margaret. That was a very welcomed purchase because it eased our one car driving situation. Almost every Friday night we had started going to the new dog racing track in Mexico. We would bet on the races and laughed and had such good times there. William and I always had fun together and still never argued. We had settled into a happy routine and by appearances everything was going smoothly. However, occasionally I could not help but get a little irritated when I wanted to make love and William did not. In order to keep my mind off the concerns I had, I tried to stay busy with other things like decorating our house and entertaining. I had become a pretty good cook, especially Mexican food. I loved to invite people to come eat and play games. Whenever my childhood friend Margaret was in town, she insisted I make my baked chicken enchiladas. We would often have my parents over, too. Daddy loved my Mexican food. I was so proud when he told me that he liked my pinto beans better than my mom's.

So basically, all those evil spirits that had hounded me growing up seemed to have disappeared when I got married. But they were not really gone, they were just lying in wait for the opportune moment to slither back in. Our sex issue was a frustration for me, and that was just what the devil needed to start making cracks in my and William's relationship. One evening we were invited to go to Mexico with a couple William knew from work. They wanted to go to one of the side streets to a place called *The Cave*. I had never heard of it because we always stayed on the main drag. The inside was very different than any place I had been before. There were no tables or chairs. There was a dance floor in the middle of the room, and everyone stood around it. There was a three-piece band over in the corner playing drums, guitar and a trumpet, but no one was dancing. There seemed to be a lot of drunk GI's hanging onto Mexican girls. Pretty soon one of the girls pulled one of the Army guys out onto the dance floor. His friends were laughing and pushed him to her. The poor guy was so drunk I was not sure he even knew what was going on. The music played, and she started rubbing her body up and down on his. The crowd was clapping and cheering. The next thing she did was unzip his pants and pull them and his BVDs down to his knees. Then she laid down on that dirty floor and pulled him down on top of her. She didn't have any underwear on under her skirt. She kept kissing him and fondling him and wrapped her legs around him. When she finally got an erection out of him, she rolled them both over and sat on him until he climaxed. Then she got up and just left him lying there with his pants down and trying to get up. His Army buddies were rolling with laughter and didn't even try to help him up. I did not see anything funny about the whole situation and wondered why the couple that brought us thought this was something to see. They were even laughing and clapping. Eventually, I realized what had just happened. That kid was a virgin, and his Army cronies had set him up! I felt so sorry for him. I cannot remember William's reaction, but I was more than ready to leave. What I also did not know was I had been set up, too, by the spirits of sexual sin. We left the couple behind, and as we walked back down main street holding hands a man came up to us and asked, "Do you want to get married?" When we said we were married he asked, "Do you want to get a divorce?" We just kept walking. After that night I felt strange inside. I felt unsettled and confused about my life. I never would allow myself to even think about a divorce. Even though William was no longer making me feel loved, I was sure that he still loved me. And, I definitely still loved him. I felt if I ever allowed myself to cross the line and even think about divorce, there would be no turning back. I was still able to maintain that decision, but those evil spirits of divorce and lustful sex had made their way through the cracks in our relationship. Then they joined ranks with those latent spirits of fear and rejection that had tormented me all of my life. Slowly over time, they would begin to alter my thoughts, my desires, and my decisions. It was not anything obvious, the devil does not work that way. He likes to be tricky and deceitful and lead you down the path of destruction without you even having a clue about what is really happening. I often wished that we had never gone to that awful place in Mexico because I could tell that something inside of me changed that night.

Ten

Death and New Life

Before long a series of events began to happen that increased my frustration about my life and my marriage and what I should do. My need to be loved and to be shown love was starting to dominate my thoughts, but William would have no part in us talking about it. As I said before, I never talked about my sex life or the lack of it with any friends at work. However, one day I was having lunch with my close friend Stephanie, who was now married, and another woman from our department. They began talking about how they got tired of having sex. Stephanie said her husband would do it every day if she would let him, but she kept him down to two or three times. I asked, "Two or three times a month?" She looked puzzled, "No, two or three times a week." I think my face must have reacted because Stephanie looked at me concerned, "How often do you and William make love?" "I will tell you later," I gasped. I did not want that other woman to know my personal business. Then Stephanie and I sat alone, and I poured my heart out. I knew I could trust her as a confidante. She really did not have any answers, but it felt so good to finally share my inner turmoil with someone. At this point William and I were now married over two and a half years, and sometimes it would be well over a month before he wanted sex. I always felt deep down inside that did not seem right, and now I knew just how bad it was. I felt so rejected and undesirable. I thought maybe somehow it was my fault. Or, was there something wrong with William? In reality, it was both of our faults, but without communication we were already in a vicious circle. The more William ignored me, the more I reacted to not being shown love; and the more I needed that love, the more he became determined that he was not going to do anything that was not his idea. Considering the short length of time we had been married, this was a major issue. We had to find a way to fix it. So, one day I approached him to talk about what I believed to be a problem. I did not let him know I had revealed our sex situation to Stephanie, I just said I had been thinking a lot about it and voiced my concern in a more desperate plea for change. He still would not admit there was a problem, and therefore no discussions were necessary. He turned and walked away, leaving me hurt and more discouraged. Thoughts of divorce were trying to enter my mind, but NO! I will not cross that line! I did not even try to discuss the subject with him again and nothing changed. I had no way of knowing that the real problem revolved around my love addiction and his unreasonable pridefulness.

Then one night a horrific event made all the other troubles in my life pale in comparison. That particular night William and I had planned to go out to eat and then go visit Daddy who was home by himself because Mom had gone bowling. We never had an opportunity to visit with him alone, so I was looking forward to it. But, for some godforsaken reason that still puzzles me to this day, William and I went instead to the bowling alley to watch my mom. That was a decision that haunted me with guilt for the next ten plus years of my life. Because after William and I had gone to sleep that night, the phone rang around 1:00 a.m. He answered, I tried to listen, but he did not say much. He hung up the phone and told me to get up and get dressed, there was something wrong with my daddy. I began to panic and asked question after question as I hurriedly threw on clothes. William hardly talked. At one point on the drive to my parent's house I was screaming hysterically, "Is my daddy dead? He's dead, isn't he? Tell me!" I was completely losing control. Then William did something that was totally out of character for him, he reached over and slapped my face. I was shocked, but I somewhat calmed down. Finally, we got to their house, and I ran in to find Daddy lying in bed and Mom in the bathroom. By now, I was screaming again and shaking my daddy to wake up and asking him to please smile! I even put my fingers on his mouth to force a smile. I didn't understand why I did that because he hardly ever smiled. As I shook him, his arm which was laying across his stomach slid off and dropped limp to the side of the bed. I jumped back with a shriek. That caused my mom's panic to intensify, and all of a sudden, a wave of compassion came over me as I realized how much she was hurting and scared. When I finally went to Mom, I saw that there was poop all over her pajamas. The shock of Daddy dying in his sleep had caused her to have instant diarrhea, and it was everywhere. I immediately started helping her clean up while William put Daddy's arms to his sides and pulled the sheet over his body. He loved my daddy, too. It was the first time in my life I had ever felt compassion for my mom. They had been married over twenty-five years, so there must have been some kind of love between them, and now my mom had lost him. And when she was sitting on the toilet covered in poop, it was the first time I had ever felt that she needed me. After I got her into clean clothes, I called a nearby funeral home and the family physician. As they wheeled my precious Daddy out of the house, Mom, William and I just stood there in silent shock. After the hearse drove off, we packed Mom a bag and took her to our home. Even with all the past episodes in my life that I had considered tragedies, my daddy's death was the most devastating night I had ever experienced. I loved him so much!

When we got to our house we settled my mom into the guest room, but none of us got any sleep. All I could do was cry. When morning came, we all cleaned up and prepared to go to the funeral home. Mom was always a strong woman, but this was more than she could handle for the moment. It felt good that she needed me, and I could be strong for her even though I was breaking inside. After William and I called our jobs, we all solemnly drove to the mortuary. While we were with the undertaker, making arrangements, a man came into the room to meet us. He was one of their hearse drivers. He offered his condolences and introduced himself, "My name is Manuel, and I knew Mr. Larry when he worked at the battery store. I was a truck driver then. I considered him a good friend, and I had much respect for him." We graciously thanked him and he continued, "I would consider it an honor and a privilege to drive Mr. Larry to his final resting place." With that heartfelt statement I totally lost it. Tears were flowing freely including Manuel's. I got up and gave him a big hug and thanked him so much. The funeral was two days later. William, Mom and I went early for the viewing. I had given the undertaker a picture of me when I was two that Daddy always carried in his wallet and instructed him to make sure he put it in Daddy's suit pocket. When we went in to see my daddy, that was the first thing I wanted to know for sure. The man promptly pulled the picture from the suit pocket, I nodded, and he tucked it back in. If you remember, I was afraid of everything, especially death and dead people. The night Daddy died I was so crazy knowing he was gone that I did not even think about the fact I was touching a dead person. But now, there he was all embalmed, lying in the casket and looking very dead. Those fears began working overtime. I wanted to touch him and give him a kiss, but I was so scared! I just could not do it, but I kept hearing a voice inside my head saying, "You will regret it." I felt pushed. I had to do it! This was my daddy! I knew I would regret it if I didn't give him a kiss. So with every ounce of courage I could muster up, I touched his cold, stiff hand and leaned over and kissed his forehead. I continually thanked that voice in my head that it had enabled me to kiss Daddy goodbye. Being an Army veteran, the funeral was in a military cemetery complete with a twenty-one-gun salute and the receiving of a folded American flag. Daddy had many friends in attendance along with my half-brother and his family. At the end of the day, after all the company had left, I began mulling over the events of the last few days. As I did, I began to cry profusely, and suddenly I realized that Mom never cried through the whole ordeal. Then I remembered she did not really cry when her father died. I just could not understand that because I could cry at the drop of a hat. I just figured that was her way of handling grief. I kind of felt sorry for her.

The next day, after things had quieted down, William and I decided that Mom should stay with us for a while because she still was not herself. I sort of wished she would stay *not herself* because I liked her better that way. But after a few weeks, she began to feel stronger and started acting like her old self. Before long the nagging was resurfacing which meant it was time for her to go back home. She threw a fit that we thought she should leave and would not talk to me for weeks. She told everyone she knew that I had thrown her out of my house. When she finally decided to talk to me, she had already moved into one of the rental apartments at their house. I thought that was a good idea, so she would not have to be where Daddy had died. I asked if she needed any help only to be rebuked with, "No. I'm fine. I don't need your help." All I could feel was, "Oh well, it was nice while it lasted." I would check on her as often as I could, but she did not seem to care one way or another, so my visits sort of tapered off to occasionally. In the meantime, William and I were able to get back to business as usual. Despite the temporary distraction and turmoil of Daddy's death, we were no closer to solving our problem than we were before. Once we were back into life's routine, I continued feeling just as rejected and insecure with no apparent answers to our problem. You know sometimes rejection is not always an action. It can also be a lack of an action. And that old serpent, the devil, was going to make sure he did not lose this opportunity to take full advantage of our situation and my emotional vulnerability.

There was another couple from William's work that we often played cards with at their house because they had kids to put to bed. On a rare occasion we would go out with them to a club to dance. William was not that good of a dancer, but her husband was. I would mention to William that he should ask her to dance in hopes that the guy would ask me, and he did. I had no ulterior motives, I just wanted to dance. Whenever we all went out, that guy and I danced a lot. After a while, on the slow dances, he would hold me real close to his body and rub up next to me. He always made sure we were hidden from our spouses by the other people on the dance floor. I enjoyed the attention. The spirit of lust was all over us. Well, one night when William and I were at their house playing cards I went to the kitchen for a soda, and he was in there, too. He grabbed me and kissed me. It was crazy! We could have so easily got caught, but we didn't. I felt sensations that had not been aroused in a long time. After that first encounter, we occasionally did it again, trying not to be obvious. There was something hot about the danger of possibly being caught. But I would lie in bed at night longing for William to give me those same feelings again. And when he did not want to, I felt so lonely even though I was not alone. When William and I first married, I thought I would never feel alone again. What had happened to our perfect marriage? Did William even love me anymore? The encounters I had with our friend never went beyond kissing, but they were something that I thought would never happen to me. I loved William with all my heart and would not ever want to hurt him. But temptation is a major tool the devil uses to destroy people's lives. And when a person is in a vulnerable state of mind, the door is wide open for the attack. I became increasingly dissatisfied with William's behavior, and more of my friends at work knew about our sex life because I needed emotional support. He and I were on a dangerous downhill spiral in our relationship, and I don't think William even realized it. I really did love him, but he was not contributing to our marriage either physically or emotionally. I had run out of ideas, and there seemed to be no resolutions for our dilemma. At the five-year point of our marriage, there was nothing William did that provided me with an ounce of knowing that I was loved. And no, he was not getting it somewhere else. He was a good man. He just was not interested. Everything else about our marriage was perfect. We continued to have fun together, he was a hard worker, we still never had an argument, but I needed intimacy. Finally, one day I told William that something was terribly wrong in our marriage, in our sex life, and I wanted to go to counseling. He was totally shocked! His pride swelled up and he angrily said, "We do not need any counseling! If I ever think we do then I will decide if we need to go. And that is the end of it!" I was so frustrated that he would not even talk to me about our issues. According to him we had no issues. The gap between love making became larger. So, one day when William mentioned something about starting a family, I'm afraid I was a little, or rather a lot sarcastic when I said, "You have to have sex to have kids!" There was not much he could say back. Actually, I had such a depressing childhood I did not really want children. I thought if I had a baby, it would be a girl, and she and I would be as miserable as Mom and I. After our conflict about counseling, it seemed as if sex became even less important to him, and I felt less and less loved. I was not sure if I was being punished for my remarks or if it was just more stubborn pride. The worse our situation became the more my frustration turned to internal anger. I tried to keep it inside, but that just caused more sarcastic remarks to pop out every now and then. Neither William or I knew how to communicate and discuss the problem, so we just glazed it over and went on with everyday life. Since we always got along so good, by outside appearances we were considered the perfect and successful little couple. However, you just never know what goes on behind closed doors.

Then during the holidays, after visiting William's family, we decided to stop on the way back home to see this older couple who were long-time friends of my family. The man had taught me to swim when I was little, and his wife was such a sweet lady. I really loved both of them. She was asking me when we were going to have children since we had been married over five years. I pridefully answered, "Oh, I never want any children." And she so kindly replied, "Isn't that being rather selfish?" Those words went through my heart like an arrow. I had never thought of it that way. Nothing more was said, but I could not forget that question. After William and I got back home and back to work, I began thinking, "I really don't want to go through life not knowing what it's like to have a baby." I also thought maybe having a family would help our relationship. Ultimately, I told William I was getting off the pill. He was shocked, but happy. For a while our sex life improved dramatically, but that did not last. After several months passed, I did not think I would ever get pregnant with the limited number of times we had relations. Then, like people say, William and I went on a mini-vacation and *voila*, we made a baby! Previously I had experienced a few false alarms, so when I missed a period this time, I was not all that excited. Then a couple of months later I was feeling absolutely exhausted when I got home from work. I would have to lie down on the couch for a while before I could fix supper. I eventually went to the doctor because that was unusual for me. He thought I was probably really pregnant this time, and the test proved him right. William was beside himself with joy and when I told the girls at work one of them jokingly asked if it was Immaculate Conception. We all had a good laugh about that, but of course, I would never tell William. I was not sure what my mom's reaction would be since she was not a baby person. She really did not have much of a reaction at all. She only smiled and said, "Well, I guess it's about time." On the other hand, William's mom was so excited when we called and told her, as well as his brother and family. I had been through so many emotional ups and downs in the past couple of years I was ready to settle down and enjoy this amazing change in my life. And, what a hundred and eighty-degree change! I had gone from never wanting children to cherishing this wonderful moment! It felt so good to be happy again.

I absolutely loved being pregnant. Perfect strangers were so nice to me. Women would ask all kinds of questions about my pregnancy and had no reservations about patting my belly. Men would open doors for me or get up to give me their seat. It was funny though right after I had the baby, I was about to walk through a door expecting it to be held open, but the guy went in first, and the door almost hit me in the face. Anyway, I really did feel special the whole time I was pregnant. I never got sick, however all the foods I loved to eat I could not even stand to smell, like Mexican food, pizza or anything fried. And I always drank Pepsi or sweet tea, but I could not stand the taste of them. All I wanted was meat and vegetables, especially mashed potatoes and milk. I had never been so healthy in my life. I only gained sixteen pounds by full term. I really did not have cravings, but one time I did have an inconvenient request. I got us up out of bed in the middle of the night to go to our favorite twenty-four-hour coffee shop to have a piece of their amazing butterscotch meringue pie. It was certainly worth the effort. The girls at work gave me a beautiful baby shower. I received everything I needed and then some. But, the downside of having a baby was I had to quit work. I know that sounds unbelievable and very archaic, but the bank had no maternity leave in those days. I had to quit three months before my due date. Even though I had worked there almost eight years, I was really okay with that because I was excited to finally get to be a real housewife. I was ready to stay home and have more kids. I was actually wishing I could have twins, so there would be no chance of having an only child like me. It was so lonely being the only one. Since I had always worked it was a novelty to stay home. I painted the nursery white with red trim and the dresser, too. I sewed red and white candy-striped curtains and blankets to match. The room looked so cute. At the shower I had been given so many baby clothes in various sizes they would last for months. I had the best time washing and ironing them and arranging them in the closet by size. I cooked wonderful healthy meals and even did some yard work. I was very happy because I was enjoying what I had always wanted to do since I was young, be a homemaker. It did not even matter that William had absolutely no desire to make love to a pregnant woman. I had someone else who needed me that was moving around inside my belly. That has got to be one of the most amazing sensations in the world. My baby loved to be active in a warm bath, and I could have laid in that tub for hours just watching the movements and enjoying the flutters.

Finally, the big day was about to arrive. On Monday I spent almost the whole day out in the yard cleaning dead bushes out of the backyard flower beds. Then on Tuesday I had a doctor's appointment. When he checked me, I was slightly dilated. I was not even sure what that meant, but I was too shy to ask because I did not want to appear ignorant. The doctor said to go home and pack a bag, and if I did not go into labor that night, I should go to the hospital at seven in the morning, and he would induce labor. In those days you just did what the doctor said and you did not ask questions, so I still wasn't sure what was about to happen. Everything was so different back then. There were no ultra sounds to know the sex of the baby, and the fathers had to stay in a waiting room during delivery. Well, needless to say, I got no sleep that night waiting for something to happen. Wednesday morning came and no labor pains, so I got William out of bed, gathered up my bag and off we went to the hospital. I was very nervous! After we checked in, I was placed in a wheelchair and quickly rushed to the maternity ward. I never saw William again until later in the afternoon. I was over-whelmed, but excited. I just knew this baby would make our marriage complete and everything would be better. William was so excited he had gone out and bought a Polaroid camera to document the occasion. And as I found out later, he had also purchased a box of cigars. So far it was a fun and glorious day, but that was, of course, about to change. When I got to the delivery floor the nurse wheeled me into a semi-private room and to the first bed. The curtain was drawn because the other bed was occupied by another woman who was moaning and occasionally yelling, "Oh no, here it comes again!" That sort of scared me. The nurses rushed me through a procedure of an enema and a quick shave. That right there was pretty traumatic. Everything was a surprise because nothing had been explained to me. I had attended one Lamaze class which had explained how to breathe during labor, but that was it. Soon they had me in a hospital gown and lying on the bed with a very thick pad under me. It was not long before I found out what that was for. One of the nurses approached my bed with a long plastic rod that looked like a giant pickup stick. Can you believe she stuck that thing up inside of me? Next thing I knew a warm gush of liquid soaked that pad I was lying on. I did not even know what it was. I know I sounded very stupid about everything, but you must understand what a different world it was fifty plus years ago. Unless you had siblings, friends or a mother to explain these things, you would be clueless because you did not hear them from your doctor. When I went for my checkups he would ask the questions, not me. Then he would say I was fine, see you in a week or whenever and he was out the door. It was not a normal expectation to question your doctor. There was also not a lot of information readily available about labor and delivery, especially if no one told you how or where to find any that might have existed.

By now, they had me hooked to a heart and blood pressure monitor and to an IV drip to induce labor. The nurse looked under my sheet and said I was at four centimeters, so it would be a few hours. My doctor came in about then and agreed, but then rushed out. I heard later that he delivered ten babies that day. Again, in my ignorance, I had no idea what four centimeters meant or what number I had to get to. I became concerned when they said hours because once the pain started it seemed to be intensifying rather quickly, and it was not intermittent like the woman on the other side of the curtain. Mine was a constant pain. I had always had a high pain tolerance, so for a while it was a bearable dull ache and not a sharp pain. I was trying to breathe like I had learned in Lamaze class, but I started hyperventilating, and my hands were tingling and getting numb. When the nurse came back, she helped me slow my breathing down, but still said it would be hours, and I was doing great. I was lying there wondering how I was going to tolerate this constant pain for several hours. The screaming woman next to me had already been rolled out to go to delivery. It seemed like an eternity before the nurse came back. I was checked again and she exclaimed, "Oh my God, you are already a ten and crowning!" She called to another nurse to alert the doctor. Then they brought in a gurney and off we went speeding down the hall to the delivery room. I was placed on another table with a huge round bright light over it. There was one important request I had made to my doctor, I wanted to see my baby being born. So, the nurses proceeded to administer a spinal block. As I laid there waiting for my lower half to go numb, the pain was becoming extreme. I thought it felt as if the baby's head was trying to push out. I was watching a clock on the wall in front of me wondering how many more minutes would it take before the block worked. As they kept pricking my feet to see if I was numb, only one side of my body had been affected by the injection. The doctor said they could not wait any longer, they were going to have to put me out with gas. I hollered, "No! I want to see my baby being born! I can take the pain! It's already on its way out!" The doctor said something about we had not talked about natural birth, and while I was still pleading with him, they put the gas mask over my face and I was out. But at the moment they did that, I had glanced at the clock, and my baby was born ten minutes later. I knew I could have done it. When I woke up in my room, I was mad that I did not get to see my daughter's birth. Yes, it's a girl! We named her Heather. The woman sharing my semi-private room told me she did not want to see her baby being born, but she did because she had a cold and they could not give her gas. I was so upset! It was just not fair! This incident was just another addition to the long list of disappointments that plagued my life. When my doctor came to see me, I told him how mad I was. He said I really could not have taken the pain because they had to sort of push her back in a little so she would come out straight and not angled. I listened, but I still believed I could have handled the pain. It was only ten more minutes.

Soon, the nurse brought my baby girl to me, and when she placed her in my arms an incredible feeling of overpowering love poured out of me to my baby. I had never felt such love for anyone before that magnificent moment. The instant bond of mother and daughter was unbelievably real as my swaddled infant just melted into my arms. I thought how could my mother not have felt that. Her face was beautiful, her hair was beautiful, her eyes were beautiful, Heather was just beautiful! The nurse brought me a bottle, and she taught me how to feed and burp her. I held her until she went to sleep, then the nurse took Heather back to the new born nursery. Now I understood what that family friend meant when she told me that not having children was selfish. I had never realized how into myself I was until I saw my sweet, innocent little baby who was now totally dependent on me for her very survival. It was a life changing moment. Just then William came into my room, he was grinning from ear to ear. "Did you see her?" I asked. Immediately, he pulled out half a dozen Polaroid pictures he had taken through the glass at the nursery. "Isn't she beautiful?" I swooned. William beamed, "She sure is!" The nurses didn't let William stay for very long because by now I was exhausted, especially since I had not slept the night before. After a bowl of warm soup and some extra blankets on the bed, I was fast asleep. I slept so sound and comfortable for over ten hours. I felt refreshingly well when I first woke up until I discovered a terrible mistake had been made by the nursing staff. And the way I found out was when it literally hit me in the head like a sledge hammer. Upon awakening, I sat straight up from sleeping on my back all night and stretched my arms, I felt very rested. My bed was by the window, so I turned my head to look at the bright, sun shiny day, and a pain hit my head so violently it threw me back onto my pillow! "Oh, my God! What happened?!" I cried. My head felt as if it had been split open from the back of my neck to my forehead and was throbbing with pain. Frantically, I rang for the nurse. I screamed as I held my head in my hands. The nurse kept asking questions, trying to find out what caused the sudden headache. Fortunately, I would not be nursing my baby so they were able to give me pain meds and a muscle relaxant. The doctor determined that because the chart showed I was given gas it did not say I had also been given a spinal block that never took. When you have had one of those injections, the nurses were supposed to get me up out of bed to walk every two hours, so my spine would not tighten up. I had slept over ten hours straight which caused my back, neck and spine to be in tight knots and my head to feel like an ax had just split it wide open. The doctor never suggested any kind of therapy. In fact, other than giving me meds, the medical staff basically ignored the problem. In this day and age, I could have probably sued the hospital, but people did not readily think like that back then. I had never had a headache in my life, but it ended up taking me over a year, constantly using pain killers and muscle relaxants, to get rid of that never ending headache.

There was always something in my life that tried to ruin my joy every time I was experiencing happiness. But this time, I had overflowing joy, and nothing was going to steal the happiness of that moment. I was in the hospital several days, and the nurses taught me how to change diapers and give Heather a bath. That was a good thing because I was never allowed to babysit to learn those necessities. Soon the day came to leave the hospital. I tried to not let my constant headache ruin my excitement about taking Heather home. In our modern days of car seats and seat belts it seems almost frightening to think that we put a delicate five-day old baby in what was called an infant carrier and sat her on the floor of the car. The carrier was just a piece of canvas material attached to a small frame. She was not strapped to the carrier nor was the carrier strapped to the car. That was just the way it was done in those days. When we got home the neighbors on each side came running over to see our new baby. Things were hectic, Heather was hungry, and my head was throbbing. I tried to be sociable, but was glad when everyone left. My mom never came to the hospital to see her grandchild, so I was supposed to call when we got home, but I had to lie down for a while. By the time I did call my mom she was upset, but she came over anyway. Heather was asleep in her cradle, so Mom did not stay long. I was sure wishing Daddy could have seen his granddaughter. He would have been so proud. William really helped me out that day. He was doing so good at taking care of our baby girl I decided to let him do it all, and I took pain meds and went to bed. It was now Monday, and William took off the whole week to help me get acclimated to motherhood. I was very glad since I was nervous about taking care of Heather by myself. I was always plagued with fear about something, and this time I was afraid I would hurt her in some way. She was so fragile and perfect I was scared I would drop her or fall asleep and not hear her. Also, with William there, I could take stronger pain pills for my headache. That was all the doctor offered, just more pills and Valium. It was almost as if they did not want to make a big deal out of it. Maybe because they were concerned about a law suit if they admitted something was wrong with me. I depended on William so much that week I was scared for him to go back to work. What if I did something wrong? What if she chokes? What if I can't get her to stop crying? What if she stops breathing? What if, what if, what if? I would worry about any and everything. I used to tell people if I did not have something to worry about, I would be worried. All too fast, that inevitable day came. I had to be by myself with Heather and I had to grow up.

My first day alone with Heather seemed to take forever to pass by.

I was so careful with her, watching where I walked while holding her, how I fed her and how I laid her in the cradle. I was so paranoid. I was worn out by the time William got home, so I quickly handed the duties off to him so I could take my headache medicines and fix supper. I was afraid to take the meds when I was alone with Heather. William was tired from work, but he took care of her. Even through the night he had to get up to feed and change her, because I was knocked out by the pills and relaxants. Each day with Heather got better and better as my confidence level grew, and I realized she was not as fragile as I had believed. I found I could bathe her without drowning her or feed her without choking her and hold her while walking around without dropping her. My fears seemed so silly, and I was actually enjoying her and motherhood. But then, I had to overcome another fear hurdle when I had to put Heather in the car and drive her to the doctor for her four-week checkup. I had purposely decided on a pediatrician just a few blocks from where we lived, so I did not have to drive too far. Again, with the infant carrier on the floor of the car, off we went to the doctor. I think guardian angels must have really worked overtime to protect all the children of that era. They were not only riding on the floor of cars, but they laid on the back seat and on the shelf by the back glass and rode in the back of pickup trucks. Anyway, Heather survived her trip to the doctor, and I was proud that I was out of the house with her. That achievement opened up more times of venturing out until I could drive her anywhere without being afraid I would cause her harm. Even though I still suffered with a constant severe headache, I began to have fun with my baby. I enjoyed dressing her up and showing her off wearing all the cute outfits and taking pictures. We played all the baby games and shopped for toys and clothes. It was like having a live baby doll. But even with all the fun I was having, I somehow felt sad a lot, sometimes bordering on depression. Looking back, I believe I could have had a touch of postpartum depression. I would not have known then what it was because no one I knew was talking about such a thing. If I did have that combined with the headaches, I can understand now why a lot of things happened the way they did. Sometimes I would stay in my pajamas and not leave the house for days. I could have taken Heather for walks in the stroller, but I did not have the energy or the desire. I still showed her plenty of attention, but I lacked initiative for anything that took extra effort. The one thing I did force myself to do was to get dressed and fix my hair before William got home from work. Even though he did not seem to care less, I always believed that was important. I had grown passive to his lack of outward expressions of affection toward me, but when William began to react the same way to Heather, the mama bear came out in me. I got on to him for not showing her enough love. Well, that was a big mistake because his pride made him do just the opposite. I asked him why he didn't spend more time with his daughter. He haughtily answered, "I guess I just got used to not having one around." That response flew all over me! I had accepted that prideful treatment against me for years, but when it came to my baby, that was a different story. I was so mad! I was sure everything I had said back just made him more prideful. I was very glad I had Heather to love, and she loved me unconditionally. She became my world where I could find peace and joy, a new sanctuary. But, battling against that place of serenity were the headaches, the depression, and William's pride. He once said being married to me was like being on a roller coaster. Well, no wonder! I was the one screaming inside, "Stop the roller coaster! I want to get off!" But even with all that turmoil, William and I rarely argued which was probably not good because everything was held inside. I was still determined to not allow myself to cross that line and think about a divorce. So, all three of us settled into a semblance of a happy family life. Besides, I also wanted to hopefully have another baby someday.

My world as a stay-at-home mom was becoming much more interesting and rewarding. I relished each and every day with Heather as she approached the moments of her life with wide-eyed wonderment. I had her on a good routine of eating, sleeping, and playing. Once I got the hang of it, Heather was relatively easy to take care of. Her favorite thing to do was sleep, so she gave me plenty of time to keep the house well organized. Since I was home every morning now, I decided it would be more convenient to have our milk products delivered to our door. Yes, Virginia, there really was a milkman. A few chapters back I had mentioned a bartender in Mexico named Armando who used to make little pigs out of limes for me. Then he quit his bar job because he had found better work, and I never saw him again. Well, when the milkman came to my door to set up the route, would you believe he was that bartender, Armando? And he was going to be my milkman! Unbelievable! Even though I had not seen him in years, I recognized him right away. When I reminded him who I was and who my parents were, he remembered me. I had changed a lot since he last saw me. I asked him to please wait a minute, I had something I wanted to show him. I went and got my little dried-up pig, the last one he had made for me when I was a teenager, and I asked him if he remembered making them. I thought he was going to cry. It meant so much to him that I had kept my last pig for all those years. It was an unforgettable moment for both of us. After he left, I thought about how unreal it was that situations in life happen like that. How could people's paths cross out of nowhere? Was there someone in charge of the universe? I dismissed it as coincidence and figured that song was true, "It's a small world after all. . ." Heather loved to be around people, so I began to get out of the house more and more and would take her with me to have lunch with my friends at the bank. Getting to go places with her was doing me a world of good. Sometimes, I would even take her by to see my mom. Even though Heather was her first grandchild, there was not a whole lot of the usual grandmotherly attention. When Heather was a newborn, and William and I took her to meet her grandmother, it was an eye-opening experience. When I handed Heather to her for the first time Mom did not even know how to hold a baby or how to cuddle her. Now granted, it had been a long time for her, but she did not even come close to doing it. My daughter started crying because she was scared, so I showed Mom how to hold her close and make her feel secure. It was not perfect, but she did get to hold her for a little while. That incident made me wonder if my mom really had ever held me at all. I knew Mom never liked me, but I hoped she would be different with her granddaughter. And for the most part, she was. Mom always appeared to be glad Heather was around, and would even keep Heather overnight after she turned three. Either Mom had mellowed in her old age, or she just liked Heather more. Either way I was happy that Heather had some attention from her grandmother. I had been a housewife and a mother about four months when I met a new friend, a woman who lived on the street behind my house. Her name was Elizabeth, and she came to my door one day selling Avon. We had an immediate bond of mutual friendship. She stayed an hour just talking and getting acquainted. After that day we saw each other all the time and often went places together. Her kids were much older than Heather, so she enjoyed being around a baby again. She also liked to bowl, so when the day time summer league started Elizabeth and I got on a team together. Heather was such a good baby. Even with all the noise around her she would just sleep right there by me in her carrier. Elizabeth's and my friendship became closer and closer to the point where we were able to confide our personal problems to each other. That was a stress relieving outlet for both of us, to have someone to talk to. However, at the same time, in some ways she was not exactly the best influence on me. She had been married a long time, but her and her husband were on the verge of a separation or even divorce. That was a subject I was trying hard to avoid, so it was difficult to be a good friend and let her vent. But because Elizabeth and I did always have a lot of fun together, I remained in our relationship.

Eleven

Life Is a Soap Opera

The first year with Heather brought so much joy into my lonely days. I could not imagine life without her. The older she became the more I enjoyed her. Seeing her smile and hearing her laugh made life worth living. I loved playing with her at bath time then snuggling her warm little body wrapped in a hooded towel. We played games like *Peek-a-Boo*, tickle monster and Mommy fetch the ball. It was so much fun! But when Heather laid down for a nap, I had started a ritual that would ultimately influence me in ways I would have never imagined. As soon as she was sound asleep, I knew I had a good two hours to plant myself in front of the TV and watch soap operas. I had always felt as if life was just a stage, and we were all acting a part in a big play, so now I was living vicariously through the characters on the screen. These daily dramas seemed to penetrate my very soul and I unknowingly began yearning to live in the stories they portrayed. The women were sassy, the men were sexy, and their lives were exciting. The love scenes were enticing and so romantic. Somehow, I overlooked the tragedies in their lives to only see a world full of intrigue. Each day I was enthralled with lives that seemed so real. The life I lived was as far on the other end of the spectrum as you could get. I had no romance, no intimacy, and no emotional interaction whatsoever. I just wanted to be held and loved in a way that I knew I was needed and important. There was a time when William fulfilled those needs, but that had become a distant memory. When the shows were over for the day I had to snap back to reality as William's wife and Heather's mother. Then I would hear her cute cooing and baby talk, and all was well with my world. She was a bright light shining through my somber skies. When William got home from work, he paid a little more attention to Heather now that she was older, but I was greeted more like a roommate. We had passed our seventh wedding anniversary as William and I were just going through the motions of a marriage. Our incompatibility was becoming clearer every day. I know we loved each other, but we both had our own big problem that did not make us suitable spouses. My unfulfilled need for manifestations of love partnered with his prideful lack of interest in intimacy was a ticking time bomb.

Soon the holidays were approaching again, only this time they were going to be really fun because we had Heather. Each event was a Polaroid moment as she celebrated her first Halloween, her first Thanksgiving, and best of all, her first Christmas. William and I never knew holidays could be so meaningful until we experienced them with a child. What a priceless moment it was as Heather's eyes got as big as the moon when we plugged in the lights on the Christmas tree. She crawled around the bottom of the tree and gently touched as many shiny ornaments as she could reach, each one producing a fresh look of awe and discovery on her face. That first look at the Christmas tree was in close competition to her unforgettable countenance as she surveyed all the toys Santa had left on Christmas morning. Making Heather so happy gave us a whole new perspective on giving. Even William and I felt happier toward each other, and we were a little more lovey-dovey on through New Year's. A month after Christmas was Heather's first birthday. Unlike my childhood I was determined to make sure she had a party every year, and they would be special. We invited two couples that had children Heather's age that she also knew. I bought her a special first birthday cake, so she did not have to wait until she was nineteen to have one (sarcasm intentional). She was gentle with her piece of cake and did not like her hands to be messy. Heather and the other kids played with her new toys and everyone had fun, including the adults. Every new year brought me fresh hope for a better marriage. This one was especially encouraging because now we had a child to find joy and love with every moment of everyday.

All the busyness and distractions of the holidays had been good for me since they temporarily took me away from the soap operas and back to real life. Not only did my mental and emotional health improve, but my physical health also. The headaches had become rare, the depression was better, and William and I were enjoying each other's company again. But I continued to feel rejected because he still was not that interested in making love. Eventually, the soap operas were starting to creep back in, but were detained when William and I decided it was time for a road trip with Heather. William's mom had not seen her granddaughter yet, and his relatives were having a family reunion. Heather was a perfect angel on the road. When she wasn't sleeping, she was fascinated with watching the world speeding by the windows. Upon arrival, my wonderful mother-in-law reacted to Heather the way I wished my mom had. While we were there, she loved on her and dressed her up and showed her off to all her friends. I wished we lived closer so Heather could have a doting grandmother all the time. In fact, they were having such a good time together, William and I actually spent a day by ourselves and had fun. We went to the local coffee shop for lunch and then took his pistols to the river bank and shot at snakes and branches in the water. And then, guess what? We went and parked at a secluded spot, laid both seats back and had sex! It was not very comfortable, but I wasn't going to complain. I told William I wanted more children and he agreed. I thought finally when we get back home, he will be different, so I could get pregnant again. It was an amazing day! His mother was very sad when we finally had to leave, but fortunately she had four other grandchildren living close by. On the trip back home, I was really happy. We had made it over a very rough spot in our marriage, but now I believed everything was going to be alright. For several months after we returned home life was better. However, better to William meant returning to the once a month routine. I figured if I was ever going to get pregnant again it would have to be another Immaculate Conception. Now that Heather was walking and talking, my mom was finally showing more of an interest in keeping her every now and then. I guess she just did not like babies. That gave William and me a chance to go out with friends or just go to a movie. As our eighth anniversary came and went without fanfare, I was still not pregnant again, and William was losing what little renewed interest he did have in making love. So, after Heather's second set of holidays and her number two birthday party, I was on a downward spiral again. In an effort to escape from reality, I went back to my old friends on the soap operas. This time my old enemy, the devil, was not going to let me get away from the clutch he had on my desperate existence. He was going to add more fuel to the flames of discontentment in his effort to destroy my marriage.

Through all my ups and downs, Elizabeth and I were still very close. She was always telling me how bad her marriage was. She had been talking about a divorce for two years. My marriage was not anywhere near as bad as hers, but I still wasn't happy. She began to go out to clubs with other girlfriends and wanted me to come, too. I completely refused to do that because I still had hope for something to change between William and me. Elizabeth and I were still bowling together, and she and some of the other ladies would talk about all the guys they had fun with at the clubs. Also, Elizabeth had started smoking marijuana. We had been friends for quite a while, and I had never known her to act the way she was now. Some of the fun Elizabeth was having resembled parts of what I watched on the soap operas. Elizabeth's life seemed exciting. Then to put another log on my devil fire, an old friend of William's moved to our city to manage the computer section of a new furniture store. When he found out I used to run the bank's computer, he offered me a part time job. I had not ever considered going back to work. Even with the lack of intimacy in our marriage, I still loved being a housewife. Besides, if for some reason I had to work again, I would have probably gone back to the bank. One of my biggest reasons for not working was I did not want to put Heather in daycare. However, the friend was offering me a few hours at night after William got home from work. That was very tempting. It would give William more one-on-one time with Heather, she would not have to go to daycare, and it would give us extra money. Plus, the idea of being productive in the work place again kind of lifted my spirit. I could meet new people, learn a new computer system, and I would be helping out a friend of my husband. William could not say, "No" to that, so I said, "Yes" and started working the next week from 6:00 p.m. until 10:00 p.m. I made sure that I had a good supper prepared for Heather and William when he got home at 5:00. Then I ate a quick bite with them, but I had to leave them at the table. William seemed okay with the idea, and Heather was fine staying with her daddy. So, with hugs and kisses and last minute instructions, I was out the door. The job was very interesting, and I was able to utilize my keypunch skills as well as learning the new computer setup. Our department was an integral part of the process of selling the furniture, so we worked closely with the sales force. Many of the salesmen were single, and some of the married ones thought they were. I tried to ignore their flirting, but it was impossible not to feel a little bit complimented by their interest in me. To make matters worse, a young girl I worked with was always encouraging me to take them up on their offer to have a drink after work. I told her, "No way! I'm married!" She retorted, "So are they. So what? Everybody's doing it." That is one of the Biggest (with a capital B) lies that the devil uses on all of us to cause us to make wrong choices. Everybody is NOT doing it, but thinking that everyone is somehow makes it okay. So, I stayed strong to my convictions, did my job, and went straight home to a good husband that unfortunately had no interest in me. However, with the influences of the soap operas, my friend Elizabeth, the salesmen at work and my co-worker, it was not easy to maintain those convictions. Especially, if you mixed in William's total indifference to our crumbling relationship. But I continued to keep my promise to myself that I would stay true to our vow to forsake all others.

I had now worked part time at the furniture store for about five months, and in a couple of weeks William and I would be celebrating our ninth anniversary. Our time together was limited except on weekends. William and Heather were usually asleep when I got home, and I would see him briefly in the mornings and evenings. Our encounters were platonic, never romantic. The situation obviously put a strain on our already fragile marriage. Our anniversary fell on a Saturday, and I was asked to work during the day since the store was having a big Labor Day weekend sale. When I got home that evening, I surprised William with his favorite pizza and said, "Happy Anniversary!" He was glad I had brought food because he was hungry from doing yard work and watching Heather. There was no anniversary salutation for me, so we just all sat down and ate our pizza. Heather was excited to play with me since she missed our day together. We had fun while William finished his outdoor project. It was getting late, so I bathed Heather and rocked her to sleep. I loved holding her close and rocking her the way my daddy used to rock me. William had showered and was in bed, but not asleep. I went over and sat on the side of the bed and gave him a kiss on the lips and said, "I love you. Happy Anniversary." He finally said, "Happy Anniversary," too, but not I love you. He was lying on his back, so I leaned over again and gave him a longer kiss which was met with very little response. I thought maybe if I joked around he would lighten up, so I started smiling and teasing with him, "Don't you want a little anniversary present?" I tried to tickle him some, but he was not smiling. I asked, "Are you mad at me about anything? Is there something wrong?" He replied, "No," so I began to cut up again and acted all lovey-dovey. He just laid there without moving a muscle. What began as fun on my part became a challenge to get a response. I had seen the women on the soap operas entice their men into a fit of passion, so I began loving on William the way they did. Then I shut our bedroom door, seductively slipped off my gown and crawled into bed. I snuggled up close and put my leg over him and started kissing his face and ears. I just knew at any moment his natural male bodily function would take over and he would not be able to resist just like on TV. Only in my dream world I had momentarily forgotten that William did not react like other men. I pulled myself over to sit on his stomach and leaned down to slowly kiss his lips again. Nothing. He did not move an inch. The challenge changed to frustration as I scooted down so I could kiss his chest. I felt nothing being aroused in the area I was sitting on as William just laid there expressionless and motionless. Frustration turned to anger as I began to kiss him all over, and I do mean everywhere. Determined to get results, I tried and tried for what seemed like forever. William continued to just lie there like a hard-hearted stone statue. The harder I tried the madder I got until finally, in complete exhaustion, I threw myself off the bed and ran out of the bedroom and rushed to the den. I felt disgusted and humiliated and rejected and angry beyond belief. I was so mad I did not even cry as all the years of putting up with William's stubborn pride and lack of interest went racing through my head. I felt like such a fool because of how I had tried to get him to want me. The more I thought about everything the deeper the hurt went into my soul, and my heart became hardened. Finally, that awful night, on our ninth anniversary, I allowed myself to cross the line. For the first time in our marriage, I said to myself, "I am done. It is over. I want a divorce." And the devil laughed.

For a while I don't think William had any idea what he had done to me that night. I was civil, but aloof as I went about my daily chores. I kept up the house and Heather and continued working at the furniture store. But inside of me, I was cold and finished with William. You know, it never was about the actual sex, it was about being wanted and needed and loved. In the beginning, William used to make me feel those things, but Heather was the love of my life now, and I was so thankful I had her. I was not real sure how to go about getting a divorce, so I talked to my friend Elizabeth. She had recently finalized her divorce and had all kinds of advice, most of which did not apply to my situation. But, one suggestion she made did sound like the right approach, a trial separation. Only at the time I never intended it to be temporary. I just wanted to let William down easy. I don't know why I should have even cared; he certainly did not have any feelings for me. There must have been someplace deep down inside of me where I still loved the real William, but not the prideful, cold, insensitive person I saw that fateful night. But as horribly hurt as I felt, I was not mean or hateful to him. That would not have been good for Heather. I just wanted it all to be over. One day I told William I needed some time away and asked him if he would take care of Heather for the weekend while I stayed at Elizabeth's house. He had become obliging about many things because I believed he was worried. So, I packed a few things and walked to Elizabeth's. My friend had been divorced for a few months, and she made it all seem so glamorous. She had planned for us to go out to a club that night, but I was not ready for that scene. She also offered me a joint, but I quickly said, "No!" Elizabeth was probably thinking that I was not very good company for a sleepover. Anyway, we stayed up very late just talking about life, kids, marriage and divorce. After staying at Elizabeth's one more evening I went back home. I had made a decision.

Being away from William and the house had helped my stress level and cleared my head. I basically told him we needed more time apart from each other so could he go stay with a friend. He asked, "How long?" I answered, "I am not sure right now. I just need some time." He never asked why because I think he actually knew the reason since the atmosphere in our house had changed immediately after our anniversary. I figured this way was better than saying, "I want a divorce, move out!" William agreed to a trial separation and moved in with a guy he worked with. People we knew were shocked when they found out the happy little couple was not so happy after all. Even my mom showed an unusual sense of concern. We did not tell William's family; we just couldn't. Not yet. Heather was almost three years old, so she did not really understand what was going on. William would still watch her in the evening while I worked and then leave after she was asleep, so her routine was not noticeably changed. Not long after we separated, I was offered a full-time day position at the furniture store. Even though I hated putting Heather in daycare, I needed more financial independence from William, so I accepted the job. He continued paying the house bills required during the separation, and I paid for daycare. The bad thing about the new situation was since William did not have to watch Heather every evening he hardly ever came by or called to talk to her. I wondered if his pridefulness had convinced him that he was being revengeful to me, but he was only hurting himself and Heather. With William gone I was mainly enjoying just Heather and me alone. I was not even that interested in going out anywhere. It was crazy though, when word got out that I was by myself, men came out of the woodwork. Even guys William knew from work called me. I had heard the term *Happy Divorcee*, so I began to see why. I was getting all kinds of attention. I guess they all figured that now I wasn't getting any, so they wanted to help out. Little did they know I was not getting any even when William was there. The callers gave me a major boost to my shattered confidence, but that was as far as it went. I explained to them all that we were just separated for now. But I told the single ones that they could call me later if William and I ended up getting a divorce. Sadly, most of the callers were married.

On a rare occasion William would take Heather and me out to eat. We would all have an enjoyable time, but I still could not find any feelings left for him. He had destroyed them all on that one horrible night. I was through being rejected and unloved. Having said that, if I could have known then what the next ten years would be like, I might have done an about face. But for now, I was happy just going to work and spending quiet evenings at home with Heather. Strangely, one night after I put Heather to bed there was a knock at the front door. William had not said he was coming over, so I cautiously peeked out to see who was there. I was surprised to see Jason, a good friend of ours. William and I bowled on league with him and his wife. He was not one of the men who were calling me because we had not told them about our separation. He seemed distraught and explained that they had a huge fight, and he wanted to come in and talk to William and me. I told him William was not home. Jason had been drinking quite a lot and begged to come in for coffee so he could drive home. I certainly did not want anything to happen to him, so I let him in and made coffee. He was very belligerent as he told me all about the big fight. He was becoming angrier and saying how she would be sorry. Then out of nowhere, he pulled out a gun! I got so scared, especially for Heather who was asleep in her room. I thought, "Please do not wake up and walk in here!" I was shaking inside, but I spoke calmly, trying to get him to give me the gun. He waved it around as he went on and on about his wife. I was afraid he was going to shoot something, or me. I finally got Jason to sit down and drink his coffee, but he still had the gun. I told him, "You really need to talk to William. I'm going to call and see if he will be home soon." I went to the phone and dialed William's apartment. I was praying, "Please be there!" William answered, and trying not to panic I told him he needed to come home because Jason was there to talk to him about their fight, and he had a gun. William said, "I'll be right over!" In no time William was in the house, "What's going on Jason?" Our friend started waving the gun around again as he began to replay the story when William said, "Hey, is that a 45? I think I have one just like it. Let me take a look at it." And Jason handed him the gun. I breathed a huge sigh of relief! William put his arm around Jason's shoulders and said, "Come on, I will take you home, and you can get your truck tomorrow." As he escorted Jason out the door, William left the gun on our couch and told me he would be back. In about an hour William came home. I was still very shaky thinking about what could have happened. He suggested, "Why don't I just stay here tonight?" I agreed. We went to bed together and unbelievably; he made love to me! And it was his idea! It must have been the damsel-in-distress scenario because it was the best he had ever done! That night probably should have ended our separation, but I did not trust that there had been any real change in him. I felt it was just a reaction to an intense situation. One night did not make a marriage. Besides, he never mentioned he loved me or he would like to come home and work on the marriage, so I just kept my thoughts to myself. The next day Jason and his wife came and got the truck, but William kept the gun for a while. They apologized profusely and said all was fine now. After William spent the day with Heather and me, that evening he went back to his apartment.

The salesmen where I worked had become aware of my separation from William and began more intense flirting. It was putting Band-aids on my fractured ego, so I finally began to allow myself to enjoy the attention. The men and women on the sales team would usually go for drinks after work on the weekends, and they were always inviting me to go with them. Well, eventually I did not see any harm in going with the group. The few times I had to work a weekend, William or my mom would keep Heather, so I was free to go out with the gang. We all just talked and laughed at jokes; it was all innocent fun. I usually had only a couple of drinks, bought for me, because I was not there to get drunk. I just wanted to relax and have fun. I was not looking to hook up because, after all, I was still married. Our separation routine went on for a few months, and I would have been fine leaving things the way they were for a while longer. I did miss William, and the deep hurt from our anniversary night was waning, but I was still afraid to recommit. Understandably, William was growing weary of the separation and called me one day to discuss it. However, he offered no solution to our problem or a path to reconciliation. As far as I could tell he was not ready to share any responsibility for our failed marriage. I heard no words that suggested he wanted to stay married or if he even still loved me. He just said he could not live like that anymore, sitting on the fence, not knowing which way he was going to fall. He said I needed to make a decision about our situation. I thought, "Why was he putting the whole issue on my shoulders? He could have a say in this, it was his marriage, too." I was not ready to be pushed into a corner and give an answer. He said he had to have an answer right then. I begrudgingly said, "If you force me to make a decision this instant, it can only go one way." William inquired, "Which way?" "I am not ready for you to come back home yet because I don't believe you have changed. And, you still are not willing to talk about our issues or go to counseling," I responded. Then William surprised me by saying, "Then I'll go to a lawyer this week and start divorce proceedings, and I will let you know when the papers are ready to be signed." Well, he certainly did decide to have a say in it, but I was not expecting that! Shaken by the thought of finality, "If that's what you want to do," came slowly across my lips. William said, "Fine. Goodbye," and hung up. The context of the conversation took my breath away. It took a moment to absorb what had just happened. I just sat there staring into space with dozens of emotions running through my head. There was sadness, relief, anxiety, happiness, unhappiness, fear, loneliness, anticipation and apprehension. I was not sure what to think or how to feel. Then Heather came running into the room and threw her arms around my neck, and I knew everything would be okay. I hugged her and kissed her and told her I loved her. Her "Me too Mommy" kept me from feeling sorry for myself right then. I was so thankful for Heather that day, even more than usual.

A few days later William called to tell me that we had to go to a marriage counselor before we could get a divorce. Hearing those words was almost laughable. I thought, "You have got to be kidding me! Isn't it a little late for that?" I had pleaded to go to counseling almost five years ago when we could have possibly saved our marriage, and now when everything had fallen apart, we had to go to a marriage counselor! Unbelievable! Our meeting was totally unnecessary because I was not looking for reconciliation anymore. William had put the last nail in the coffin when he filed for divorce. I went for two reasons. Because we had to go, and because I hoped maybe the counselor could help William understand why our marriage had gotten to that point. So now William and I were sitting at each end of a table, facing one another, with the marriage counselor sitting on the side between us. He said he would submit a report to the lawyer for the judge to see. He asked a question for us both to think about our own answer, "What do you see as the biggest problem in this marriage?" The man called on me first. I replied, "He only wants to have sex every two or three months." Just as William was about to sip his coffee, the counselor turned to him with a surprised look on his face and exclaimed, "What is wrong with you man?" It so caught William off guard that he spewed coffee all over the table and started coughing. I thought finally he will realize what I had been trying to tell him. If only we had done this years ago when we both cared. The counselor turned to me and asked if William was physically capable of having sex. I said, "Of course, he just does not have any interest in it." Then he turned back to William and suggested he seek out further counseling with a psychologist. He surmised that William could have what was called a *Mother Fixation* which hinders men from seeing women in a normal way. William was in shock! After all that, the counselor did not even ask him what he thought was the biggest problem with the marriage. I wished he had because I would like to have heard William's answer. In fact, the counselor did not even ask any more questions or offer any counseling advice. The man just filled out some information on his paperwork, and we both signed acknowledging our participation in the meeting. William and I left in silence and went our separate ways. As I left, I was mildly gloating over the fact that I was right about William having a problem, and he was going to be sorry he had not listened to my pleas for help with our marriage. But I knew William did not have a *Mother Fixation* problem, he had an extreme pride problem. And it had become a vicious circle with us. The more starved I was for affection the less his prideful heart wanted to give it and so the more I needed it and so on and so on. It was so sad that it was too late to repair the enormous expanse that had formed between us.

Three weeks had passed, and the lawyer called William and me to his office to sign the divorce papers. He commented that he had never handled such a friendly divorce. The details were agreeable to both of us. I gave William the house because I did not feel as if I could maintain it. But Heather and I could live there free in lieu of child support until she was eighteen or until I remarried. He had to pay for the utilities and the upkeep. If we did move out then William would have to pay child support. It was a perfect setup. Heather's life would not be further disrupted by moving, plus I had very supportive neighbors. At the time it seemed to be the best choice for me and Heather. I was extremely nervous as the lawyer read the documents aloud. Then he told us if we had any reason why this divorce should not be finalized, we should speak now or forever hold our peace. Every fiber of my being wanted to get up and run out of that office, but for some awful reason I sat silently glued to my chair, as did William. After what seemed an eternity, the lawyer finally spoke, "The signed divorce papers will be filed at the courthouse and copies will be sent to both of you. As of today, for all intents and purposes, this marriage is dissolved." My heart sank to join the knot in my stomach. It was over. I felt so incredibly empty. We thanked the lawyer and rode down in the elevator together in total silence. I felt sick to my stomach. I was sure hoping we had done the right thing. Heather was still at daycare, so I went to see my friend Elizabeth. I started crying, "How did this happen? I really loved William so much, but not once during this whole ordeal did he say he did not want a divorce. So, I guess he really did not love me anymore." Elizabeth said, "Come on now, cheer up. We are going to have so much fun. You will be so glad you went through with it." "Are you sure?" I sobbed. "Listen, leave Heather at your mom's Friday night, and we will go out and celebrate!" Elizabeth suggested. "Okay, I guess. Right now, I need to go pick Heather up, but I will see you Friday." Driving to the daycare I felt so alone, and then I saw Heather's smiling face. Oh, what would I do without her hugs? We had a nice peaceful night at home. I rocked her to sleep and held her tight in my arms. The house seemed extra quiet and extra empty. As I watched Heather sleeping, so free of the cares of this world, I began to sob, "God, if you really exist, I hope she will be alright through all this. Please keep her safe and happy." Then I felt some words just bubbling up from my insides to my head, and the words began to form a poem. I rushed to find a pencil and paper and quickly wrote down the first of what would be several poems that would be birthed out of emotional upheavals in my life. This is the poem that came to me on the night of my divorce.

HER WORLD IS A TOY BOX

A fat Pooh bear without a care,
holding hands with Raggedy Ann.

There's Baby Beans, she pulls the string,
and I know her day's began.

A broken phone, she's calling home,
to a Daddy who isn't there.

A tick tock clock that teaches time,
why's growing up so unfair?

Her world is a toy box,
full of dreams and fantasies.

Children learn to play their games,
just like you and me.

Skates and blocks are all her riches,
and love is in her heart.

We make a toast over tiny dishes,
Lord, please never tear her apart.

Twelve

It's Party Time!

I was not too sure if I really wanted to go anywhere, but Elizabeth was adamant about us going out partying on Friday night. My mom was always glad to have Heather stay with her now that she was not a baby anymore. Elizabeth said she wanted to show me all the good places where there were lots of men. She said, "You need to put yourself out there and see what you've been missing. Be friendly and the guys will buy the drinks." So, I figured if I was going to all the trouble to do this, I might as well try to have some fun. We stopped in at several clubs, but finally stayed at Elizabeth's favorite hangout, a large country western dance hall named Crazy's Place. I loved watching all the different dances, and everyone seemed to know how to do them. I had never danced to anything but rock music which did not really have any specific steps. You just stood there and did your own thing. But these people looked like professional dancers. They were doing waltzes, polkas, the two step, swing and several other unusual dances. I was practically salivating with a desire to learn how to do all those dances! I knew that I had inherited my parents love for dancing, but I had not been exposed to real dancing. Elizabeth introduced me around to all of her friends and told them I was celebrating my divorce. They were all nice and took me right into their group. Eventually, one of the men asked me to dance. I was not sure I could. I told him I had no idea how to dance to country music, and I was not wearing cowboy boots. He assured me that did not matter, and he would teach me the dance steps. "You have to learn some time, and now is the time," he responded as he pulled me out of my chair. The people on the whole dance floor seemed to all move in a circle going the same direction as each couple weaved in and out of each other like a well-oiled machine. I was sure if I went out there, I would be the proverbial monkey wrench thrown into the gears, and everyone would fall all over each other. But thankfully, the guy took me over to an empty corner of the big room and patiently began teaching me a slow two step. It felt so weird because the girl spent most of the time going backwards. You certainly had to trust the guy to lead you away from running into someone. I never realized that I actually had the ability to learn how to really dance. I picked the steps up quickly, so we ventured out to the dance floor. That was scary! I was relieved I made it through the song without falling down or causing a train wreck. Then he said he wanted to teach me the country waltz. It was a bit harder to learn with the one-two-three, one-two-three step process, but he was incredibly patient. I don't think my legs had worked that hard since high school drill team.

As the night went on, my dance teacher became friendlier and friendlier. He always had his arm around me, holding me close when we were sitting at the table. When I looked at Elizabeth, she gave me a big smile and a wink. It was getting close to closing time when the guy told me he was not always there; his work made him travel a lot. He said he sure hoped I would be around the next time he was in town. Then he kissed me, and I kissed him back. It was exhilarating! He explained he was staying in a motel nearby and asked me to come to his room. I said, "I don't know. I came with Elizabeth." He kissed me and whispered, "Just let me know before closing time." I grabbed Elizabeth and told her we needed to go to the restroom. I relayed to her what the guy had proposed, and she excitedly answered, "Of course, go! Isn't that what you have been missing out on?" I nervously responded, "But it's too soon. I just got divorced. It hasn't even been a week!" I was beside myself with emotion. "And, how will I get home?" I asked. Elizabeth said, "I will just wait in the motel parking lot. Take your time." "You would do that for me?" I queried. "I'm your friend, and this is what you need to get past your feelings of uncertainty about the divorce," Elizabeth insisted. "Okay, if you are sure," I replied apprehensively. "I am sure," answered Elizabeth. So, I went back to the table and told my new acquaintance, "Yes," and we left together for his motel. He held me close to him as we rode in his truck and would lovingly kiss me at every stop light. I had no idea what to do when we got to his room. I had never been with a man who was so excited about having sex. When he approached me, he was as patient there as he had been on the dance floor. I told him, "It has been a while for me, and I have never done this before." He calmly said, "No problem," as he took my hand and led me over to the bed. As we stood there by the bed, he took off his shirt and belt. Then he pulled me close and slowly and ever so passionately kissed me on the lips. I kissed him back as I put my arms around his neck. I thought, "This is just like I've seen the people on the soap operas do it. SO romantic!" But on TV, the action always ended there. I was excited to see what was coming next. As he kissed me, he slowly undressed me, and my head started spinning. I began to respond seductively, the way I thought the women on TV would. I could not believe how patient and romantic he was. Then he picked me up and gently laid me on the bed and stared at me like I was a goddess or something as he finished undressing. He told me to just lie there and enjoy it. The way he made love to me was nothing like William ever did. When he finished it was not, "Okay, I'm done." He continued loving on me for a while afterwards. Then we both just laid there in silence as he held me close. I was so relaxed I was afraid I might go to sleep and leave Elizabeth waiting in the parking lot all night. It seemed as if he might doze off, so I quietly said, "That was amazing, but I really need to leave." He said okay and quickly got me a towel from the bathroom to clean myself. I thought, "That was so nice of him to be concerned about me like that." He was about ten years older than I was, so I figured men his age must be more gentleman like. I got dressed, and we kissed goodbye. I told him to just stay there, I would walk myself to Elizabeth's car. When I got to the car, Elizabeth was sound asleep, so I startled her as I knocked on the window. She inquired, "How was it?" I oozed my answer out, "It was incredible! I never imagined someone would actually make love to me like that! It only happens in the movies!" We both giggled and shrieked with joy. However, the devil was also shrieking with joy because his plan was now in full force. I could not have known that I had been given the ultimate sex experience, like the first time high from a drug, to get me hooked. Or, that I would spend the next ten years unconsciously trying to replay that euphoric love making. That one-night stand had ushered in spirits that would gradually intensify my unknown love addiction. In order to try and replicate that extraordinary feeling of being loved, sex would become my drug of choice and men would be my suppliers. When I got home, I was totally unaware of what had really happened to me. As I lingered off to sleep thinking, "Maybe the single life will be alright," I almost felt happy again.

Monday at work I relayed my exciting evening to the girl who was always wanting me to go out with the salesmen. The way she reacted you would have thought I had been with a movie star. She exclaimed, "Well, now you are ready for the whole sales department!" We both laughed, but I had never before considered going out with a guy just for sex. All I knew was you go out on a date to dinner or a movie, and after a while the dates might lead to making out. Before Friday night I had never had intercourse without being married. This was a whole new playing field. Imagine having sex like that all the time. I caught myself daydreaming instead of working. They played a song at the dance hall, "I'm having daydreams about night things in the middle of the after-noon . . ." That was me, and it sure put a smile on my face. I could not wait for the weekend, so I could go back to Crazy's Place to dance and meet new guys. But before I went back, I just had to get me some cowboy boots. I went to an outlet store and found a very comfortable pair of gray leather boots. At home, after Heather was asleep, I put on my new boots and practiced the dance steps I had learned. By Friday I was so excited, but also a little nervous, as Elizabeth and I entered the dance hall. I knew my dance partner would not be there, so I was on my own. Since I was not a regular at the place no one was asking me to dance. Everyone was such a good dancer they only wanted to be with someone they knew could dance well. Elizabeth was one of those good dancers, and every now and then when she finally made it back to our table, she would see how I was doing. "No one will give me a second look," I whined. Elizabeth said, "You need to flirt with the guys. Smile at them when they walk by." And off she went again to the dance floor. I didn't know how to flirt. I had never needed to flirt before. Again, I thought about the women on the soap operas. They knew how to flirt. They would walk into a room, pick out a guy and smile and make eye contact until he finally came over. That was what I needed to do. I looked around and saw a cute guy standing at the bar. I coyishly tilted my head a little, smiled and looked him right in the eyes. It took concentration to hold that pose, but lo and behold, he picked up his drink, walked over and sat down beside me! I was elated thinking, "It really works!" He bought me a drink and then we danced. He was a so-so dancer, but that was okay because I was still learning. He invited me to breakfast at the truck stop where everyone went for food and coffee after closing time. I told Elizabeth I was leaving, and I had a ride home. She gave me the thumbs up. The guy was nice, a semi-regular at the club. After breakfast we went to his apartment. It looked like a bachelor pad, messy. I was expecting to be made love to like the first guy, but this one just wanted to get after it. There was limited kissing and foreplay, and it was mostly all for him, not for me. After he finished that was about the end of it. He was not mean or rough or anything like that, he was just selfish. He drove me home, gave me a kiss good-night and said, "Maybe I will see you around." As I went to sleep, I was puzzled by the complete difference of the two sexual encounters. I was not feeling important or loved this time. I figured this guy was just a dud, and there were more out there like the first one. My plan was to find that unselfish love again, but my search would eventually evolve into a fanatic fixation, like a drug addict looking for their next high. I was constantly trying to feel loved. In time, I would be anything for anybody so they would want to come back, and I could get my next *fix*. I know you could not drink it, smoke it, swallow it or inject it, but in every way my addiction was just as destructive. The journey would take me farther and farther away from reality. But who knew? No one knew because I did not even know. I would be fooled into thinking that I could find what I needed through sex. True love will never be found in one-night stands or in meaningless relationships built on lust. But I did not see it that way. Sadly, at this point of my life the devil had me hook, line and sinker. So, as the saying goes, now for the rest of the story.

I not only became obsessed with men, I could not get enough of country western dancing. I absolutely loved it! I could hardly wait for Friday and Saturday night to come. I devoted all my time to Heather during the week, so I could have my weekends. I would take her to my mom's house to spend two nights and would pick Heather up on Sunday afternoon. One time Mom commented, "I may not always want to keep her every weekend." I sarcastically retorted, "Okay, I'll just find a sitter." I really did not want to do that because my mom was free, but I was becoming very self-indulgent, so nothing was going to stop me from going dancing. Mom never brought it up again because she had fun with Heather. Mom was a lot nicer to her than she had ever been with me. She seemed to genuinely like Heather. Every weekend, I was at Crazy's Place even if my friend Elizabeth could not go. By now it didn't matter because I had become one of the regulars, so I went by myself. Since I was one of the good dancers now, I was quite popular with the guys who came there for the same reason, we loved to dance! I usually danced to every song that was played by the live band. I was losing so much weight that my jeans were practically falling off of me, and I had to buy new ones. My ego was through the roof because I was looking good. I enjoyed the flirting and the teasing as much as actually having sex because it was more about the attention than the act. And there were plenty of guys to flirt with. There were even some younger ones who could really make me feel special because they wanted a woman with experience. I wrongly thought I had found a new sanctuary.

Then one night two guys that were very different looking and not dressed in western attire walked into Crazy's Place. They were staring at the dancers and the dance hall with amazement on their faces. One of them was short and very cute. I liked short guys because I was short and they were easier to dance with. However, these two did not look like they knew a thing about country western dancing, and by now I would not give a guy the time of day if he was not a good dancer. Surprisingly though, there was something intriguing about them. I went over close to where they were sitting and overheard them talking in what sounded like German. For some reason they aroused my curiosity and my interest. I kept staring at the short one hoping he would look my way. Then our eyes met, and he had the most gorgeous blue eyes. Then he smiled the biggest grin and he had dimples! I melted! I was a sucker for dimples. He got up and came over to me, and with an adorable German accent he asked me to dance. Ordinarily, I would never dance with someone unless I knew for sure they knew how, but this guy was just so darn cute and had such gentlemanly manners. And those blue eyes and that accent and those dimples! I was twitterpated! I could not resist, so in an instant I was up and on the dance floor. The band began to play a slow country waltz, and to my surprise, he started doing the waltz step. He was not doing it country style, but he knew the one-two-three, one-two-three. Boy, was I surprised! When the song was over, we went back to my table, and he pulled my chair out for me. Wow! That had never happened to me before. Especially the guys at Crazy's, half the time they wouldn't even walk you back to your table. He politely asked if he could sit down, and then he introduced himself, "My name is Warner, what is your name?" When I told him he smiled that big grin and repeated my name with that beautiful accent. My name never sounded so good. He continued, "My friend and I are here from Germany. We are in training at the Air Force base. We are in the German Air Force." I could only make small talk while swimming in those amazing blue eyes. He said they had heard about the country music and the dancing, so they came to see what it was. I could not believe I heard myself ask him, "Do you want to learn the Texas Two Step?" He was so excited, "Yes, of course!" Warner was a quick learner, so we were able to dance to several songs. Then the band started playing a country polka. He got really excited, "A polka! I know how to do this one! We dance polkas all the time in Germany!" His polka was a little more exuberant than I was used to, but we had a lot of fun. At closing time, he charmingly asked permission to call me. I loved being treated so nicely, so I said okay and gave him my number. He gave me a big hug and said goodbye. He was refreshingly different and such incredible manners. I really hoped I would hear from Warner before next weekend.

Usually, guys would not call for several days or a week after getting your number. They had to play their little game of not appearing too anxious. But Warner called me the next morning! He invited me to lunch. It was Saturday, and Heather was still at my mom's, so I said I would love to. He showed up at my house right on time in a Volkswagen beetle. What else, right? He said he had a special place to take me and hoped I would like it. The place was a small German restaurant near the base. I had lived in that city my whole life and probably drove past there a hundred times, but I had never noticed that restaurant. The menu was in German, so Warner patiently explained all my options. I chose something called Wiener Schnitzel, and it was so good, only I gave him the sauerkraut. We talked and laughed and had such a fun time. This guy was perpetually happy, and I was happy being with him. Warner had only been in town about a month, but he sure knew his way around. He took me to meet some of his Air Force friends from Germany, plus some Germans who were permanent residents in my town. That was when I found out Warner was an officer in the German Air Force. His friends told me how smart he was, but Warner was so humble. I was thinking this guy was really something. After spending the whole day with his friends and enjoying more delicious German food, Warner drove me back home. I had never allowed a guy to spend the night at my house, but I did not want our time together to end. Since I would not pick Heather up until Sunday afternoon, I invited him in for a drink. We sat on the couch and talked and drank and listened to music. It was so peaceful. We got up and began to slow dance to a dreamy song. He was such a gentleman I thought he would never kiss me. Finally, while dancing, he gently kissed my lips. That was all it took. I whispered, "Would you like to stay the night?" He flashed that big dimpled smile, picked me up and asked, "Which way?" Warner was incredible. I actually felt very wanted and important again. The next morning, after I made him breakfast, I told him I needed to clean up and go pick up my daughter. Warner said he worked long hours during the week, but wanted to spend all next weekend with me. I said I would, just call me to be for sure. We lovingly kissed goodbye and he left. I was nervous and embarrassed that the neighbors probably saw him leave and therefore knew he had spent the night. But it was a wonderful night, and why should I care about what they might think. Everybody does it, I rationalized. By the time I arrived at my mom's place, I had convinced myself that all was well with my world and my life. And to have Heather run up to me and jump into my arms with a big hug, sealed the verdict. I loved my daughter so much! I was feeling very happy as I tried to go to sleep that night, but could hardly wait for next weekend and another chance to be with Warner. I was finally feeling loved again.

Every weekend I had with Warner was like living a fairy tale with a knight in shining armor. Being with him could not be compared to any soap opera, it was so much better. Warner was definitely unique. I tried to not think about his time at the base would come to an end soon, but just enjoy the precious weekends we had left. I had not even thought twice about Crazy's Place nor did I miss anyone I knew there. I did not want this dream to end. I did not want to have to go back to where I was before. Warner and I had such incredible fun together, always with his friends. I never did introduce him to Heather because I knew she would love him as much as I did. And since he would be leaving, there was no point in doing that to her. Every time Warner and I were together was a special moment, but there were two unforgettable evenings that stood out from all the others. One night Warner drove us in his Volkswagen across the border into Mexico. I was nervous because I considered it risky to drive a car in the older section of that town. He sped that little car down the narrow back streets like a Mexican cab driver. I trusted him though because he said it was just like driving in Europe. Pretty soon we stopped in front of an old bar. Warner was beaming as he introduced me to the woman behind the counter. Then they started talking in German which shocked me because she was Mexican! He later explained that she was married to a German man who had died a few years ago. They had run that bar together for the German Air Force guys to have a home away from home. Warner put money in the juke box which was loaded with all German records. The beer was flowing, and all the Germans were singing and making a toast to everything they could think of. They were a happy bunch of people. Then Warner led me over to the longest part of the counter. In that wooden bar top was carved hundreds of names or initials of the people who had patronized that obscure little bar. Warner reached in his pocket, pulled out a small knife and began etching our first names into the wood as a lasting memory of our wonderful night in a place I never knew existed. I was always amazed by Warner. I began to realize that he could have fun anywhere. He was just that type of guy. The second special evening with him was our last night together before he had to leave the next afternoon. He had told me to dress up fancy because he was going to wear a suit. He also informed me that this time I was spending the night with him on base. I didn't know I could do that. He said it did not matter now because he was leaving. Warner was always full of surprises, but this night topped them all. It all started when he drove us to a quaint fancy restaurant. It was lovely inside with cozy round tables with white tablecloths and napkins and elegant silverware and candles. The waiter, dressed in a black suit with a white cloth over one arm, pulled out my chair for me and then shook out my napkin and placed it in my lap. There was a man in a nearby corner softly playing romantic music on a baby grand piano. On the walls were beautiful paintings and small chandeliers hung from the ceiling. Warner had done it again! I had also never heard of this place. He was unbelievable! How did he come up with all these unique establishments when he did not even live here? Warner kindly asked if he could order for me. I figured by now he should know what I liked, so I agreed. We began with shrimp cocktail and then had prime rib that melted in your mouth along with scalloped potatoes and a vegetable medley in cheese sauce. Our dessert was cherries jubilee followed by an after-dinner liqueur. I felt like royalty. But the next surprise was unimaginable. Warner got up and went over to the piano player, I thought to request a song. But the piano player got up, and Warner sat down on the bench! What was going on? Then he began to play this beautiful melody as if he was a professional! And if I was not shocked enough, he began to serenade me as he played! Warner had an incredible singing voice that was much different than when he was singing his German beer drinking songs with his friends. No one had ever treated me that special, not to mention I had never been sung to. I was at the apex of feeling important and loved, and it had nothing to do with sex. What a wonderful moment in time! Warner was the most amazing man I had ever met. My head was in the clouds, but the evening of surprises was not over.

We drove back to his room on base, so we could spend some alone time together before he had to leave. We changed into comfortable clothes and then he said, "I want to show you my home in Germany." I was expecting a picture album, but he pulled out a movie projector, a screen and a reel of film. Warner never did anything small. The projector began with scenes from the town where he lived. It was beautiful. Then the camera turned towards a street sign as Warner said, "This is the street where I live." Curiously the street sign was the same as his last name. That was puzzling. Then the camera moved along a tree lined road which showed a large brick and wrought iron fence on the left side. The fence continued to two tall wrought iron gates that opened as the camera passed through. Then Warner announced, "This is my home." I know my mouth dropped open as the camera continued up a brick driveway lined with colorful plants and flowers and stopped in front of a gorgeous mansion! No kidding! A real honest to goodness mansion. You could have pushed me over with a feather. The film ended there. Warner turned the lights back on. I was speechless. He teasingly said, "Say something." I said, "No wonder you can play the piano and sing like that." I don't know what that had to do with a mansion, but that was what came out first. He laughed and said I was sort of right. He had studied voice and music at a conservatory in Germany. Then to top it all off he added, "And my father is a famous opera singer in Germany." Well, that took the cake! I definitely knew I was dreaming now! Warner hugged me tenderly and whispered, "I just wanted you to know before I leave because I will write to you, and I hope this will not scare you off." I was still at a loss for words, but I smiled, "Of course, I will write back." We made love, but never mentioned love. We were so comfortable together. It was wonderful. I certainly did not want him to leave. He said he would find a way to come back. The next afternoon came too fast. I was able to go out to the plane with him. We both had tears in our eyes. But I had to laugh when he put on that big sombrero hat that he bought in Mexico. He still had it on as he walked up the steps to board the German Air Force transport plane. He stopped at the door, threw me a kiss, and waved goodbye. I felt a big empty hole in my heart that day as I watched the plane fly away. With huge tears in my eyes, I walked slowly back to the car. We had used my car the night before so I would have it on base. I was crying so much I wasn't sure I could drive. I was still very sad when I picked up Heather. She could tell something was different, "What's wrong Mommy?" I held her tighter than normal and thought to myself, "What would I ever do without her?" I said, "Mommy's just a little sad because a close friend of mine left town." "Will they come back?" she sweetly asked. "I don't know. What do you say we go get ice cream?" I inquired quickly changing the subject. Heather clapped her hands, "Yay, let's go!" As I drove to the ice cream parlor, I realized at least I did not feel rejected. Warner really cared for me, so maybe I will see him again. But life always had to go on for the sake of Heather. I hoped she would never have to feel sad or alone or rejected, ever.

After Warner left, I had no desire to go back to Crazy's Place. He had been a sanctuary where my addiction was not welcomed. I was never even obsessed with needing sex to feel loved because Warner showered me with so much heartfelt attention that I was always satisfied that he really wanted me. The short time I enjoyed with him was like heaven where I had no anxieties and no loneliness or insecurities. I felt clean and renewed and wanted to stay that way. It had been so nice having one man who genuinely cared about me and respected me. He left me feeling loved and in love. Now, I just enjoyed spending quality time with Heather while I reassessed my single life. During the time I was with Warner none of my so-called friends from the dance hall had bothered to call and check on me, not even Elizabeth. I decided I would not go back there now that I really didn't miss it, and obviously they did not miss me. Just two weeks after Warner left, I received the cutest card from him from Germany. The front of the card had a drawing of a pretty girl with reddish hair and in part German and part English said, "You are my First Lady." He wrote the sweetest message inside. After saying his flight was good and his parents were very happy to see him again, he wrote, "You can believe me, it was very hard to say goodbye, and I would like to say thank you very much for the beautiful days we had together. I am proud to know a girl like you, and I think all days of you. Next week I start to work, and I can ask my chief what is going on for the coming time. I want to plan to come back to see you. I send you 1,000,000 kisses and hope you think of me. I miss you very much. All my love, Warner." Well, you can imagine how elated I was to receive such a romantic letter. As I clung to the words "All my love," I was definitely convinced that he was for real about his feelings for me." I was so glad I had some snapshots we had taken, so I could look at him as I read the card over and over. My heart was overflowing with happiness as I immediately began to write a letter to him. I told Warner how excited I was to hear from him and how much I loved the card. I continued to relate to him that I too missed him so much and wanted to see him again. I conveyed how I had showed Heather his picture, and she liked his uniform. I asked if he could ever call me or was it too expensive? I made sure he knew I genuinely cared about him, also. I closed with "All my love" and kissed the letter with a lipstick imprint. When I mailed it, I felt completely confident I would hear from him again.

I continued to stay away from Crazy's because my thoughts of

Warner were such a better place to be. But the days turned into weeks and no letter came and no phone call. After a month of no response, I knew I would not hear from Warner again. I was heartbroken. My mind was working overtime trying to make sense of it. Warner was a dreamer and a romantic, so he would never consider the possibility of any issue that could cause us to not have a future together. But as a realist, I was always concerned about it. We were from two different worlds, and whenever I would voice my fears, he was always so patient with me. He would say, "You think too much," and then with a big hug and that dimpled smile all my worries would melt away. But now he was not here, and he was not writing and he was not calling, so what I believed was that all my concerns had come to fruition. I kept hearing a voice in my head saying, "You do not deserve a man like Warner. Look at what you are, a failure, and he is rich and extremely educated." The scenario I played out in my mind was when Warner received my letter at his parent's house, they wanted to know why there was communication with this American woman. I pictured his father as this wealthy and powerful German man who had Warner's future all planned out. Warner had been educated at the best schools, graduated college and then trained at a prestigious conservatory of music. He was a commissioned officer in the German Air Force and was probably being groomed to marry into the proper social level. And on top of all that, Warner had been raised to be a devout Catholic, and he had fallen in love with a poor divorced woman with a child. I could just hear his father as he forced Warner to give him my letter so he could read it. I knew Warner thoroughly respected his parents and would be totally obedient to his father. I imagined how furious his father was that Warner would have the audacity to think that he would be allowed to throw his future away on some common American divorcee. I could feel Warner's heart breaking as his father forbade him to ever contact me again. And being the kind and humble person I loved, Warner understood and obeyed his command. Even though my heart was broken, too, the one act play I created in my mind helped me to rationalize an otherwise hopeless situation. But that did not help the loneliness and the depression I felt from realizing I would never again see the most wonderful man I had ever known.

It was not long before I could not take it anymore, and I had to go back to Crazy's Place to get my *fix*. There was an unbalanced pseudo therapy that emerged from being around other losers and dancing to songs about broken relationships. I was finally beginning to understand why they called the place Crazy's. So, I called Elizabeth and told her I was back in action and would be there Friday night. She was excited and said she would plan to go, too. When I walked into the dance hall I felt a huge empty feeling, but familiar faces began to fill the void. It helped when people came up and asked, "Where have you been? We thought you left town." Before long I was back on the dance floor two-stepping my sorrows away. In my make-believe sanctuary, I relied on my obsession with country western dancing because that made me popular, something I had never experienced before. Every now and then I would even get to dance with one of the Arthur Murrays of Crazy's Place. One of our best dancers, Jake, had a girlfriend he always danced with, but one night she was not there, and he kept me on the floor with him for every song. I felt so honored that he had picked me to be his dance partner for the evening. He asked if he could take me home, which translated meant, "Do you want to have sex?" I said, "Sure." So, since Heather was gone, he spent the night. It's twisted, but I felt privileged that he had chosen me to spend the night with in place of his girlfriend. And so began my downward spiral into a decadent world designed by Lucifer himself. He laughed in my face every time I sunk a little lower into the pit.

One Friday night my friend Elizabeth had an idea. She said it was about time I smoked some pot. I was not for that at all because I did not even like to smoke a cigarette. She said if I would sip some wine then the smoke would not burn. So, I agreed to try. As we sat at my kitchen table, Elizabeth lit up a joint and passed it to me. We had poured glasses of wine in readiness of my impending doom. I sucked in on the marijuana, choked on the smoke and started coughing. I grabbed my wine glass and took a big gulp to sooth my burning throat. Elizabeth was laughing as she took another hit. She said, "Here, try again." This time I took a big drink of wine first and then puffed the joint. It still burned, so I downed some more wine. Because I did not usually drink much, all that wine mixed with a few hits of pot were beginning to take effect. Everything became really funny, and I started laughing with Elizabeth. I didn't want any more marijuana, but we finished the bottle of wine. I was supposed to go to a disco club several miles from my house to meet a couple from work. That night became one of the many times someone must have been praying for me because it was only the grace of God I did not kill someone or even myself. My life could have gone from bad to worse in an instant because by the time I got in my car to drive to the club, I was unbelievably drunk and high. Elizabeth should have never let me get in the car. But I guess she was so high she didn't care. She left and walked home as I was leaving for the club. I had no memory of backing out of my driveway or parking at the club or any idea how I got there. The only memory I had of driving was when I ran a red light, and there were no cars around. Can you imagine how devastating that scene could have been? Totally out of it, I found myself standing in a crowded room that was spinning out of control. When my friends found me, I could hardly stand up. "What's wrong?" they asked in a puzzled tone. They had never seen me that way. As I tried to find a place to sit down before I fell down, they grabbed my arm and said, "Come on, we are taking you home!" I argued with them, "No, I came to party with y'all. I am not leaving!" Suddenly, I was outside with one of them on either side of me, pushing me along the sidewalk. With my head still spinning, my legs finally gave way completely. My friend's husband, a rather large guy, picked me up and carried me to my car. He laid me on the back seat, and she drove my car as he followed in theirs. No matter how hard I tried I could not stop the world from spinning. I hated feeling that way because I had no control over my mind or my body. He carried me to my bedroom and laid me on the bed, then left the room so she could get my clothes off of me. She said they were going to stay in the guest room overnight to make sure I was okay. I immediately passed out, but it was not long before I was up and hugging the toilet where I promptly passed out on the floor. Morning came and I woke up in my bed, so they must have helped me during the night. I had a horrible headache, I was still sick to my stomach, and my mouth was like cotton, but at least the room had stopped spinning. She helped me get in the shower, so I could get clean and wash my hair because I had thrown up all over myself. After some juice and toast, I thought I might live, but I was not convinced. When my friends felt it was safe to leave me alone, they went home. It was unbelievable what all they had done for me! They were amazingly true friends who had gone above and beyond any normal friendship. I always held them in high esteem after that night. Thankfully, Heather was staying one more night with my mom, so I went back to bed and slept until Sunday morning. By the time I picked her up I was back to normal and very thankful I was not in jail or something worse. God cares about us even when we don't care about Him. That weekend I certainly learned my lesson. When I would think about what could have happened, I shuddered. After all that had transpired, I just did not have the same feelings for Elizabeth anymore. We remained close friends, but I always felt disappointed that she had put me in a vulnerable position. I know, I chose to smoke the pot and drink the wine, but she knew I was a novice, and she did not take care of me. That made me sad about our friendship. The couple that had helped me so much were not even as close to me as Elizabeth, and look at the difference. I thought Elizabeth was a true friend, but that assessment changed overnight. She no longer had my trust. And that was the last time I ever allowed anything to cause me to lose control of all my faculties. That was a horrible feeling! I did not see how people enjoyed being drunk or high because there was absolutely nothing about it that resembled fun. My drug of choice, men and sex, was certainly more fun, or so I thought at the time. And unlike other drugs, my drug was free and in abundant supply. Plus, it would not cause me to lose control. Well, that was a lie from the pit of hell. Little did I know then just how out of control I would eventually become.

Thirteen

Why Say No?

During the months I spent with Warner, it seemed as if the rest of the world had been on pause. Like in a movie when a couple in love are in a dream sequence, and everything around them stops and fades from existence, and all that's left is the two of them. That was how I felt about the magical moments Warner and I shared. During that time none of the salesmen at work hit on me, and the girl I worked with kept her crude humor to herself. It was as if I had been in a bubble. But now the bubble had popped, and someone yelled, "Action!" and all the players moved back into position to continue the story.

One of the salesmen, Becker, had flirted with me ever since I started working at the furniture store. After my divorce the timing was never right to get together until one Friday night when we all had worked late during a sales event. He invited me for some food and drinks, and this time I was eager to say yes. While having after dinner drinks Becker began to look sort of sad. Puzzled, I asked, "What's wrong?" He answered, "I'm glad you came with me tonight. I sure did not want to be alone." He looked down at his drink and continued, "You see, it has been two years ago today since my wife and child were killed in a car wreck. It is still difficult to get past the date it happened." "Oh my God!" I exclaimed. My heart went out to him as I took his hand and held it tight. He looked up with a small smile and said, "Thank you. I really hate to be alone tonight. Do you think you could stay with me? I will be glad to sleep on the couch." "Of course," I quickly agreed. On the way to his apartment, I kept thinking how horrible it would be to lose your child. We started out watching TV on the couch, but of course one thing led to another and we had sex. We slept together so he would not feel alone. The next morning, he was fine as he drove me back to the store to get my car. Becker and I got together several times after that, but not really for dates, just sex. Then all of a sudden, his interest in me stopped completely. Although our relationship was only physical, I had begun to count on those intimate rendezvous to feed my addiction. I was feeling very despondent and rejected, but he never gave me a chance to confront him. A couple of weeks later when the store had an employee bowling night, I found out the reason for his about face. Becker and I happened to be bowling on the lanes next to each other. After finishing his frame, he would always go back to the gallery seating area and sit with a woman and two kids. I thought, "Now I know why he has cooled things off with me, he's got a girlfriend." That was fine. I had finally resolved my rejection issue because I had plenty of guys at Crazy's that were interested in me, for sex anyway. I was sitting with another salesman and just making small talk. I laughed, "Looks like old Becker has got himself a girlfriend and with kids to boot." The guy responded, "Oh, that's not a girlfriend, that's Becker's wife and kids. They finally moved here after school was out." Shocked was not a strong enough word for how I felt! I was floating somewhere between anger and pity. Anger, that he had conjured up such an elaborate lie to get me to have sex with him and pity, for his poor wife and kids that they had to live with such a jerk. I wanted so badly to go up to her and tell her what a low life she was married to, but she looked like such a nice lady and the kids, too. I rationalized maybe she knew he cheated on her, and she was okay with it. A lot of couples were doing that in those days. But that awful story about the wreck! I did not know what to do, so I did nothing. I just hoped his family would not really be killed because he had said that. I learned a valuable lesson from his lies. You cannot trust anything a man tells you when he wants to get you in bed with him. And, the really ridiculous point about the whole thing was all Becker had to do was ask, and I would have gladly complied. He did not have to make up that horribly tragic story about losing his family. Evidently, he thought I was a nice girl that had to be coaxed. If that was the reason then he thought better of me than I thought of myself.

Then there was salesman number two, Enrique, a very good-looking Mexican man with a capital H for handsome. He was everything you would picture a Don Juan to be. When he would bring his sales ticket to me, I could hardly think. Enrique just oozed with personality and sex appeal. I knew I would never have a chance with him. But then, I found out he only dated Anglo women, non-Mexican. So, whenever he brought his sales ticket up front, I started flirting with him and would just melt when he began to flirt back. Then, unbelievably, one night he asked me to go dancing with him! Me? He actually asked me? I was on cloud nine all night. He was such a smooth disco dancer and a real charmer. When he took me home of course he expected to have sex. My libido was racing! This amazing specimen of virility, this Latin lover wants to have sex with little ole me! There was just one problem. I had recently been taken off my birth control pills because of a hormone issue. When I told Enrique that, he got even more turned on. He had no condoms. He said he didn't use them. I could not resist his romancing, so we had sex. The fact that I might get pregnant was a moot point. Enrique wanted to be with me almost every night if I had let him. He was like a dog after a female in heat. Then one night while we were making love he whispered, "I can feel you getting pregnant. I just know that this time we are making a baby." We had never talked about being in love or getting married, Enrique just wanted to have a baby. As our love making continued, he described in romantic detail how my egg was being pierced by his sperm and how it would grow into a beautiful baby. By the time he finished I was totally convinced I was pregnant. I even ended up missing two menstrual cycles. So, another lesson was learned about how strong the power of suggestion can be on a person's mind and body if you allow it. It was like mind control. Well, as it turned out, I was not really pregnant. When Enrique found out, he decided that I was a waste of time in his quest for fatherhood, and that was the end of our relationship. About six months later I went to a party the store was having in the warehouse. In walked Enrique with an Anglo woman who looked to be at least five months pregnant. I went over to congratulate him, "I didn't know you got married." He said, "I didn't. We're just having a baby." I thought, "Wow! Thank goodness I never got knocked up by him. What kind of future does that poor girl have with this baby?" Thankfully, I was back on birth control pills, so I would not ever have to be in her position.

There was never a shortage of guys to have sex with. My unrealized addiction had a steady supply chain whenever I needed a fix. Usually, I did not have one of my freak out moments if the guy turned out to be just a one-night stand. But, if I was with him twice, my expectations were high. For instance, I had been with a guy from Crazy's Place just two times when I called him at his trailer. The night before I had intentionally left my bracelet and a ring on his counter in order to guarantee another chance to be with him. I told him I wanted to come get them. He said, "Sure, come on over." Those were exciting words, and I was hyped up for another intimate evening. However, when I got there his truck was gone, but the trailer was unlocked. I let myself in. My bracelet and ring were on the table. He was not there. I thought maybe he ran to the store because he was expecting me. But as I looked around, I noticed the place looked bare. I began to get that freaked out feeling as I found out the cabinets and closets were empty! Panic filled every part of me because this was not in the plan! As I drove home, I frantically stopped at every pay phone along the way to call his number. My hands were shaking nervously as I dialed, hoping he had returned to the trailer. My mind was going crazy as I tried to wrap my head around what had just happened. The only way I could calm the rejection storm was to go to the club that night and find a replacement. It never crossed my mind that my reactions were not normal. I just kept rationalizing that I was not doing anything wrong because I thought everybody was doing it. And besides, I felt justified because of all the years I had done without.

The sad part was I did not realize how long my list of sexual encounters was becoming. And, it was not like I was that crazy about the sex. Most of the time I just made sure they enjoyed it so they would come back, and I usually pretended to have an orgasm. The whole affair just seemed to fill a void for a short while. Then the emptiness and torment would prevail again, and I would have to find another guy over and over and over again. There was Darrell, you might say a boy, who was at least ten years younger than I. He did not even have hair on his chest. After a few sex dates I realized he was not fulfilling my deep needs because he was so inexperienced. I did not want to be a teacher. I was too self-indulgent for that. Bradley was a ninety-day wonder Army officer who was short in stature, but big on ego, too big. I thought I was in love. He broke my heart. Daniel, a really good dancer, was married, but would often spend time with me when he was in town on business. After a fun Saturday night, we would enjoy a quiet Sunday morning just hanging out and reading the paper. Momentarily, I felt like a wife. Then there were more one-night stands than I care to remember. Keith was a male model who cooked me a gourmet breakfast while dressed only in an untied smok-ing jacket. Then there was this, Oh So Cute, drunk cowboy who asked me to hold his watch while he fought a guy in the parking lot. I thought I was so special when he chose me out of the crowd. Then we ended up in Mexico where he smashed his truck into two parked cars while trying to leave a parking spot. I don't even remember his name. I used this cute guy Derek, an excellent dancer from Crazy's Place, to show off my dancing skills at a formal Christmas party. I thanked him with sex. I was so full of myself. Then there was another cowboy named Stephen. He was younger, but a really good kisser. He took me to a party some-where way out in the desert. We were definitely planning on having sex, but on the way back to my house he ran out of gas on the highway. Two cop cars pulled over to check us out, and one stayed with him while the other one took me home. I never heard from him again. I guess he was too embarrassed. Unfortunately, the list goes on and on and on.

Then I came across Ronald, a very peculiar person. I read my horo-scope one day that said, "Beware of a good-looking man, he is stranger than he appears." Well, if you read those things the devil will make sure he uses them to his advantage and will make you think that junk tells your future. That night I met Ronald who was extremely good looking. I mean Hollywood good looking. He was from out of town. He was temporarily working downtown doing construction work for an electronics company. He asked me out for the next night, and I went with him to Mexico for dinner and, as it turned out, to watch him down drink after drink. I had never seen someone consume that much alcohol without getting drunk, at least noticeably. He had no problem driving to his apartment where we promptly had sex. But then, he immediately passed out cold on the bed. He was breathing, but he was dead to the world. I had to get to my house because my mom was bringing Heather home first thing in the morning. I tried everything to get him to wake up, but I could see I had an impossible situation. It was too far to walk home. I had no money for a cab and neither did he. I checked his wallet. Plus, it was 3:00 a.m., so I could not call anybody to come get me. The only solution was to take his truck keys and drive home. I left him a note, locked the door, and proceeded to his truck. I had never driven a truck before, and it had been at least eight years since I had driven a standard. It was a miracle I was able to get home. I parked down the street from my house so Mom would not ask questions and then managed to sleep a few hours. Around noon I received a call from Ronald. He wanted his truck. I asked a neighbor to watch Heather for a little bit while I ran an errand. I drove my car to pick Ronald up and take him to his truck where I told him I did not care to see him again. He was so upset and apologetic, but I said goodbye and drove away. For weeks after that he kept calling me all the time, especially in the wee hours of the morning when he was drunk. He would mumble a few words about wanting to see me and pass out with the phone off the hook. That made me so mad because it tied up my phone line, and I could not use the phone until he hung up. In those days there were no answer machines or caller IDs to monitor your calls, and there were no Robo calls, so you always answered the phone. Then one day he showed up at my house with this enormous wooden galleon ship with tall masts and insisted I keep it. He barged in and set it on my dining room table. He had bought it in Mexico. I had to admit it was a beautiful work of art, but he was still begging me for another date. I tried to get him to take the ship back, but he refused. I asked him to please not come back to my house. I was starting to get scared that this was some kind of fatal attraction. Then after a while the phone calls finally stopped. About a week later I received an out-of-state letter from him that made our encounter sound like a lot more than a one-night stand. I was worried again. But then, he said he was leaving for another job in another state, and thank goodness I never heard from him again. So, beware of reading horoscopes. They are as bad as Ouija boards. What they say may just happen. And even if things look good in the beginning, there will always be a bad ending because of the evil spirit controlling the situation. They should be called Horrorscopes.

In the meantime, I had met another salesman, but not from the store where I worked. Travis was a medical supply Rep who regularly came in and out of town on his sales route. Our eyes met across a crowded dance floor at a disco club. He was nice looking, so I kept staring into his eyes as he seemed to come closer to me. When I went back to my table, he came over to buy me a drink and the rest, as they say, was history. We were together the rest of the night, the entire next day and that night. Travis was such a gentleman and took me to eat at really nice places I had never been before. He was a very decent guy, but married. He and his wife were separated, but trying to reconcile. They had children that he really missed. Travis was so sweet that I found my-self encouraging him to stop running around with other women and go back to his wife. Our dates became like counseling sessions, but I would always spend the night with him. Travis was a very tender and loving man, and I looked forward to when he was in town which was quite often. But our last encounter came one day when he called me at work and wanted to see me right away. The girl I worked with laughingly said I should go and get some *afternoon delight*. I had a feeling Travis had not called about that at all, but he sounded as if it was important. I asked my boss if I could leave for the rest of the day and he said okay. I went to Travis's motel room where he was waiting for me. When I walked in, he grabbed me and hugged me for a long time. He looked happy as he related his news to me. Travis told me that he and his wife had totally reconciled and were going to marriage counseling. He continued to say how everything I had told him was what had made the difference in how he felt about his marriage. I was honestly excited for him because I knew he really loved his wife. I felt proud of myself that I had done a good deed for somebody. He was on his way back to his home and, being the caring individual he was, he did not want to just leave me hanging and never show up again without a word. I told him his wife was a very lucky lady to have him. With another big hug, we said good-bye forever. That experience had given me such a wonderfully unselfish feeling that many times after that you could find me sitting on a bar stool listening to some guy's sad marriage problems and encouraging him to go home and make it better. However, Travis was my one and only success story that I ever knew about.

After I no longer had Travis to look forward to, soon loneliness over took me again and turned into depression which sparked my addiction. Without realizing just how far away from normal conduct I had drifted, I willingly fell deeper and deeper into the swells of darkness. Nothing seemed out of the question or too lurid to be a party to. This period of time in history was when *swingers* would have key parties where husbands and wives changed partners and had sex with neighbors. Free love was all the talk, but there was nothing free about it. You paid dearly with the price of your soul. Oversexed men wanting strange encounters were easy to find, and women like me were always willing to join in on anything they wanted to do. I decided one day that I needed to get away and have a change of scenery, so I planned a short trip, by myself, to visit my girlfriend, Margaret. She lived in northern California. One of the guys at Crazy's Place over heard me talking about my trip and said he had a friend who lived where I was going to be. He called him, and the friend said he would show me the town. I agreed since that way I would not have to spend my money. Margaret picked me up at the airport, and after a few days with her I called this guy. He was ready to drop everything and spend the weekend with me. I packed a small overnight bag, and he came and got me the next morning. He drove me everywhere on a sightseeing mission that any tourist would envy. He was fun and appeared to have money. He dressed nice, had a nice convertible car, and a gourmet appetite for food. There was just one small detail I was curious about; he wore a wedding band. When I finally felt comfortable enough to ask about it, he just laughed. "Oh, that. Don't worry about a thing. My wife and I have an arrangement, an open marriage. She goes out with other men, and I go out with other women. We always tell each other where we are going. It makes our marriage more exciting and increases our desire for each other." I thought, "How weird? Oh well, if they are crazy enough to live like that, I will just reap the benefits because he was treating me like a queen." The guy showed me an amazing day, but it was not over yet. He said, "Why don't we just spend the night here so we can get an early start tomorrow. I have many other places to show you. We will probably be gone an extra night, so if you need to buy any toiletries or clothes, I can take care of that. I'll just call my wife, and you call your girlfriend so they won't worry." Talk about double weird! Anyway, we both made our calls, and he got us a nice room. It was the first time I had ever slept on a water bed. Sex was definitely different. After getting up the next morning, I still felt like I was rocking back and forth on the water. We had another two very fun days shopping, eating at amazing restaurants and being regular tourist. When he took me back to Margaret's place, he was so matter-of-fact about the whole adventure. We had a fun weekend and that was that. The experience just confirmed my opinion that everybody was doing it, but I did not think I was as crazy as he and his wife, not yet anyway.

Soon after returning to work at the furniture store, I was surprised to receive a phone call from my old boss at the bank. He had heard about my divorce and offered me my old job back. I would not have imagined in a million years that he would do that. Of course, I said yes immediately. I loved working at the bank, and it was a lot more pay. So, the first of the month I started back doing what I had done for years, running their large check processing computer system. I felt as if

I had never left. But my boss soon found out that I was no longer the meek young lady who used to bow to his every mood. I was a woman of the world now and would not put up with some of the stuff he liked to dish out. It was not long before he realized there were boundaries and mostly stayed away from me and let me do my job. Being back at the bank gave me a whole new group of party friends, but I drew the line at having sex with any co-workers from there. As depraved as I was, at least I had enough sense to know that was not a good idea. The bank atmosphere was much more G rated than the furniture store, which was a good thing. My new job afforded me enough money to buy Heather more things, but it also gave me more to party with. And now, the elements surrounding my sexual adventures were becoming more bizarre or even perverse. The darkness that engulfed my every decision was leading me into situations where I would have never thought I would go. I lived in a constant onslaught of emptiness and fear. Some of the women at the bank had been going to an old lady who read palms and Tarot cards. I also went to her and received *permission* from the cards to live my life doing whatever feels good. Imagine that. Wonder where that came from? I'll give you three guesses. That green light to sin and degradation was from the pit of hell, but I just received it with an anxious anticipation for future pleasures.

Right on cue was my new temptation to, "If it feels good, do it." With the extra money I was making I was able to join a bowling league again. I thought it would be a more wholesome alternative to Crazy's Place, and Heather would have fun playing in the child care room they provided at the bowling alley. Well, lo and behold, the devil was waiting for me there, too. I reconnected with a married couple that William and I used to bowl with before our divorce. I guess you could say we were friends, and I had actually known the guy in grade school. He was a jerk then and an even bigger jerk as a grown man. When William and I were married he would flirt with me when no one was looking, but I always just ignored him. Once he found out I was divorced, he came on to me even more this time. Only the difference between then and now was I had also become a jerk. One day he called me and asked me to meet him, so I did. We parked somewhere and made out in the car like a couple of teenagers. He said he wanted to get together again to have sex, but it had to be during the day so his wife would not get suspicious. Well, that was no problem since I had a floating day off during the week because I worked on Saturday, and Heather still went to daycare to keep the routine. He would come to my house every chance he could, and there was something about all the sneaking around that made our sex even better. We managed to carry on this charade for quite some time until one day his wife called me, and she was crying. She told me she thought her husband was having an affair, and she didn't know what to do. I just listened and consoled her. I could not tell if she knew it was me or if she was trying to find out for sure. Whatever her reason was, she had accomplished her mission. After that conversation I felt so guilty, I told her husband I was stopping. I often wondered if she did really know that I was the one or that she just needed a shoulder to cry on. Frankly, I believed she knew because although we were friends, we were not that close for me to be someone she would have called and confided in. The lady had guts. We all continued bowling together on the league, always acting like we were friends. I sometimes thought to myself, "She was a very clever woman."

The *having sex for fun because I had been without so long* excuse had by now, gone totally by the wayside. Sex had evolved into an addictive need to be with a man. My actions in that area of my life were spiraling out of control while I maintained the perfect picture of motherhood to my friends and neighbors. I was not much different than a weekend drunk who kept a steady job, took care of a house, and raised a family. Only my vice was not booze, it was sexual encounters. There was one girl at the bank who knew me well because we always went to Crazy's Place together. Then after closing time, we would continue to party across the border in a new modern area that had built upscale clubs which stayed open all night. Anglo women were very popular with Mexican men, and many of them had money. It was easy to feel wanted over there. For instance, this one night the owner of the club was being very friendly towards me. There was just something about a Latin lover that really made me melt. I was his the rest of the night, dancing until dawn. My friend had already left because he was taking me home. After he closed the club, we left in a taxi to go to my house. We had made out the whole time on the way, so we were both ready for sex. The taxi waited in my driveway for seven hours because we both fell asleep. That really made me feel wanted when I thought about how much he was going to have to pay that taxi driver. It did not even bother me that it was just a one-night stand because my need had been filled to the brim for the time being.

But eventually, having sex with so many men was taking a toll on my psyche. One would say, "It's about time!" It had now been about a year of this degrading lifestyle. Although I was not happy, my flesh did not want to quit. Addictions are hard to stop. I thought, "It's time to settle back down into a serious relationship." But there was no way the devil was going to let that happen. He was having too much fun with me. So, he put Jackson in my path. Now, when I met Jackson, I was fooled into thinking I could have what I wanted a relationship to be. He was a hardworking, good old boy type much like William, but Jackson enjoyed sex. We went out a lot, mostly dancing, which I loved. We got along great, and I thought things were moving along pretty normal until one day he asked me how I felt about a foursome. A foursome? I didn't know what he meant. Then he said there was a guy at his work who wanted to have couple's sex, all four of us together. On one hand I was shocked, but on the other hand I did not want Jackson to lose interest in me, so I agreed and he set it up at his place. I had never been to where he lived, so it was quite a surprise. Before his divorce he had planned to build a house, but only finished an enormous garage/shop area, and that was where he lived. One big room with a cement floor and a toilet and shower in one corner and no privacy. There was a small bed, a table and a refrigerator. No stove, just a hot plate. Jackson had put a large camping mat on the floor, covered with a quilt for padding and a sheet over that. I felt as if I had to disconnect from reality to go through with this, but I was ready. The other couple finally arrived, and I could tell right away that the guy's wife was extremely nervous. She was more the doting housewife type. You know the kind that might always wear a dress, high heels and pearls at home. It was obvious this was all her husband's idea, and she was just going along with it to please him. Jackson and his friend started taking their clothes off, so I did too. By now, I had zero modesty. The other woman stood frozen in place. Jackson went over and started kissing on her and tried to help her undress while her husband and I were already on the mat. Nothing about this situation turned me on because I kept watching her reaction to her husband being with me. I felt so sorry for her and was sure she had probably never had sex with any man other than her husband. She only had her blouse off when she pulled away from Jackson, so he joined us on the mat. Then she started crying, "I want to go home!" She was sobbing uncontrollably as she tried to hurriedly put her blouse back on. After they left, Jackson was apologizing to me that the evening was such a disaster. My mind was in a fog. I was not sure how to feel other than filthy, and I don't mean because we had been on the floor. I was just so concerned about that poor lady and wondered if their marriage could withstand such a traumatic event. I told Jackson we were never doing that again.

If I'd had any sense, I should have been concerned about me, that I had stooped so low to even do such a thing. But when you are addicted to something you don't exactly think straight. Jackson and I continued to date because I figured that episode was the end of that scene. Then one night he took me to a popular movie called *Bob and Carol and Ted and Alice*. It was a comedy about two couples who jointly agreed to indulge in a foursome. Even though the foursome bedroom scene ended with only kissing, it gave Jackson new motivation. He left the movie saying that was the way that awful night should have been. He observed the problem could be solved if all parties involved were in agreement to have sex. I basically ignored him, not realizing he wouldn't let it go. One evening when he picked me up for our date, he said he had a surprise for me. He drove us to a house in an ordinary middle-class neighborhood and parked in the driveway. I asked, "What are we doing?" "You'll see," he grinned. The door was answered by a couple a little younger than us.

After introductions they ushered us to a back bedroom filled with wall-to-wall mattresses. The room was painted black with erotic pictures on the walls that were illuminated by a black light. The man guided me into the room and began to kiss me and undress me while Jackson and the woman did the same. The scenario was quite unreal, and I could not help thinking, "Where did Jackson find these people?" I figured the movie was right, foursomes were the *IN* thing. The sex was intense as partners were switched back and forth. It was obvious this couple were pros at this. I have no idea how long we were there, but it was quite an unnerving experience. Jackson was thrilled, but I was tired of being weird or kinky or sexually perverted. That was not the kind of sex that fulfilled my need for love. I was at war with myself, and I did not like the person I had become. I wanted to be normal again with a normal lifestyle! So not long after that escapade, Jackson and I parted ways.

Just in the nick of time, before my sanity was totally depleted, an opportunity arose for another change of scenery. The bank where I worked was sending several employees out of town to train on a new computer system. Naturally, since I was the main computer operator I was getting to go, and I was thrilled! An all-expense paid trip out of this godforsaken town was just what I needed. We would be there for five days. But just because you change your location, does not mean you change your sin. So wouldn't you know that my old friend for sex, Jake, the best dancer at Crazy's, heard about my upcoming trip. And conveniently, I was going to be in the exact same town in the exact same week that he would be there for a business convention. He asked me where I was staying because he wanted to take me dancing at some big well-known country western place. How could I resist that! A whole night of dancing with the Fred Astaire of Crazy's Place and not have to share him with anybody was like a dream come true. So, we set it all up to get together. The plane ride to our destination was a blast because the group that went was all about having fun. We worked by day and played by night. We each had our own room in a luxury hotel in the downtown convention center area. It just so happened that week was a big coaches convention, and there were hundreds of men in our hotel. It was a virtual male buffet. Wherever we went in the hotel, we just could not help but tease. We would yell, "Hi, coach!" and the whole room would turn around. It was hilarious! In the club I finally zeroed in on this one cute guy that was kind of shy and married. I think it was the challenge. He sat very close to me at my table in the hotel lounge where my friends and I would go after work. One night he had a lot to drink which emboldened him to be very snuggly on the dance floor. When the party broke up, he followed me up to my room. I took his hand and led him over to the bed. I had the definite feeling he had never cheated on his wife before. But what are out-of-town conventions for, right? All the guys were doing it. No one would ever know. Sadly, that is how we all thought. We were right in the midst of tremendous sex when the phone rang. I thought, "Who in the world would be calling me here?" Then I thought about Heather, with my mom, so I had better answer it. I whispered to the coach to not talk, and I picked up the receiver, "Hello." It was Jake. I could not let him know I was with this guy because he might get mad and cancel our date. So, I had to lie there and make small talk for a few minutes. He told me the time he would pick me up the next night, and I hung up the phone. I knew the coach had heard every word. I felt like a prostitute lying there having sex with one man while filling my schedule with a different man for the next night. Although the atmosphere on the bed changed and seemed uncomfortable, I made sure coach got what he came for; then he left right away. I convinced myself that at least he knew I was not a prostitute because he didn't pay me anything. However, I still felt cheap. The next night I met up with Jake, and we danced to every song played by a fantastic country western band. I felt like Ginger Rogers. We ended the night in my hotel room. He didn't stay until morning because he had an early meeting the next day. As I laid there alone in my bed an awful feeling came over me. "I am a prostitute," I thought. I am always available for any man, and I make sure they have great sex even if I don't. I was afraid to even count up how many there had been. What have I become? An unpaid prostitute? The thought made me nauseous. Then I rationalized the whole thing, "I'll bet most of the women at Crazy's do the same thing I do. I am no different than they are." Thinking like that somehow gave me enough peace to drift off to sleep, but my turmoil was far from over.

When I got back to my home, I was so glad to see Heather and feel her little arms around my neck. She was my anchor, and the only true joy I had to look forward to. She was four years old now and always a pleasure to be around. If it were not for my week days of sanity with her, my weekends of craziness would have already done me in. I wanted so much for her and me to get away from all this, but I did not know how to make it happen. I found myself becoming more and more depressed, but I still kept going to Crazy's Place. That was a perfect name for it because most of the people there were crazy, including me. One night Jake said, "Let's go out back." I followed him out the club's back door. It was dark and deserted. He pushed me against the wall, pulled my jeans down, unzipped his and proceeded to do a *Wham, bam, thank you ma'am,* only he did not say thank you. He finished quickly, zipped up and went back inside. He just left me there with my pants down, dripping with semen, and feeling like the total slut I had become. Just a discarded piece of trash left next to the dumpster. I thought I had hit rock bottom, but there was still more room to fall before I was completely there. I continued my downward spiral one night in Mexico. My girlfriend and I went back to the club where the rich Mexican men hung out. It was easy to find one that would show you a good time. This particular man was older and very charming, good looking and well dressed. I was feeling especially depressed that night, so when he invited me to his motel room, I went. The next morning, I was awakened by a knock on the door, and the guy was gone. I wrapped the sheet around my naked body and opened the door. A large body guard looking dude was at the door. He said, "You need to get dressed and leave now. There's a taxi waiting downstairs to take you home. Here's some money to pay the driver and a little extra for you." He shoved the money into my hand and shut the door. I was furious, "How dare that jerk treat me like this!" Now I felt like a real prostitute. I wanted to throw the money back in his henchman's face, but I needed it to get home. As I dressed, I was steaming mad, "The nerve of that guy leaving without a word, then sending his goon to pay me off! Who did he think he was anyway? Or worse, who did he think I was?" I left the room and slammed the door hard. The big guy was waiting for me and escorted me to the cab. I guess he wanted to make sure I was gone. I was fuming all the way home. I wasn't sure if I was madder at the rich guy or at myself. You would think that incident was finally rock bottom, right? But unfortunately, darker days are yet to come.

My depression worsened. I hung desperately to the lyrics of a song they played at Crazy's, "Help me to take one day at a time sweet Jesus, that's all I'm asking of you." I was not religious by any stretch of the imagination. And I was not even sure if there was a God or a Jesus, but there was something about that song that gave me hope. The closest I came to hearing the Gospel was as I waltzed to "On the wings of a snow-white dove He sent His pure sweet love, a sign from above, on the wings of a dove." To me it was just a great song to waltz to. I was so self-absorbed, but afraid of everything, especially death. There was no way I would ever go to a funeral or even visit someone in the hospital, even when a dear friend from work got real sick. She was the most loving person I had ever met; her name was Patricia. She was always smiling, never got mad or upset, was not judgmental, and never gossiped. Every day she was so nice to everyone; you could never tell that Patricia had leukemia. One day her doctor told her the stupidest thing you could imagine. Patricia looked healthy and felt great, but according to tests he had run on her, he told her she should not be feeling that good. Can you believe a doctor would say that? Well, it was not long before Patricia was in the hospital. I wanted to go see her so badly, but all my fears kept me away. Then one night I had a very unusual dream. I saw Patricia lying on a hospital bed. The room was all white, and no one was with her. On the far wall by her bed was a door. The door opened, and Jesus walked in. He came around the foot of the bed to the side I could see, and He took Patricia's hand. She got up out of bed and began to walk with Jesus, still holding His hand. When Patricia got out of bed, she had on a hospital gown, but when she walked through the door with Jesus, she was wearing one of her favorite pantsuits she often wore to work. They just disappeared into the brightness on the other side of the door. I suddenly woke up and for some reason looked at my alarm clock. It was exactly 2:00 a.m. The next day at work, I found out that Patricia had died earlier that morning at 2:00 a.m. I quietly freaked out! I could not believe it! Why did I have that dream? Had I seen Patricia slip into eternity? Does Jesus really exist? It was all so bizarre to me I did not tell anyone, but I certainly never forgot it. The dream seemed so real.

I believed the lyrics of those songs and that dream kept my nose above water. I still went dancing every chance I got, but for a while I was not having sex with anybody. Then along came Frank. He was the sweetest, funniest, most sincere guy you could meet in a bar and had dimples. We met one night when I was shooting pool at Crazy's Place, and Frank put his quarter on the rail. The person I was playing left, so Frank and I played. There was just something about him, besides his winning smile. I liked him immediately. We shot several games of pool, danced, and then he took me to breakfast. When he took me home, he did not even try to come in. That was refreshing. A few nights later I was in the den watching TV when there was a knock at the side door. It was kind of late, Heather was already asleep, so I cautiously opened the door. It was Frank! He came in with a six-pack of beer that I put in the fridge. He didn't know that I did not like beer, but I opened one for him. We talked and watched TV while he downed several cans. Then he got romantic, and we ended up having sex. That weekend he took me to Crazy's, and we had a wonderful time. I spent the night at his trailer. It seemed as if our relationship was really progressing, and then it all went cold. He stopped calling, so I called him. He was friendly, but that was it. I asked if I could come over, and he said maybe another time. I really liked Frank, and I was starting to feel panicky that I might not see him again. One night the panic turned into an overpowering, almost obsessive desire to be with Frank! I needed him for my *fix*. I just had to see him, immediately! Out of the darkness came the spirits of manipulation and control and set my imagination on fire with a plan to make it happen. I conjured up a devious idea to force him to see me. It was after midnight when I drove by his trailer to make sure he was home. A few blocks from there was a phone booth near some houses. I made up a detailed story of how I had been at a small party at one of those houses, and everyone there decided to leave and go to Mexico, but I didn't want to go. By the time I realized I had left my car keys in their house all the people had driven away, and I was stuck! There I was all alone on a dark, deserted street, and I was scared. Sounded pretty good, I thought. I had a spare house key hidden at home and spare car keys in the house, so I was safe to initiate my nefarious plan. I wanted my desperation to sound authentic, so I opened the trunk of my car, threw my keys in there, and slammed the lid closed. Crazy, right? I was truly stuck. I walked to the nearby phone booth, called Frank, and proceeded to relay my diabolical story of a damsel in distress. Being the nice guy he was, what else could he say but yes, he would help me. My plan had worked! He picked me up and took me to my house to get my spare key. I had won! I was with Frank! I had never before felt such power to make something happen. I loved on him all the way back to my car; you know, to show my appreciation. Before I got into my car, I gave him a passionate thank you kiss that he could not resist. "Let's go to your trailer," I beckoned. We did, and I spent the night. Mission accomplished! I felt good, but my elation was short-lived when the following weekend Frank showed up at Crazy's with another woman. I was devastated! How could he do that to me? I was freaking out again. Frank had a friend at the club named Gabriel that I had started talking to a lot. I was trying to find out what was going on with Frank and this woman. Gabriel had a girlfriend that worked at Crazy's, so he was always around. Sometimes he would go dance, but mostly he just sat at the bar waiting for his girlfriend to get off work. So, I always went crying on Gabriel's shoulder about Frank. That was how Gabriel and I became friends. I never thought anything about Gabriel except he was a friend of Frank's. I kept bothering Gabriel because Frank kept coming every weekend with the same woman, and there was gossip they might get married. I felt like such a fool when I thought about the crazy stunt

I had pulled with the car keys. It was like it wasn't really me that did that. Was I having a mental breakdown? Heather was even starting to act out because I was not showing her enough attention. Finally, after weeks of mental turmoil, my obsession with Frank subsided. My life desperately needed a change. I decided I would stay home more with Heather, so I sold all my living room furniture and bought a regulation size pool table to put in that space. I loved to play pool and having my own table would allow me to have friends come to my house to have fun, and I would not have to go out as much. For the time being, that was my best plan.

Fourteen

A Second Chance

There was a small country western club near where my mom lived, and sometimes I would stop in for a few dances on Sunday afternoon before picking up Heather. There I met three young girls that were in the Army and stationed at the local base. We would talk a lot about their lives in the military, and they all three hated living in the barracks. They were nice girls, so I unassumingly said why don't you all rent my spare bedroom. I figured there was no way all three of them would want to be in a small bedroom with a double bed. But they jumped at the chance! They alternated sleeping on the bed with one on the floor. They shared Heather's bathroom and had full access to the rest of the house. All three were good kids and they spent time playing with Heather and enjoyed the pool table with me. It was wonderful having people in the house like I had a big family. There was never a dull moment with those ladies around. They always had interesting stories to tell about their adventures in the Army. The joy they brought to my home greatly helped my vulnerability to depression. But I really missed dancing, and it was good exercise. So, when I saw an ad in the paper about square dancing lessons at the YMCA, I decided to check it out. There was child care for Heather, and I could be around decent ordinary people. The only problem was you had to be a couple. I was so longing for wholesome fun that I decided to ask my new friend Gabriel if he would consider being my partner. Surprisingly, he said yes right away. So, once a week Heather and I would meet Gabriel at the YMCA for our lessons. It was so much good clean fun. Gabriel was very funny in square dancing class; he had everyone laughing. Now that I had somewhat cleaned up my act, I thought I had been doing better as a mother until something odd happened one night in class. It had been quite a while since I had experienced an event that could be added to my list of unusual occurrences. I was sitting and talking to some people during rest break, and for some reason Heather was there in the class with me that night. Suddenly, this old man I had never seen before came up to me and said, "You only pay attention to her when someone is looking at you." He was motioning towards Heather. I turned and looked at her, then quickly turned right back to speak to the man, but he was gone. I searched the room for him, and he was nowhere to be found. We were sitting at the opposite side of the room far from the only door. There was no way he could have made it to the door that fast, even running. Although I always thought I did a good job of giving Heather attention, she was still being mischievous. I knew I was spending too much time on the telephone. So, after that creepy encounter, I made sure my attention for her was genuine and not for show. Years later I realized the old man was probably an angel on assignment to help me be a better mother. For some crazy reason I always took to heart what people said and did it. But unfortunately, I also did some things I was told that were not good. After a while Gabriel began to pick us up for class, and sometimes we would go eat afterwards. We were both getting pretty good at square dancing. One Sunday afternoon our class even got to do some exhibition dances at the airport. Heather and I were really enjoying ourselves and began spending more and more time with Gabriel. She liked him because he was funny and made her laugh. Even Mom liked him, but she was always partial to Mexican men. Personally, I still just thought of him as a good friend. I finally seemed to be in a pretty good place emotionally, and I wanted to keep it that way.

Having the girls around all the time, plus having fun with Gabriel was definitely helping me to not feel so lonely or unloved.

After a few months of dance lessons, Gabriel began to come around the house more often. I thought he just enjoyed being around Heather because his ex-wife would not allow him to see his boy and girl, or so he said. William could see Heather anytime he wanted to, it just seemed like he seldom wanted to. So, it was nice for Heather to have Gabriel around to give her attention. But then, Gabriel began to ask me out on dates. That was a pleasant surprise in our friendship. Especially because, the few times I went back to Crazy's Place Gabriel still waited for his girlfriend to get off work. I asked him if they were breaking up, and he said he was working on it. That was new for me. Now I was the other woman. Usually, men left me for someone else, so it was a big ego booster. A few weeks later Heather went with William to visit his mother and would be gone for two weeks. That was when the relationship between Gabriel and me really started heating up. Until then I had not even thought about going to bed with him. But now, Gabriel and I were hooking up on a regular basis. He was practically living at my house. The Army girls didn't care; they were so whatever. Gabriel was very passionate in the bedroom. He wanted me to talk dirty to him, like I was a whore or something. Whether it was true or not, he made me feel like I was the best sex he had ever experienced. By the time Heather returned home, Gabriel and I were getting pretty serious. However, he went back to stay at his trailer for Heather's sake. But, doing that created major problems because Gabriel's old girlfriend kept coming over to see him, and he was not doing much to put a stop to it. He and I would get in big arguments about her, but he swore he was not interested in her anymore and only wanted me. Gabriel would tell me, "The worst of you is the best I've ever had." I wondered how many other women had heard that line. But amazingly, after a fight, we would have the most incredible sex. I was definitely hooked.

Then one day Gabriel came to see us and he looked rather sad. He said the union was sending him on a construction job in Houston that could last up to a year. Well, this time it took a while, but here we go again! I held it together because Heather was there and feeling very sad. She had got used to having him around, too. My insides were doing flip flops, getting ready to panic when Gabriel said, "Don't worry, I will be back to visit. I love you guys!" Those words seemed to create a ray of hope that appeased my fears momentarily. The day he left we had a tearful group hug, and off he went to drive all the way across Texas. In the weeks that followed I knew I felt a void in my life, but I was not devastated like when other men had left. Maybe because he really had not left me, but because of the job. Maybe I believed he would come back. Gabriel called us as often as possible which really helped my uneasiness. After he had been gone a few months, he called and said he was really lonesome for us and wanted me and Heather to come to Houston. I said I would check vacation schedules, so we could go for a visit. Gabriel said he didn't want us to visit, he wanted us to stay. That was when he added, "Will you marry me?" I was speechless! I never saw that coming! I slowly sat down on a kitchen stool. Gabriel wondered, "Are you still there?" I said, "I'm here, but I am not sure what I just heard." He repeated, "Will you marry me?" Thoughts were racing through my head, "He's not bad looking, he is great with Heather, he makes good money, he's a good dancer, he is excellent in bed, and I could leave this town." That cinched it. I said, "Sure, why not." Gabriel was excited! I was elated at the thought of settling down. I was really tired of the single life, and I always liked being married. I asked, "When do you want the wedding? I do want to get married in a church." I don't know why that was so important to me when I never really acknowledged God. It just seemed the right thing to do. Gabriel answered, "I will get time off for Thanksgiving, let's do it then." "Do you care which church?" I inquired. "No, I will leave all the planning to you since I'm not there. I'll send you a check to cover expenses." Now, I am starting to feel excitement as I asked, "Can we have a small reception at the church?" With that he answered, "You know what? Let's get married the Sunday afternoon before Thanksgiving. We can have the church reception then invite all our guests and family to go directly out to Crazy's Place for a party and dancing." "But they are not open on Sunday," I queried. "Exactly," Gabriel answered. "I can rent the place for a few hours for the party." I thought, "Wow, he does have money." I said, "Okay, I will get to work on everything. Can I tell people right away?" "Of course. Invite anyone you want, and I will call my family and friends," Gabriel replied with joy.

After I hung up, I was beside myself with anticipation. I could not believe what just happened! It was an ordinary phone call which turned out to be an extraordinary turn of events. My thoughts were overloading my brain thinking of all I had to do, and I only had two months to plan. Well, William and I did it in one week, so two months should be easy. This time I wanted to have a real wedding. I wanted to walk down the aisle to *Here Comes the Bride* and have someone give me to the groom. I wanted music as the guests were being seated and a bigger wedding cake. I wanted to carry flowers and have a professional photographer. And of course, Heather would be my flower girl. But who would give me away? My daddy was gone! I had so much to think about and plan. Most importantly, I had to tell Heather first. She was in her room coloring at her little desk. I walked in and sat in the rocker, "Are you ready to show me your picture?" She nodded happily, then climbed up on my lap while proudly holding her masterpiece. After she explained all the shapes and the story I asked, "Do you ever miss Gabriel?" She said, "Yes, I wish he would come back." "What would you think if we went to see him in Houston?" I replied. "When can we go?" she answered excitedly. "Well, what would you think if Gabriel and I got married and we moved to Houston?" Heather looked puzzled. I was not sure she understood what getting married meant. Then she asked, "Where's Houston?" I smiled, "On the other side of Texas. Do you know what it means to get married?" She said, "No." I explained that we would have a wedding in a church and wear long dresses and lots of people would be there. Then Gabriel and I would be husband and wife, and she and I would move to Houston to live with him. Heather was quietly absorbing all the information. Then I asked, "Would you like that?" She responded, "Yes, Mommy. I like Gabriel. Will my dress be pretty?" I laughed, "It will be beautiful! Any more questions?" She put her finger on her chin as if in deep thought, "What will my room look like?" With that question I instantly decided that we would take all of Heather's furniture, toys, curtains and decorations. "Your room will look almost the same as this one because everything you have will be going with us. Will that be okay?" She smiled and nodded an okay then went back to her desk. "I'm going to draw a picture of the wedding," she announced. I giggled under my breath thinking, "I wonder what that's going to look like since she has never seen a wedding?" I answered, "I'm going to fix supper. Show me your picture when you finish." When I went to bed that night I thought, "What a difference a day makes!" I had already started my to do list that evening after supper. It was overwhelming, but surely I could pull off a small ceremony. I was a born organizer, so I knew I could do it. I would start tomorrow.

The first person I called the next day was my mom. She liked Gabriel, but was mildly reactive to my marriage news. When I told her we were moving to Houston she strongly responded with, "When will I get to see Heather?" You notice I was not mentioned in the request. "We will come back as often as possible because all of Gabriel's family is here, too," I explained. Then she wanted to know when and where, so I laid out all our plans. As expected, there was no offer to be involved and no real excitement. "I just wanted you to be the first to know, and I will give you more details later." I hung up and called Rosemary, then Elizabeth, and the excitement began to build. About then my doorbell rang. It was Gabriel's older sister, and she did not look very happy. She began to explain, "Gabriel has told all the family that you are getting married." "That's right!" I announced joyfully. She still looked serious, "Why don't you just date and remain friends or even just live together until you know for sure?" "Because he wants to marry me," I said, not sure what she was getting at. "You know he was divorced, right?" "Of course. I'm divorced, too," I retorted in his defense. She continued, "Do you know he has two children he never sees? And do you know why?" "I know Gabriel has two children, but we never talk about that, nor do we talk about my marriage and divorce. That was all in the past!" I was starting to get a little perturbed. Then she said, "It's because Gabriel used to beat his wife." "I do not believe that!" I rebutted. "It's true. His wife finally had to get a court order against him because it happened a lot during their marriage. And that's why she does not want the kids to be with him." I was appalled at her audacity to assume that Gabriel would ever treat me like that! I fumingly responded, "Well, if there is an ounce of truth in what you say, they were very young when they got married, and Gabriel is different now! He treats me very well. We have even had some big arguments, and he has never made a motion to do something like that. So, I think you need to leave now." As his sister got up to leave, she added, "I just thought you should know, as I was sure he had not told you. Why don't you ask him about it?" "Don't worry. We are fine! Goodbye!" I could not believe the nerve of her trying to rain on my parade. I was not about to ask him such a thing or even tell him she came by. Because then, she and Gabriel would be mad at each other, his whole family would get upset, and my beautiful wedding would be ruined! Besides, he had never shown any signs of abuse. He was soft spoken and hardly got mad even when I was furious. As far as I was concerned that was the end of that.

All I wanted to do was concentrate on our wedding and get out of that godforsaken place. Gabriel called almost every day to keep up with the progress and to see if I needed more money. I was always frugal and searched out good deals, so he appreciated my efforts. Finding a church proved to be somewhat difficult. Neither Gabriel or I went to church, so they either would not marry us because we weren't members, or they didn't have weddings on Sundays. I wanted to find one in our part of town for everyone's convenience and to be relatively close to Crazy's Place for the after party. I must have gone through the entire phone book list of churches when finally, I found one near my house that said, "Yes." That was a big hurdle out of the way, so the rest should be easy. I found a gorgeous off-white full-length dress with long sleeves for me and a beautiful long dress for Heather that almost matched mine to a tee. Being a winter month, flowers in November were very expensive, so I had the bouquets, corsages and boutonnieres made with artificial flowers. They were perfect. We were expecting a lot of guests, so I ordered a three-tiered, heart-shaped wedding cake for the church reception. As I mentioned before, this time I was determined to walk down the aisle to a resounding wedding march. I could not think of a better person to escort me in place of my late father than my dear friend and neighbor, Mr. Watkins. He and his wife had always been incredible neighbors, but even more, they had been like parents to me after my divorce. They were always there to lend a hand of support and helped with anything I needed. Then I was informed by the church that the organist would not be available for music. I panicked! I had to have the wedding march played! Everything else was falling into place, but no one I knew could play an organ. Then one of my girl roomies suggested I ask the couple that played the music at the small club where we all met. So, I did. They said, "Yes," and I said, "Whew!" He played keyboard and they both sang. They agreed to play soft music while the guests were being seated, sing a couple of love songs to start the ceremony, and then put forth a robust wedding march. Unfortunately, it was a pretty small church so my grand entrance would be limited. But everything was working out perfectly. The rings were bought, Crazy's Place was reserved, hair appointments were made, the photographer was scheduled, and invitations were hand delivered with one week to spare.

Now all we needed was the groom to come to town. Gabriel's plan was to leave his truck in Houston and fly home after work on Friday. We would have to bring my car back with us. He arrived at his mom's place in plenty of time to rest and clean up in order to make it to the rehearsal that evening. I was so excited that I was going to be with him permanently. After the church rehearsal, the entire wedding party and relatives went to my future mother-in-law's house to celebrate. Our festive evening was complete with delicious homemade Mexican food and lots of dancing. Gabriel wanted to stay at my house that night, so I kept telling myself, "I will not have sex with him. That way our wedding night will be more special." Yeah right, famous last words. When we returned home from the party, Heather went fast to sleep. Then Gabriel picked me up and carried me to my bed where all the weeks of waiting were enthusiastically satisfied. I was overwhelmingly happy. The next day was a much needed down day because everything was done and ready for Sunday. My room renters had already found other places to live, and they were missed. As we all enjoyed our time together, I imagined this was how it would be every day after we were married. Gabriel and I made a real effort to get to bed early that night, so we would all be rested for the big day. Sunday finally arrived! After breakfast I left Heather with Gabriel while I went to get my hair done. Before I returned Mom came over to watch her so Gabriel could go to his mom's house to prepare for the wedding. I also did not want him to see me in my dress until I walked down the aisle. The entire day was terrific. Even Mom and I were having fun getting dressed up and fixing Heather's hair; a rare moment of togetherness. We three arrived at the church way before Gabriel got there. The photographer began taking behind-the-scenes pictures as more of the wedding party arrived. Heather and I were having so much fun! This was like a real wedding! Wait a minute! It was a real wedding! We laughed joyously! Then the time came to get quiet and composed. Everyone was in their places, including Gabriel. Then I heard the beginning of *Here Comes the Bride*. I almost cried! I took Mr. Watkin's arm, the doors opened, and just as I had always dreamed, I walked down the aisle to my smiling groom. When Gabriel saw me, his expression made it worth all the work. The double ring ceremony was relatively short. We said our vows, a special love song followed, and we lit a unity candle. As the final words came, "You may now kiss the bride," I heard Heather happily giggling as she stood beside me. After the procession exited the sanctuary, we all gathered in the fellowship hall for our reception. Our photographer did a great job capturing every special moment from the walk down the aisle to the cutting of the cake, plus pictures of family and friends. I was especially proud of all the cute posed and candid shots he took of Heather. I could not have asked for any part of our wedding to have gone more smoothly.

Now it was time for the real party to start at Crazy's Place. We had arranged for Heather to go home with my mom for a couple of nights, so Gabriel and I could have some alone time together. Our favorite waitress had readily agreed to work our party, and we hired a D.J. to play music. The normal band would have been way too expensive. We had around thirty people in attendance, and all were having a great time cutting up and dancing. Even Gabriel's sister, who did not want us to get married, was enjoying herself. Gabriel, on the other hand, never liked being the center of attention. He was quiet and withdrawn around a lot of people, so we spent most of our time together on the dance floor. However, as for me, I had always been a people person. I liked to mingle and visited with our guests. But something was different about Gabriel's usual reaction to my normal friendliness. For some reason, I was sensing an animosity of sorts that I had never felt from him before. I just blew it off as an overload reaction to lack of sleep, the stress of the wedding, and too much attention. All was fine when we got home. And unlike my first wedding night, this one was passionate and fulfilling. But there was no way I could have known that night would be the last time in our marriage for me to fully enjoy the freedom of being friendly.

Gabriel and I had the next two days to ourselves, but we spent most of the time arranging my and Heather's move to Houston. He had already been living in a two bedroom apartment in the southeast part of town, so that part was taken care of. We had to rent a small U-Haul for Heather's furniture and toys, plus all our clothes, linens, dishes and so forth. All my furniture remained in the house for the time being to be used by a single mother who rented the place from William. That Tuesday night Gabriel and I went back to Crazy's one more time to tell everyone goodbye. Frankly, I was so glad I would never have to go there again. On Wednesday we picked up Heather, so she could help in the packing of her room. It was a difficult decision as to whether Gabriel and I should pack her room ourselves and not have her come back to see it empty. Or, to let her experience the move and have closure by saying goodbye to the house she had known since birth. I chose the latter, and it was the right decision. Heather was all into the excitement of moving. Gabriel had already spent more quality time with her than William ever did, so leaving her daddy did not seem to be an issue. Leaving her Grammy, my mom, was a little more emotional for Heather, but we planned to return at Christmas, so that helped. That night Heather had to sleep with us in my room. She giggled herself to sleep with Gabriel making jokes, plus she thought it was humorous that we were all three sleeping together in the same bed.

Thanksgiving finally arrived. Heather and I got our cereal and snuggled in front of the TV to watch the Macy's Thanksgiving Day Parade. That had been a tradition for me since I was a kid, and now I was passing it on to Heather. Gabriel eventually woke up. I had let him sleep since we had a long drive to accomplish the next day. I said, "I'll get you some cereal and you can join us." Gabriel answered, "That's okay. I'll get it." When he got his bowl, he didn't come into the den to join us, but instead he sat down at the table in the kitchen. Then I asked, "Aren't you coming to watch the parade?" "No," he answered. "Why don't you guys come in here so we can all eat at the table." I was puzzled, "Normally we would, but it's the Macy's Parade," I explained. "Our family tradition is to watch the parade together, and now you are part of the family so come watch it with us." "I don't think so," Gabriel replied. I thought, "Well, that is kind of strange, but whatever, suit yourself. Maybe he doesn't like parades. He could have just said that." Do you know Gabriel sat at that table, drinking coffee, the entire time the parade was on. One time I went in the kitchen to get Heather some more cereal, and I asked him if I could get him something. He halfway acted like he was not going to talk to me, but finally answered, "No." That was the only time he spoke to either of us during the parade. I didn't know what was wrong with him. In the past he was always ready to be a part of whatever Heather and I were doing. Anyway, she and I finished watching, then ran to the kitchen and gave Gabriel a big hug and kiss and yelled, "Happy Thanksgiving!" Heather always made him smile, so he seemed a lot better. We all got dressed up, and off we went to Gabriel's mom's house for her big Thanksgiving meal. My mom was invited to meet us there.

Now, a Mexican Thanksgiving dinner is a little bit different than your traditional meal. Oh, they had the usual turkey with all the trimmings, but they also had a big pot of pinto beans, Spanish rice, homemade tamales and tortillas, guacamole and a dozen desserts. However, with Gabriel and his large family, including me, Heather and my mom, there was not much left by the end of the day. The party was still going on when we had to leave and get to bed. We had an early morning the next day and a long drive ahead of us. We were hoping to make it at least halfway to Houston. We said all our tearful goodbyes to his family and my mom and then returned to my house for a bittersweet last night there. It seemed as if we had just closed our eyes to sleep, and it was time to get up. Gabriel and I showered and packed last-minute items. I did a final run through in the house and headed out the door. My neighbors were out in the yard talking with Gabriel. The most difficult goodbye for me was Mr. Watkins. He had been like a father to me. I knew I would cry, and he teared up, too. Mom and I had said our final goodbye the night before. So, with my car securely fastened to the small U-Haul, we pulled out of my driveway, and I left my home of nine years. I had a brief moment of sadness. But as soon as we were headed out of town, I felt such a release in leaving all the bad memories behind that nothing but pure bliss filled my heart and mind. What a wonderful feeling it was to be out on the open road, like a newly found freedom. We all seemed relaxed and happy. Heather sat between us sweetly hugging her dolly and coloring in her book. I looked over at Gabriel as he drove, and suddenly this thought popped into my head, "I can learn to love him." I was somewhat shocked that I would think that. But then, I realized the whole time we dated, planned the wedding and got married, love was assumed, but not clearly mentioned. Neither Gabriel or I had ever actually said the words, "I love you" to each other. That surprised me! I had never really thought about it. We got along great, had awesome sex, were perfect dance partners, so love was a given. Right? How could we have even arrived at a point in our relationship to decide to get married if love had not been a part of it? Anyway, I was committed to this marriage now and was thankful that Gabriel had no problem making me feel like I was wanted and loved.

The trip was long and tiring even though we spent one night in a motel. The closer we got to our destination the greener the landscape became. I never knew Texas was so beautiful. I fell in love with the Houston skyline. Some of the building's architectures were so unique. Then we passed by the Astrodome and Astroworld Theme Park, so exciting! As we drove down the freeway there was green grass on each side of the road with gorgeous landscaping and trees, and this was the end of November! It certainly looked nothing like the drab desert where we were from. Soon we came to an older part of town that was not as pretty. The area was cluttered with several small businesses and an unremarkable apartment complex which was our new home. Gabriel had lived there for two months and said it was a safe place and not real noisy. If I had been picking the apartment, I would not have chosen this one, but then again, I didn't know what was available or the price of things in Houston. The complex was rather plain with a few green bushes, and the exterior surrounding was mostly asphalt and cement. Our apartment was upstairs, but I was young and thin, so I didn't mind the climb. When I walked in, I saw a small two bedroom, one bath dump with ugly rented furniture. So much for letting a man pick out a place to live and furnishings. But I figured I could fix it up and made the best of it. I sure did not want Gabriel to think he had messed up. Heather was excited as we unloaded her furniture and toys and fixed up her bedroom. After emptying the U-Haul, we set out to find a place to eat and then somewhere to buy groceries. Gabriel had not yet installed a phone in the apartment, so I looked for a pay phone to call my mom. I wanted to let her know we arrived safely and to tell her about the trip, the apartment and so forth. Well in those days, way before cell phones, if you were calling long distance, you could call collect which meant the person you were calling would pay for the call. That was especially handy when using a pay phone for a long-distance call. Otherwise, you would have to obtain a ton of change to keep feeding coins into the slot. Mom would be charged, but I could pay her back if she needed us to. The operator would ring the number, and you could hear her asking the other person if they would accept the charges for the caller, and when they said, "Yes" you could start talking.

Only guess what? I heard my mother say, "No. I'm not paying for any long-distance call," and she hung up. I tell you as many times as she hurt me, it never got any easier. It was as if I had been stabbed in the heart with a knife, and my whole body ached. Tears welled up in my eyes as I stood there motionless with the receiver in my hand. I fought hard to compose myself, and with a big lump in my throat I returned to the table where we were eating. I tried to not have a strange look on my face as I told Heather and Gabriel that she wasn't home. I hated lying, but I knew if I spoke the truth out loud, I would fall apart and cry a river. I did not want to upset Heather and ruin the fun we were having. We found a grocery store, but only bought essentials. We were all so tired. Heather got her bath, and as I tucked her into bed with a big hug and kiss, she was already sound asleep. Gabriel was also out like a light. When I finally laid down, I was exhausted, but all I could think about was that awful phone call. How could a mother turn down a call from her child? Anything could have happened that I needed to call her! For crying out loud, we had just driven clear across the whole state of Texas! Something could have happened to Heather, or Gabriel, or we could have had a wreck! Or Gabriel could have turned out to be a crazy person, and Heather and I needed help to get back home! My imagination and my pain were running wild. I was so glad Gabriel was sound asleep, so I could cry myself to sleep. I knew I would never be like her. I would never turn my back on Heather, no matter what!

The next day was Sunday and the last day off for Gabriel. We all slept late, then after breakfast and showers, he said he wanted to show us Galveston. So, off we went down the big freeway and on to a bridge over a lot of water with boats everywhere, and by the water there were picturesque houses built on stilts. Visitors were welcomed to Galveston as they drove down the main road lined with towering palm trees and enormous oleander bushes with beautiful flowers. Soon we came to the famous Galveston seawall and a view of the vast Gulf of Mexico. I had once seen the Pacific Ocean, so the Gulf was by no means a comparison, but it had a beauty of its own. The atmosphere of the unique buildings, the history it proclaimed, and the seawall itself provided an essence of charm that could only be found in Galveston. Through the years, that city became one of my favorite places to go. Heather had never seen that much water or sea gulls or for that matter, a beach. We parked along the seawall and let her run in the sand. Then she got brave enough to get her feet wet at the water's edge. We searched for the prettiest sea shells to fill her pockets. Later, Gabriel took us to the most incredible sea food restaurant I had ever been to. It was built way out in the water at the end of a long pier, so when you looked out the windows all you saw was water. Plus, they served the most delicious jumbo fried shrimp imaginable. The whole town saturated you with a desire to return because there was so much more to see and experience. I just loved that whole area.

When Gabriel went back to work, life settled down to normal. I was finally able to clean the place from top to bottom which helped me like it better. Heather and I enjoyed quality time together, and I had supper ready every night when Gabriel got home from work. It was a good month and we all got along well. It would be much later before I realized that all was well because I stayed at home as a good little housewife and did not know anybody. Before we knew it, the time had come to pack our bags for another long trip. Heather was excited about Christmas and now that we had a phone, I called my mom to tell her we were coming and that Heather wanted to stay with her. I had not called her since the collect call incident, but neither of us mentioned it. She was glad to have Heather spend time with her. Gabriel and I would stay with his mom because she had more room. Interestingly, as we drove back across Texas, I realized I had already grown accustomed to the abundant vegetation in the Houston area, so as we traveled west across the state, the change in scenery became obvious. After we went through San Antonio, I decided it was greener in east Texas in the winter than west Texas in the summer. By the time we drove back into the town I was glad to leave behind, everything looked dead, there was no color. I thought, "This place is terrible!" My eyes had not seen it quite that way before. I knew right then that I would never want to go back and live there again. We arrived at my mom's place on the 23rd in time to take her out for her birthday. Then we left Heather with her and went to Gabriel's mom's house. My mom would bring Heather there early Christmas morning to see what Santa brought her. Christmas Day was wonderful being around a big family. Heather was loaded down with presents to take back to Houston. It was a good thing we drove Gabriel's truck that had a shell over the bed, so all of our gifts would be safe. After spending four days visiting everyone, we had to get back for Gabriel's work. We hit ice and snow in San Antonio which made for slow travel, but finally made it safely back to Houston without incident. New Year's Eve was quiet and uneventful since Gabriel and I could not go out because we didn't know any sitters. We just made popcorn and watched the ball drop in Times Square. I was happy and hoping for a peaceful, loving new year. But, the enemies of my soul were not going to let that happen. It would not be long before they showed up in full force.

After Gabriel went back to work, I was running out of things to do in that small apartment, so Heather and I started exploring. We found a mall and a movie theater and a good Mexican restaurant. Since Heather was about to turn five, I also began to look for a kindergarten in the area. I found a nice one that seemed ideal and not far from our apartment, so I enrolled her there. She started even before her birthday and seemed to fit right in. On her birthday I sent a small bouquet of flowers to her at the kindergarten. She felt so special now, a big girl of five and going to school. I had always worked since graduating high school, so the natural thing to do was to think about getting a job. My youthful dream of being a housewife never even entered my mind. I could have probably stayed home, Gabriel made plenty of money, but I never thought about that as an option. Besides, I assumed that Gabriel wanted me to work because he liked having that extra money. Now that Heather was in school, I began looking in the area for job possibilities. There was a public bank near where Heather went to kindergarten so I thought, "Why not? Maybe my experience at my old bank job would mean something." Well, it did. Two weeks after I applied, I got called for an interview. The woman I talked to was the manager of accounting, about my age and very nice. She hired me on the spot! I would start the next week. Gabriel was glad I got a job because Heather's kindergarten was costing extra money. The bank was just past her school which was also a daycare, so that worked out perfect. I also felt secure in knowing that I could reach her in minutes in case of an emergency. With both of us working now, adjustments had to be made in scheduling dinner, grocery shopping and free time, but all seemed to be going smoothly. I was enjoying learning new aspects of banking in the accounting department and making new friends. Up until then I had not met anyone because the people at the apartment complex were not exactly the type I wanted to be friends with. I had only been at the bank one month when Heather got chicken pox from her school. I had no choice but to stay home with her for one week. Then not long after returning to work, I received news that my dear sweet grandmother had died, she was 90. Again, I had no choice, I had to fly home for her funeral. Mom had no one to be with her except me. So, I was off from work another week. I was sure I would get fired since I was still in the probation period. But thankfully, my boss, who would later become my best friend, saw potential in me and kept me employed. Several months later she told me just how close she came to agreeing with the officers of the bank that she had made a mistake in hiring me. But it was meant to be that I stayed there because we both were destined to become very instrumental in each other's lives.

Even with all the transitions and interruptions, Gabriel and I were getting along pretty well. My only concern for the moment was he just seemed as if he wanted to be catered to all the time. And when we were with friends from the bank, he would withdraw into himself, not in a shy way, but more like, "I'm not going to join you, everyone else needs to come join me." It was really hard to understand because I was such a people person. Sometimes he acted like he was jealous because I was friendly and seemed to be mad at me. I tried to make him feel wanted and welcomed in our circle of new friends. For instance, when Gabriel's birthday came around, I planned a small party for him at our apartment. Three couples came and brought presents for him which I thought was so nice of them. I had food and a cake and everyone was talking and laughing except Gabriel. He hardly said a word, sometimes even standing off to the side, making everyone uncomfortable. Then I asked Gabriel to open his presents and he said, "No, I don't think so." It was like ice water was poured on the festivities; everyone got quiet. It was not so much the words, but how he said it. More like, "Are you stupid, why would I want to do that?" I was very upset at his rudeness towards our guests and their generosity to bring gifts. I tried to blow it off and keep the fun going, but one by one the couples started to leave. What followed was our first argument since we had been married almost five months ago. I let Gabriel know how what he had said was rude and the reason why everyone left. He said he didn't care, and that made me even madder. He was coming towards me, and I pushed him away. Then it happened! In a heated exchange of words, Gabriel reached out and slapped my face very hard! I was dumbfounded! Not knowing exactly how to react, I momentarily thought of what I had seen in the soap operas, so I slapped him back. Now on TV when the man and woman slapped each other they would immediately embrace with a passionate kiss. But that was not what happened in reality. Gabriel started roughly hitting my head and face with both hands. I screamed for Heather who was in her room playing. She came running out and he stopped. My heart was racing, and I was shaking with tears running down my cheeks. Heather ran to me, "Are you okay Mommy?" I was thinking in panic mode, "What should I do? What should I do?" Gabriel just stood there glaring at me. Finally, I grabbed my purse and told Heather we were going for a ride, just her and I. She was excited. I had to get away and clear my head. When we got in the car, I asked her if she wanted to go see the water? Fortunately, Gabriel had not tried to stop me. Probably because Heather was there. So, she and I went to Galveston and walked along the beach. It was so peaceful. I could not even think what I should do. I had never been confronted with anything like that before. I was scared, I was mad, and I was confused. I thought about what Gabriel's sister had said about him beating his first wife. He and I had arguments before we got married, but he never hit me. It was starting to get late, so I knew we had to go back to the apartment. I had no idea what to expect, but I knew if I kept Heather close to me Gabriel would not do anything. Somehow, I just knew he would never hurt her. When we got back Gabriel had cooked supper for us. Heather ran and gave him a hug and showed off her new sea shells. He picked her up and came over to me and gave me a hug and kiss. "Are you guys hungry?" he asked. Heather clapped her hands in acknowledgement. "Well, go wash up, supper is all ready." There was no apology. Gabriel just carried on like normal, as if nothing had happened. It was really creepy. I was totally quiet the rest of the evening. When we went to bed, he wanted to have sex. I was honestly afraid to say no. I complied although for the first time with Gabriel my heart was not in it. Life did go on as usual, but it took a while before I felt comfortable with him again.

Then a couple of months later was my birthday. My boss, Beverly, who was now my closest friend, said she would keep Heather if Gabriel and I wanted to go out to celebrate. Heather loved going to Beverly's house because she had two girls around Heather's age. They all three got along great and had a lot of fun together, so we let her stay over-night. Gabriel and I went to our favorite bar-b-que place to eat and then decided to go see Gilley's, a famous country western dance hall. I was excited because it had been months since we had been able to go dancing. After we found a table Gabriel left to go to the restroom. He was walking back, but still a distance from our table when a cow-boy stopped and asked me if he could have the extra matches laying in the ashtray. I didn't think anything of it. He was not flirting and I sure wasn't flirting, so I just handed him the matches and he walked off. Well, Gabriel had seen him talking to me. When he sat down, he asked, "Do you want to go home with him?" I thought, "What? Where did that come from?" Deeply confused, I asked, "What are you talking about? Go home with who?" He answered, "You seemed to like that guy you were talking to." I was thinking, "What? Did I accidentally smile at him or be friendly?" I said, "He just wanted the matches. That was all!" Gabriel sulked for the rest of the evening. We stayed and danced for a while, but did not talk much. Then when we got in the truck Gabriel started up again. He was insanely jealous! I had never seen that side of him when we were dating. I began to realize the reason for all these personality changes was that before we got married, I was only a girl-friend, but now I was his possession. His expectations had become un-realistic and unreasonable. We had both had a few drinks, and Gabriel seemed a bit meaner than usual. When we got back to the apartment I was really scared because Heather was not there to hide behind. He got even angrier, saying all kinds of crazy jealously stuff he was making up in his head. Then he started hitting my head and slapping my face just as he had done before. I ran to our room and fell to the floor as if I had passed out. I thought it might scare him into stopping because I could really be hurt. He came over and cussed at me to get up. I just laid there motionless as if I was unconscious, barely breathing. He stood by me for a few minutes and then left the room. I stayed on the floor for the longest time, until everything was quiet. Then I heard snoring coming from the living room, so I got up. Gabriel was passed out on the couch. I locked the bedroom door and laid down on the bed. I thought, "What if I had really been hurt? I could have laid there on the floor and died from head injuries while he was asleep on the couch! This was not the man I thought I had married. This was Dr. Jekyll and Mr. Hyde." As sleep began to finally overtake me, I thought if I lived through the night, I could not wait to go pick up Heather tomorrow.

The next day Gabriel again went on with life as if nothing had happened. Still no apologies, no discussion, no acknowledgement that anything had taken place. I was leery to bring it up and talk about it for fear he might get mad and hit me again. I had once wondered why women stayed with men that hit them. In my case, I had nowhere to go, and you always think maybe it won't happen again. I was normally a friendly person, but I was beginning to feel the pressure of having to watch what I said or how I acted, especially around men. I was afraid to be myself and was becoming very unhappy. In the meantime, our apart-ment complex was on the verge of being an unlivable nightmare. The roaches were out of control, sometimes we had no hot water, and gen-eral maintenance was nonexistent. What finally became the last straw was totally disgusting! There was a raw sewage leak on the side of our unit that had gone unnoticed until one day when a big storm flooded our entire parking lot with over a foot of water. The whole area became a cesspool of stench and filth because of the leak. Gabriel had to put on rubber boots and carry me and Heather to my car and back to the stairs for a couple of days. That was our chance to get out of our lease because they did not uphold their part of the contract. I was so glad to leave there and thought we would be happier in a better place. We decided to buy a new mobile home because that could be done quickly. We found a mobile home park close to Gabriel's work, but had to wait until they cleaned the apartment parking lot before we could get our things out. It was wonderful moving into a brand new clean place with new appliances and no roaches. We fumigated the apartment before moving our stuff, so we didn't bring the roaches with us. Heather loved the fact that the trailer park had a small swimming pool. It did not even matter that I had to drive farther to work, it was worth it. I was optimistic that everything would be different now. At first it was a nice transition. Gabriel seemed happier. He spent quality time with Heather teaching her to swim and ride a bicycle. He built a very nice front porch deck with steps that were safer to climb. I was feeling more relaxed and comfortable and had let my guard down. One day I came home from work, and the trailer had no electricity. It was all electric, so Heather had no water for her bath and I could not start supper. Gabriel was still at work. I was out in the yard looking at the lines going to the trailer without a clue what to do. The man next door saw me and asked if I needed help with something. He was not a stranger; Gabriel and I had talked with him and his wife several times. I told him the problem, and he went over and opened a door to a panel on one end of the mobile home that I did not even know existed. I had already checked the breaker box inside, but this switch was something different. He showed me what the problem was, fixed it and said it could happen again, so I should let Gabriel know what to do. I was grateful I could go on and let Heather get her bath and have supper ready when he got home. Gabriel was in a good mood when he walked in the door, and thankfully we had hot water so he could shower before we ate. While we were eating, in general conversation, I asked him if he knew about the breaker panel on the outside of the trailer. He said, "No, what panel?" Then I innocently explained what had happened and how our neighbor helped and said I should tell him about the switch. With the look on Gabriel's face and his total attitude change, you would have thought I had just told him I'd had sex with our neighbor. He had this way about him that he would calmly ask deliberately leading questions while you knew there was a seething bomb about to explode. Condemningly, Gabriel said, "What business is it of his to fix my trailer? Why were you asking him for help? You should have waited until I got home, so I could take care of it." Now I was upset. "I told you how it happened. I did not ask for help, but the man was kind enough to be neighborly. Otherwise, we would be eating PBJ's and you and Heather would still be dirty!" Gabriel just sat there fuming and did not say a word, which was a danger signal. The rest of the night I kept Heather close to me until he calmed down. Finally, he let me explain about the panel which he knew nothing about either. Fortunately, I survived that round without getting hit.

As time went on, Gabriel and I decided to join a bowling league. Life was going pretty well, and we were actually having lots of fun. The lanes had a child care room so Heather had fun, too. But, with Gabriel you just never knew what would set him off. Every week during league play, we would each buy a raffle ticket for the prize of the night. Most of the time it was a fifth of bourbon, and whoever won would share it with the other players. Well, this one particular night I won a bottle of Jack Daniels. So as was the custom, I opened it to share with whom-ever wanted some. The team we were bowling against consisted of four really nice black men. They were very funny guys, so we started cutting up, and I filled their cups several times. I had a lot of fun that night. So much fun that I had not noticed that Gabriel had gone into his sulking quiet mood. He did not speak a word to me on the way home. I thought he was just tired. I got Heather bathed and put to bed, and I still didn't realize I had made a big mistake. Gabriel had already gone to bed and continued not talking to me as I crawled into bed. I leaned over and kissed him goodnight and turned out the light. I stretched out onto my back and was about to doze off when all hell broke loose! Gabriel had been fuming on the inside for hours, and he finally blew. He hit my head so hard I literally saw stars as he yelled, "So, you're a nigger lover! This is what you get nigger lover!" He kept hitting my face and head harder than he ever had before! I was screaming and trying to protect myself as he kept yelling, "You want to go f--- that nigger? Is that what you want?" Finally, I was able to get off the bed. I was beyond terrified! I thought he was going to kill me! I ran into the living room, he grabbed me and kept hitting me, all the while I screamed for him to stop! I lunged for the front door and tried to unlock it, but I was shaking so much I could not get it open. Gabriel turned on the light and started hitting the back of my head. Then he spun me around and was poised to beat my face some more when all of a sudden, he stopped. I had not realized that he had cut my face, and when he saw the blood, he got all compassionate. He brought me a wet paper towel and began to gently wipe my face. I was still shaking and crying and thinking, "This guy is psycho!" He looked so sad and said, "I don't know why I do this. I do not want to hurt you." Unbelievable! Did he honestly think I was supposed to feel sorry for him? He put his arms around me and held me, I was still trembling. Talk about being confused, my mind was going ninety to nothing. I had never been that afraid of him before. Gabriel was all calm now. I was not, but I kept quiet. The bleeding had stopped, so he said let's go to bed. I pulled back from him then he said, "I promise I am not going to hit you again." I hadn't heard that before, but I was not convinced. He was so crazy this time I was even afraid for Heather. When I ran for the door, I had hoped to get Gabriel to chase me out of the trailer and get him outside, away from Heather. Thank goodness she was such a sound sleeper. She never got up because of the noise. But now, there he sat on the couch with his head in his hands wanting my sympathy. I began to understand even more why women stay with wife beaters. You continually grasp for that little glimmer of hope that they will stop. As I continued to stand by the front door I said, "You cannot keep doing this to me. You need to get some help." Gabriel nodded in agreement. He said, "Could you find me someone I can talk to?" "I'll check the phone book tomorrow," I replied. He asked if I wanted to get some sleep. I said, "I guess, but I am afraid of you right now. Will you sleep on the couch?" He agreed, so we both tried to get some rest. The next day at work my head and neck really hurt, and I was surprised I did not have a black eye. I guessed the reason Gabriel always hit mainly on my head was because it didn't show as much evidence. I covered the cut on my face with makeup. I was not sure what type of person I should look for in the phone book. Did Gabriel need a psychiatrist or a family counselor? I just picked one that appeared to do both. He was near where Heather took ballet, so we could go there while she was in class. That night I showed the ad to Gabriel, he approved it, so the next day I made us an appointment. The minute I met that guy I thought he was a weirdo. We explained Gabriel's problem in detail. The man just sat there with a dumb look on his face while listening to our horror story. Then he began to ask really strange questions about our relationship and our sex life. I was purposely vague with my answers. I could have done a better job of counseling than he did. The one and only sensible comment the guy made was when he told Gabriel that whenever he felt like hitting me, he should try to hit something else instead, like the wall or a pillow. We never went back to the counselor. However, one night Gabriel did put a hole in the living room wall to keep from hitting me. We hung a picture over it. So, the advice seemed to be working for a while.

Although sometimes Gabriel seemed to try to be different, he was still jealous, sulky and prejudice at the drop of a hat. I could not be myself. I never knew what would set him off, so I was always afraid I would say or do something to make him mad. Even when Beverly would have a party at her house with only couples from the bank, Gabriel would get jealous if I danced with one of the other husbands. They were all people we had both known for months. But of course, it was perfectly fine if he danced with the wives. When we got home, he would push me around and chew me out, but so far no more hitting. I never felt I could trust him not to blow up at any second. One night while getting ready for one of Beverly's parties, we had an argument before we even left home. Gabriel was already on the warpath about me being friendly, so I decided I would be a wallflower that night. I told Beverly about the fight and that I would not be dancing or talking to anyone but Gabriel. She understood completely because her husband was the jealous type, too, but not as much as Gabriel. So, I just sat on a chair most of the night, turning down dance invitations while barely talking or looking at the men. Occasionally, I danced with Gabriel when he asked me and then sat back down like a good little wife. I was not even drinking, but Gabriel was drinking enough for both of us. I did not speak unless spoken to and mostly to the other women. I made sure I did not smile at any man or give any indication I wanted to talk to them. Gabriel was getting drunker and more belligerent by the minute. I was still just innocently sitting in my chair when Gabriel came over to me, stood right in front of me and purposely poured a full glass of booze right on my chest! Then he said, "Oops," and laughed. I jumped up madder than a hornet yelling at him for messing up Beverly's upholstered chair! I went to get wet towels to clean me and the chair, and Gabriel started saying, "Come on, we're leaving." "Not until I clean this up!" I retorted. He was getting angry and more insistent as he tightly grabbed my arm and began to pull me away. I yelled, "Let go, you're hurting me!" and jerked my arm loose. Gabriel raised his hand as if preparing to back hand my face when he realized everyone was watching. About then Beverly and her husband came over and tried to calm him down. By now, I was afraid to go home with him. It was obvious he wanted to beat me up. I asked Beverly, "Can Heather and I stay here tonight?" She answered, "Of course." Gabriel was furious. They offered him some coffee, but he stormed out of their house and sped off in his truck. I was so relieved to see him go, and Heather was excited about a sleepover with her friends. Beverly was a really good friend, my best friend.

The next morning, we all had a wonderful breakfast, and I helped Beverly clean up the party mess. Her girls and Heather were having a blast enjoying their extended play time. It was approaching noon, and I had not heard from Gabriel. I called our house, but he was not there. We all had lunch and still no answer. Now I was starting to get a little concerned because Gabriel was very drunk when he left last night. Beverly said we could stay as long as I needed to, but if I wanted to go back home, she would take us. I did not want to overstay our welcome, so I tried calling our house one more time, and with no answer I gathered our things to go home. Beverly and I were both concerned about what we might find at the trailer. But when we got there, Gabriel's truck was nowhere around. Inside the trailer, everything looked fine. I told Beverly, "I don't think he has been here." Now we were both getting worried. I told her to go on home and I would be in touch. It was getting to be late afternoon when I finally heard Gabriel's truck drive up. I was not sure if I should be glad or scared. When he walked in the door, he looked surprised that we were there, and he was a mess. His clothes were all wrinkled and his hair was in disarray. I asked, "Where have you been? Why haven't you called?" He answered, "I did call here, but then I remembered you were at Beverly's, and I didn't know their number." I repeated, "Well, where have you been all night and all day?" Gabriel said, "You might as well sit down, it's a long story. When I left the party last night, I was so drunk I could not see straight. I knew I was weaving all over the road, so I decided to pull over on the shoulder before I hit somebody. I turned off the lights and the ignition thinking I would get forty winks and be able to drive home. But I completely passed out. I'm not sure how long I was parked there when I heard a banging sound on the door and saw a light flashing in my face. It was a policeman, and he was not in a good mood. I don't know how long he had been trying to wake me up. He dragged me out of the truck. I could not stand up and I reeked of alcohol, so he knew I was drunk. I kept telling him I thought I had done the right thing by pulling off the road instead of driving. The cop became more agreeable to that line of thinking, but he still had to take me to jail for public intoxication, and my truck was towed to the impound lot. At the police station I had to pay a large fine for public intoxication, a charge for towing the truck, and another fee for getting the truck out of impound. My breathalyzer test was off the chart, so they said I would have to call someone to come get me and the truck.

Well, this is where I had another big problem. After I called here and remembered you were at Beverly's, I was in trouble because I was still too drunk to remember their last name to find their phone number. So, I had to spend the night and most of today sleeping it off in the drunk tank. Finally, they gave me the okay to drive my truck out of there. I was starving, so I drove through a fast food and figured I would come home and shower and then go pick you guys up. But I am sure glad you are already here because I really feel lousy." As he sat there waiting for a response, I found it quite amusing that Gabriel had spent the night in jail. I hoped it had taught him a lesson. I didn't say that though, and I hoped I had not smiled when I thought it. We sort of made up, and I just kept on hoping that this would be the last incident.

A few months passed, and Gabriel seemed to be really trying to change again. It was strange that through all the chaos of the past nine months I was never plagued with not feeling loved. Even though Gabriel and I had our battles, our sex life withstood the fray, and physical intimacy was how I felt loved. Then he got word that his job was moving to another location a few hours from where we lived. This change was only going to be for three months, so it was not necessary for us to move everything there. He would be finished with it by Christmas. Gabriel decided he would stay in that town all week, come home on Friday evening and drive back early Monday morning. Actually, the separation did Gabriel and me a world of good. We were all so excited to get back together on Friday that the weekends were fun and happy times. There was no room for arguments or jealousy. Our first anniversary, the holidays and Heather's sixth birthday came and went with quality family time in our home. We could not travel to go back to west Texas for a visit because of Gabriel's work schedule. The job's original schedule had been extended a few more months past Christmas, so after a while the routine started to get tiring for all of us. Everything was still good between Gabriel and me, or so I thought. Then I began to realize that the itching and burning sensation I had been having in my vagina was not going away. In fact, it was getting worse. So, when the problem spread, I finally went to a doctor. I had not mentioned the itching to Gabriel because I thought it was just some female thing, and it would eventually go away. The doctor did some scrapings for a lab test and gave me some cream. This was on a Tuesday. The very next day the office called and said I needed to come back immediately for a shot and a prescription. That really scared me, and I began asking a throng of questions. They said the doctor would explain when I came in. I took off work Thursday morning and nervously went to see the doctor. Needless to say, I was worried. The doctor gave me the shot and wrote out a prescription and then sat down on his stool. With a somewhat serious look he asked, "Are you married?" What a funny question, I answered, "Yes." He continued to inquire, "Do you or your husband participate in extramarital activity?" "What?!" I exclaimed. I was insulted and getting upset, "Of course not! Why?" The doctor proceeded to tell me that I had a type of STD that could only come from sexual intercourse with a man who had the same STD. Now, it was not the doctor I was getting mad at, "You mean to tell me my husband has this STD!" The doctor replied, "If he is the only one you are having sex with, then yes." Trying to give Gabriel the benefit of the doubt I asked, "Could this have been dormant in either of us and just now showed up?" He answered, "No, this form of STD shows evidence relatively soon after coming into contact with it. Your husband is probably having symptoms, too, and he needs to be treated as well. I am sorry to tell you that if you are not being unfaithful, then your husband is." I just sat there in dumbfounded silence.

I left the doctor's office with so many emotions I did not know whether to scream or cry. I never saw that coming. We had a wonderful sex life, only now just on weekends. Of all the things Gabriel had done, him cheating on me never ever entered my mind. I could not believe it! He would be home the next day. I vacillated between having all his belongings out in the yard, to changing the locks, or to Heather and me permanently being gone when he got home. I was so confused, but it was time to go back to work and finish the day and then what should I do? Where could I go? I didn't even share this news with Beverly. I had to figure things out first. When I went to work Friday, I was still no closer to deciding what to do. There just were not any viable options.

After work I got Heather from daycare and drove back to the trailer. She needed supper and a bath, and before I knew it, I heard Gabriel's truck. When he walked in the door, he knew right away something was wrong. I did not join Heather in our usual hugging and kissing welcome home routine. I barely talked to him or looked at him during supper. I tucked Heather into bed, and when I knew she was sound asleep I let him have it, "Who are you having sex with, you lousy son-of-a-bitch?!" Gabriel acted shocked and laughingly said, "What are you talking about?" His laughing and obvious denial made me furious! I continued, "Are you having itching and burning on your penis?" He really looked funny when I asked that. Without answering my question, he chuckled and said, "Why are you asking all this?" I was enraged that he knew that I knew, but was playing innocent till the end. And laughing about it! "I know you are having sex while you're gone because your little whore has a STD, and she gave it to you and you brought it home to me!" I was ready to throw something I was so mad! Gabriel just sat there denying the whole accusation and even had the nerve to try and put the blame on me! "Maybe I should ask you where you go when I'm not here," he smirked. I wanted to hit him so bad, but I knew that would just end in me getting beat up. I kept trying to get answers, but Gabriel never admitted to his indiscretion. However, there was no doubt in my mind that he had cheated on me. It took me a long time to even want him around. Not long after our confrontation a statement came in the mail from a doctor in the town where he worked. I could also track his doctor visits with the insurance statements. Plus, one day I found a tube of ointment similar to mine when I was replacing some articles in his toiletry bag. We didn't have sex for weeks. When my doctor gave me the all clear, I figured his did, too, but I was not anxious to return to our normal routine. He never wanted to talk about the incident. I don't know why I continued to stay with him considering I had gone through beatings, lying, cheating, and a STD. Maybe it was for security, if you can call it that. There just did not seem to be a clear alternative. I knew I did not want to be by myself or be single again. I wanted to be married, but at what price? I also was not completely comfortable in my surroundings where we lived. I could not imagine me and Heather living in that trailer park by ourselves. So, I guess for the time being, those were the reasons I stayed. Maybe they were not good reasons and were rather poor excuses. Unfortunately, at that point in our marriage my options seemed very limited.

Fifteen

The Final Move

Now that Heather was six years old, I had to start thinking about where she would start first grade in the fall. I did not like the town where we lived. It was too transient, too big and always had an awful stench in the air from the local chemical plants. Plus, living in a trailer park forever was not my idea of having a home. I wanted Heather to grow up in a house in a nice neighborhood where she could have friends nearby. Whenever we would visit my friend Beverly and her girls, I felt at home as soon as we entered the city limits of her small town. Even though she was only about thirty miles from south Houston, the place had a warm and cozy hometown atmosphere. Every time I drove down the main street, I felt like we belonged there. So, I asked Gabriel if we could move by summer so I could get Heather registered for school in September. I think he also realized that the place where we were now living was not a good environment for her, so we decided to look for a house we could buy in that peaceful little town where Beverly lived. Well, as soon as we made that decision, Gabriel had to go to work out of town again. I was no longer concerned about him cheating because I felt he had learned his lesson, but now the whole load of looking at houses was on my shoulders. So, one day after work, I drove to that town and stopped at the first real estate office I came to. I immediately liked the broker and the agent he assigned to help me. We looked at a few houses that were vacant, but I didn't like any of them. She said she would line up some more to look at on Saturday when Gabriel would be back home. A few days later Gabriel and I spent all day looking at houses, but he was no help. He mostly just stood in the background while offering no opinion or real interest. When I asked him what he thought about a particular house he would just answer, "It's fine. Whatever you want." That day none of the houses we saw felt right. I was frustrated with him because he didn't seem to care, and he was frustrated with me because I didn't just pick something. The agent said there was a couple of new listings that would be available on Monday if I wanted to come by after work. I set up a time to see them, and Gabriel was happy to put the whole thing in my lap. Monday came and the agent was driving me to see the first new listing. When she turned left into the subdivision and I looked down that street, I felt like I was home. She drove a little farther down that street and pulled into the driveway of the perfect brick house. As I walked from room to room everything inside me was saying this is the house. I loved everything about it, plus there was a grade school just a few blocks away. When I got back into the agent's car, I told her we did not need to look at the other house. I wanted to write up a contract on this one. I called Gabriel from the office and told him I had found the perfect place at a good price and needed earnest money so we would not lose it. I was so excited! He calmly said he would go see it Saturday and put money on it then. He had said it was up to me, so now he cares, terrific! In the mean time we could lose this perfect house! I asked him to at least come in earlier on Friday, and we could go see it then. I was so afraid they would sell it out from under us. Gabriel said okay to Friday afternoon, so I told the agent we had to wait until then. She knew how badly I wanted that house, so she suggested we write up an offer to present to the seller to try and stall for time. Writing the offer had worked, they had countered so the ball was back in our court. I was on pins and needles all week and finally Gabriel got home. I took him on the tour of the house saying, "Look at this and isn't this nice." Thankfully, Gabriel actually liked the house and the neighborhood, so we went back to the office and finalized the deal. What a relief! With Gabriel still working out of town, I had to deal with jumping through all the VA loan hoops and getting him to step up when he was needed. I certainly did not mind though; we had a house! Plus, I was learning a lot about real estate. Finally, the wonderful day came for Gabriel to again return early on a Friday to attend closing, and the perfect little brick house was ours! Out of all the other places I had ever lived, that house felt more like it was meant to be my home than anywhere else.

For the next couple of weeks my daily routine was to load Gabriel's truck with as much as I could at night after work, get up and work all day at the bank, drive thirty minutes to our new home, unload the boxes and drive almost an hour back to the trailer. After feeding Heather and getting her to bed I would pack more boxes and reload the truck to do it all over again the next day. It was exhausting! On the weekends Gabriel would move some of the larger and heavier items I could not carry. Finally, I had moved all the small stuff, so Gabriel was able to clear out the rest of the mobile home, and we were completely in our new house. Even though the place was a mess, I was so happy. As always, I had high hopes that life would be better for us in this new place, and there would be no memories here of physical abuse. Gabriel had even transferred to a job closer to home, so he could be with us every day. After one more long trip to west Texas to pick up all the furniture I had left in my old house, I finally felt complete. It was very comforting to have everything I had left behind now settled in to our new home. It was not long before neighbors began to come by to introduce themselves and offer any help. Some had children Heather's age, so she was glad about that. It had been a long time since we lived where there were kids she could play with. Everyone was very friendly and made us feel welcomed. I worked on organizing the inside of the house while Gabriel repainted the outside trim and spruced up the yard. Since Gabriel and I got married we had not lived in a place I could have fun with. In my old house I made all the decorating decisions, and William took care of the yard and house maintenance. We worked well together in that area. But Gabriel had other ideas I knew not of until I began to purchase items like pictures, mirrors, etc. It was not the cost because I was always careful with money. It was a matter of control. That issue had not come up before because we hadn't lived in a place worthy of decorating. Now, I understood that Gabriel and I should discuss buying a refrigerator or a washer and dryer, but a picture for the foyer? And his reprimand was not because he didn't like the picture, it was because I did not ask permission. Gabriel's attitude was never about the money or the decor, but everything to do with a "Mother, may I?" approval for every little thing, even down to the ridiculous, like groceries. This was the first time since we married that we had lived in a place where I actually felt comfortable going grocery shopping by myself. The other two locations were not conducive to feeling safe, so Gabriel was always with us. It had never dawned on me that he basically did the shopping while I pushed the cart. Now I was able to enjoy getting back to normal for me. One day after Heather and I came home from grocery shopping she proceeded to eat one of the popsicles from a package of them I had bought for her. Gabriel asked, "What is Heather eating?" "A popsicle she picked out," I replied. He said, "I don't like popsicles." "Okay, sooo?" I was puzzled. Then he said, "Well, I think we should only buy things we can all three enjoy." I thought, "Are you kidding me? Now, I need permission to buy my daughter a popsicle!" It seemed as if when Gabriel got his castle, our house, he thought he was now the king. This new wrinkle in our growing list of incompatibilities birthed a whole new set of problems.

We lived in a picture-perfect neighborhood. People were genuinely friendly and nice with no ulterior motives. It had been a long time since Gabriel had a jealous spell. Maybe he was better or maybe I was just towing the line. Anyway, I began to let my guard down again and was enjoying being a friendly neighbor, too. One day I was on the front lawn laughing with the man next door about some trivial occurrence when Gabriel pulled into the driveway. He came over and spoke and was friendly and smiling, but I could sense he was thinking, "Wait until I get you in the house." As soon as we got inside the interrogation began, which led to a big argument. At least he didn't hit me that time. Since I was determined that Gabriel was not going to stop me from being a friendly neighbor, his jealously seemed to be making a comeback. I was beginning to feel the prison doors creaking shut. My body began reacting to the stress, and everything I ate came out as diarrhea along with severe stomach aches. I was eventually diagnosed with a spastic colon. In an attempt to help my system get healthy, I just stopped arguing with him. I would just let him make accusations, but I would not say a word. That gave me more peace, but it made him even madder. One night he and I were sitting at the dinner table, Heather was taking a bath, and he started in on me about who knows what. I just sat there calmly and quietly eating my soup. All of a sudden Gabriel picked up his soup bowl, turned it over and slammed it down on the table. Soup and broken dish pieces went everywhere. I just stared at the table for a second and then got up to go check on Heather. Normally, I could not stand a mess and would immediately start cleaning it up. But this time, I just stayed with Heather until she was ready for bed. Then I sat and watched TV in the living room. Gabriel had gone in the garage after he broke the bowl and stayed there awhile. When he finally came back in, I think he was shocked to find the mess was still there. Without a word, he cleaned up the whole thing. Something changed in me that night. Gabriel could sense it, too. I was not going to take the abuse anymore, but he still tried. Our whole neighborhood was so friendly that we all decided to have a block party. We were actually able to block off a large portion of our street, and one neighbor who worked for the electric company put up a huge street light for the occasion. Everyone brought out food and drinks from their homes, and tables were set up in the street with dozens of lawn chairs circling the food area. The kids were able to play in the street which was a rare opportunity for them. Everyone was cheerfully visiting and laughing, as was I. It was a fun and festive time. I was walking back to our front door to get more food from our kitchen when Gabriel came out carrying a big watermelon with both hands. I am not even sure how he did it, but when we passed each other, he jerked his elbow up and smashed it into my chin and jaw. Then he laughed and said, "Oh, excuse me." Believe me, that was no accident. It was intentional because I was having so much fun. When I came back out to the street I went over to where he was cutting the watermelon and looked him straight in the eye. Without even caring that he had a knife in his hand, I emphatically said, "Don't you ever touch me again!" I walked away and had an amazingly good time with my neighbors. That night Gabriel never said one word to me. It was as if I had taken down the school yard bully, and he knew he no longer had power over me. At that point I was done with this relationship. I was done with the pressure, the intestinal problems, and all the mental and physical abuse. I did not even want to have sex with him. I didn't care if Gabriel beat the snot out of me for ignoring him, I was through. He kept trying to have sex, but I refused. I figured he would hit me, but the opposite happened. He became meeker and finally stopped trying. As far as I was concerned, we could live that way forever because Heather and I were not leaving. I was finally in happy surroundings and, if need be, I now had the confidence to be on my own. I loved my house, my neighborhood and the town. I felt that where we lived was a safe and secure area for a single mom, so Gabriel could just leave if he wanted to. Plus, Heather would start first grade in a couple of months at a great school that just happened to be only blocks away. There was no way I was going anywhere!

After almost a month of going through the motions of a marriage, Gabriel finally told me he was moving back to west Texas, and I could keep the house. A feeling of relief flowed over me like warm water. Even Heather knew there had not been happiness in the house for a long time, so I didn't think she was completely surprised when we told her. The next morning Gabriel mowed and edged the yard and cleaned out the garage. Heather and I helped him pack all his clothes in suitcases, and I made us all a good supper. Considering the recent tensions, our last hours together were enjoyable. Then came time for Gabriel to say goodbye. I will never forget when Heather and I walked with him to the front door. We were all crying and hugging. But as emotional as it was, not one of us said, "Don't go", not even Heather. We all knew this had to happen for everyone's well-being. I don't know if any of our neighbors had a clue because he didn't say goodbye to any of them. After Gabriel, Heather and I finished our long tearful goodbye, we waved as he drove away. Back inside, on the couch, Heather and I sat holding each other. Then I noticed it. The house felt so peaceful it was almost tangible. The moment was magnificent! Then Heather asked, "Mommy, will you read me a story?" "Sure," I smiled. "Go get your favorite one." So, like the final scene of a dramatic movie, as the camera pulled back from Heather and I sitting cuddled on the couch with book in hand, we wondered if the ending was a happy one or a sad one. Incredibly, after Heather was asleep, another poem flooded my head just like when I split with William. Again, I could barely write it down fast enough. Even though this one was not near as good as the first one, it seemed as if extreme emotional upheavals somehow triggered these poems. It's an interesting one, but only the first two lines really applied to my situation, so I'm not sure why it came out that way.

SECONDS

My second husband said, as he hit me in the head.
I just can't seem to find that you give me peace of mind.

The hang-ups are all yours. Go get me another Coors!
Your kids are just like you. What they want you know I'll do.

I just can't find the time to go out and earn a dime.
Don't gripe at me you hag or I'll leave you with the bag.

I'm not through talking yet! Who drove up in that Corvette?
You can't walk out that door! Oh, well, I can find one more.

An amazing change happened almost immediately after Gabriel left. My spastic colon completely cleared up! I could eat again without everything running through. I had called Beverly the next day to let her know Gabriel was gone for good. The neighbors found out one by one, and eventually I told my mom. Everyone except my mother offered help if I ever needed it. For some reason I was not overwhelmed with the prospect of taking care of a house this time. Even though my payment was bigger and my salary was smaller, I had no doubts I could handle the challenge. I was determined that Heather needed to grow up in a nice house in a family friendly neighborhood with good schools and fun activities. When William and I divorced I had never been on my own, so the responsibility of a house scared me. This go around I was much more mature, and I felt where there was a will, there was a way. However, I had no idea just how much my will would be tested throughout the years ahead. Gabriel agreed to make the house payments until our divorce was final. I filed for child support from William, but he never sent any. Then Heather started first grade, and the extra expenses stretched my paycheck even more. I still was not too worried because I had learned how to *Rob Peter to pay Paul* as the saying goes. Also, every now and then if I was in a bind, Beverly would lend me money, and I would always pay her back. She was still my boss, but so much more. Eventually, I began to realize I needed a way to make more money. I remembered how I enjoyed doing the real estate stuff when we bought the house. I knew my agent had received a big commission check, so I decided that was what I wanted to do. I lived very near a community college where I could take the night classes required to get a real estate license. Beverly kept Heather for me as I attended one semester of night school while still working days at the bank. I had not studied for anything in so long that making my brain do homework was like trying to crank start an old car. But I stayed focused and was able to make straight A's in all subjects. Then I passed the three hour state licensing test with flying colors. I was really proud of myself as I proved I could still ace school work. And, even while holding down a full-time job and caring for a child and a house! Now, I was officially a real estate agent. I just had to find a job. I liked the people at the agency we dealt with for our house, so I went there first. The broker was very encouraging and said I could start right away. Wow! That was exciting! It turned out to be the absolutely best real estate office in town with the best people you could ask to work around. But there was just one unforeseen problem. I really did not understand how the getting paid part of real estate worked. I just knew the agents got nice big checks. I was so naive I thought they also earned a regular salary while waiting for those commissions. So, I made one of the stupidest decisions in my life when I quit my job at the bank to work full time at the real estate office. Beverly was shocked and worried, as somehow no one explained the reality to me. I guess they all assumed I knew what I was doing. The magnitude of this mistake was right up there with deciding not to go to college. However, the economic impact would be extremely worse. I foolishly assured Beverly that even if I sold one house a month, I would make more money than working at the bank. She reluctantly agreed.

On my first day as a real estate agent, I woke up raring to go. Now I could sleep a little later before taking Heather to school, then go back home and shower and dress for work. And, I so loved the fact that I did not have to drive in all that traffic to the bank. I walked into that office ready to sell a house. But everyone was just sitting around drinking coffee and visiting with each other. I wanted to get to work making that money! After meeting everyone an older woman took me under her wing and asked if I wanted to go with her to preview houses. Dorothy would eventually become one of my dearest and closest friends. I rode with her in a nice luxury four door sedan. Most all the agents had new cars. Mine was an eight year old two door sedan. I never thought about people would have to crawl in and out of the back seat. There would be a lot of things I had not thought about. I noticed all the female agents had husbands, which I would come to realize equated to a steady income. Dorothy and I drove from house to house to check out the properties. As we toured the places, she instructed me on what to say or questions to ask the prospects. Doing all that was so much fun. Then I asked Dorothy, "When do we start working?" She replied, "We are working," and I am sure my face showed my surprise. Then she said, "Let's go to lunch. I'm buying." I was glad she offered to pay because I did not have any money. While we were eating, I inundated Dorothy with one question after another. One very important question I asked was when do we get paid. With a puzzled look she answered, "When a house you sell or list closes." "So, you don't get money when you sell the house? You have to wait until it closes?" I queried. Dorothy still looked confused, "That's right." I was getting nervous, "How long is it between the sale and the close?" Dorothy said, "It varies. Anywhere from twenty to thirty days, sometimes more if there are problems." Now I was in panic mode, but tried not to show it. I had a few dollars in savings, but it would not last long with my bills. I told Dorothy, "Can we go back to the office now. I need to sell a house." Reality hit me hard! I started thinking and worrying, "What have I done? Even if I sold a house that day, which was not going to happen, it could take one or two months to get paid! Plus, I had to have gas money to drive people around! I began working very hard trying to get listings and calling off old prospect lists. The other ladies seemed to be having fun selling because their husbands brought home a paycheck. I was freaking out trying to make a sale. Eventually, I found out if you sold land only it closed faster, so I went after the buyers who were looking for property to build on. But even with all my hard work, I was getting deeper in debt. Then one day the young office secretary said she needed a place to live, so she rented my spare bedroom for $100.00 a month. That helped a little, but there was still not enough to live on while waiting for commission checks. I was talking and crying to Beverly about what a mess I had created. Now that she was a bank officer, she suggested a way to help. She said every month they had businesses that operated in the red and then made big deposits to get back in the black. They used the money until it was gone and then would go back in the red. That was how several of them ran their business month after month. And, the bank never returned checks when there was no money because the owners were always good for it. I had no idea businesses did that! Anyway, Beverly said she could do that for me. None of my insufficient checks would be returned as long as deposits were made periodically. That was unbelievable! I tell you even though I never included God in my life, He always took care of me and Heather.

I worked even harder, sometimes running contracts to other nearby towns to get signatures late at night with Heather asleep in the back seat. I wanted to make sure money would come in as much as possible, so Beverly would not get in trouble. I took on other odd jobs to make ends meet. On Sunday morning I watched children at a local church. I started selling Avon door to door. I cleaned apartments for a friend who managed some units. I even cleaned a house I sold. How many real estate agents do that? I was worn out and still could barely stay out of the red. Beverly said I needed to have some R & R. I told her I could not afford it. One day she called to tell me there was a guy at the bank taking family photos, and she would pay for Heather and I to have one made. The guy was my age, cute, and funny. We enjoyed the photo session, and he took a lot of pictures. Beverly called me over and said, "That guy was flirting with you. I think he likes you. He didn't take that many pictures of anyone else." I told her she was silly, but he was kind of cute. I had been working so much I had not even looked cross-eyed at a guy or taken time to think about one since Gabriel left. Besides, this guy was like a traveling salesman with a camera. Beverly said, "Go ask him to have drinks." "No! You can go ask him to have drinks," I exclaimed. She calmly said, "Okay," and proceeded to tell him what a good job he had done, handed him a twenty-dollar bill and said, "Go have drinks on us, and she will escort you." I thought, "What are you doing?" She breezed by me and whispered, "I've got Heather. Go have some fun." I could have rung her neck. The guy came right over with a big smile on his face and asked, "Where shall we go?" I could not believe I was doing this, "There's a nice place down the street, not far from here." He asked if we could go in my car since he had a company van full of camera equipment. I said sure and off we went. We ordered appetizers and drinks and made small talk as we tried to get acquainted. His name was Gary, and he seemed like a nice guy, but he traveled a lot. He said he had a few retakes to do the next day, and he wanted to take me to dinner after work. He was fun and interesting, and I knew Beverly would keep Heather again, so I said yes. Besides, it felt good to relax a little and get my mind off work and my money problems.

Beverly was very excited for me, but I reminded her that he would be gone in a few days. She said, "Just live in the moment and have fun!" The next day, I picked Gary up at his motel and let him drive my car. He had found a super nice restaurant. I was impressed at the efforts he had made for our date. We had a great time. When we got back to his motel he parked and pulled me over close and began kissing me. It had been months since Gabriel left, so I was definitely turned on. But I knew he was leaving soon, and I had left one-night stands in west Texas, so I said no more. Then what he said next was totally unexpected, "I'm leaving in two days for Dallas, and I will pay your way to fly there next weekend and I'll show you around. You can come Friday and leave Sunday because I have to drive to Tulsa that afternoon. How about it? Wouldn't that be fun?" Needless to say, I was very surprised. I told him to call me the next day, so I could figure it out to see if I could go. Maybe this was not a one-night stand situation, and other trips might be in my future. I had a lot to think about, so we kissed good night and I left. Beverly said, "Of course you can go! You need a break, and Heather can stay with us. I will take you to the airport and pick you up." So, when Gary called, I told him I could go. Later he called again with the flight information, and the weekend rendezvous was a done deal. I was nervous and excited at the same time as my plane touched down in Dallas. When I got off, there was Gary smiling that big grin. Then he grabbed me and kissed me hard, a little too hard I thought. I was like okay slow down some, we are in a public place. He had cleared the camera equipment in the van to make a spot for me and my suitcase. We went straight to his hotel room where he wanted to immediately have sex. He seemed different, almost obsessed with me. It gave me a weird feeling. I said, "You know I want to, but I am really hungry. Can we go eat first?" Gary apologized and said of course, so we left the room. He took me to the tourist section with many nice places to eat. We had a delicious dinner followed by a walking tour of downtown

Dallas at night. We had a good time, but I could tell Gary was anxious to get back to the room. It was getting late so we had to. Gary was all over me in the elevator and once we were in the room there was no stopping him. We had sex, and it was not long before he was wanting to do it again. I didn't think that was possible. I let him go for it one more time, but I was very tired. It had been a long day, so I practically fell asleep as he was finishing the second round. Early the next morning Gary was at it again! I began to wonder if he was on something. He was very different than he had been in Houston. He began talking about how we could just stay in the room all day and order room service and have sex continually. I was getting concerned that Gary was a looney sex pervert, and it kind of scared me. I tried to make light of what he was saying and reminded him of his promise to show me the town. That sort of snapped him out of the marathon sex mode and back to being the Gary I had first met. I quickly got dressed before he could change his mind and excitedly drug him out the door to explore Dallas. It was a big relief to not be trapped in the hotel room, but I still had to make it through the day and one more night. I encouraged the tour guide side of Gary and managed to keep him busy all day. Eventually, we had to go back to the room. That night was wall to wall sex. We did it on the floor, against the wall, in the shower and finally, on the bed. I was afraid to say no to any of it. I just wanted to make it through the night in case he was a psycho. I could not wait for morning to come, so he would have to take me to the airport. Thank goodness I had a red-eye flight, so with promises that he would send for me again, we kissed goodbye. I breathed a huge sigh of relief when I was finally sitting in the plane. I felt safe. During the flight back to Houston I kept thinking, "Stupid, stupid, stupid! What were you thinking, running off to another city with a guy you knew for two days? What if he had freaked out and was psychotic? You could have been an unidentified dead body in a hotel room in Dallas!" I could not wait to get back to Heather and back to normalcy. I was too ashamed of my stupidity to tell Beverly about the weirdness. I just said it was fun, but I would not do that again.

Anyway, even if it had not been a weird weekend, I realized I could not afford to be running off anywhere for three days whether it was fun or not. I could have sold a house or got a listing in that length of time. I had to work somewhere constantly and stretch every dollar to make ends meet. However, many people helped us, too. Both Beverly and Dorothy had Heather and me over to eat multiple times. And, they both would lend me money whenever I had no other options. I always paid them back as soon as I got a commission check. My broker's wife would let me preview her garage sales and buy Heather really nice clothes for fifty cents apiece. Heather's school mates thought we were rich because she wore outfits that were originally very expensive. And, poor Beverly continued to stand up for me at every weekly bank meeting. I had some really true-blue friends. It was now approaching almost a year of financial struggles with no light at the end of the tunnel. It seemed the harder I worked, the behinder I got. I was so far over my MasterCard credit limit that my number was listed in their warning book. That's the way it was done before stores had computers. It was horribly embarrassing to have a cart full of groceries at the checkout and be turned down by the cashier. I would go home in tears. Plus, it was a Catch 22. Because, I had to use the card to buy gas for my car in order to show clients and to sell Avon door to door, so I could make money to pay the card payment. One time I ran out of gas on a country road while showing property to a couple. I managed to find a nearby farmer who kindly siphoned some gas out of his tractor so I could get back to town. Unbelievably, they bought the land! Maybe they felt sorry for me. I was also three months behind on my house payment, and Beverly said the bank was really putting pressure on her to close my account. I was constantly getting calls from creditors. My electricity would have been turned off for lack of payment if it had not been for my neighbor who worked for the electric company. One day he knocked on my door to collect payment. He said he usually did not do collections, but the regular guy was sick. He asked if I could pay the bill right then. Of course, I did not have any money. He told me he was supposed to immediately cut off my electricity if I could not pay, but if I would promise to go pay the bill the next day, he would leave the meter on. He was really sticking his neck out to help me because he knew it would cost me even more to reconnect. I had no idea how I could pay it, but I said I would and tearfully hugged him. He knew he could trust me. I always kept my word. I would get the money if I had to beg on the street corner. That was one of those dire situations where I turned to Dorothy for help, and she lent me the money. You know if the regular collections guy had not been sick and if my neighbor had not been the one that took his place, my electricity would have been cut off, and it would have cost me even more money that I did not have. As always, I thought I was so lucky that everything happened the way it did. I was totally ignorant of the realization that it was not luck; it was Devine intervention.

Finally, an opportunity arose to make a huge commission check which would catch me up on all my bills. I had shown this really nice lady several houses, and she decided to buy one of my listings. That meant I would receive almost all of the entire commission. The contract and all the paperwork were going smoothly. My buyer was happy, and my sellers were content. The closing was to be in two more days, and I would soon get my big paycheck. But then, the bottom fell out! The man who owned the house, my listing, suddenly died of a massive heart attack! I cannot even put into words how devastated I was. It was like getting hit in the gut with a two by four. I could not even properly feel sympathy for his wife because I had been thrown into a financial panic! Understandably, she was trying to handle her own grief, so feeling insecure she decided that she wanted to keep her home. My buyer could have pressed for the closing, but she was not a heartless person. So, the contract was voided, closing was cancelled, and I was at the end of my rope. Everyone in the real estate office knew my plight and were equally concerned about my future. I left the office that day with my bubble of expectation completely flattened. I could not think of any way out of my financial disaster. All of my usual avenues of assistance were exhausted. I could not even rob Peter to pay Paul because Peter was flat broke. As I laid in my bed that night, my mind was racing, trying to come up with some kind of solution. After Gabriel and I divorced, I started real estate thinking I would make a lot more money for Heather and me. The exact opposite happened. Even with working four jobs and renting out my spare bedroom, I was now on the verge of bankruptcy. Then unexpectedly, in my moment of panic, another one of those out-of-nowhere poems began forming in my head. As the words quickly came, this is what I wrote.

THE QUESTION

Have you ever sat in wonderment
of how and why the day was spent?

Have you shot a thought into the air,
but couldn't find an ear to care?

Have you walked along a moonlit night
to only share with birds in flight?

Have you been with friends and felt alone
because your pair is missing one?

Have you hugged your child and quietly sobbed,
"A family's gone; have we been robbed?"

Have you laid alone at night too long
to smile as morning sings its song?

Have you danced and loved and dreamed a dream
then woke the night wanting to scream?

Have you then shook at problems you face
and asked yourself, "What is my place?"

Have you wondered if there soon would be
someone to share eternity?

Have you finally felt that you've been forced
to have to say, "I am divorced?"

Even as depressed as I was, when I thought back over the past year that Heather and I went through almost in poverty, I was somewhat encouraged by the fact that we still had a roof over our heads, we had not starved, and we were healthy. It seemed a whole lot longer than just a year, and being an agnostic, I was not exactly looking for an answer from above. But I just knew deep down inside that somehow there would be an end to this incredible struggle. When I went back to work the next day my broker had an amazing idea. He said the chemical plant on the outskirts of town was building a large new unit and were hiring a lot of people. My concern was I had absolutely no idea what a chemical plant did. My broker assured me that they would probably need to hire women, and they would train me. It just so happened the man who was head of personnel at the plant had some subdivided land listed with our real estate office. I had sold several of his lots and had talked with him a few times. My broker suggested I talk to the man immediately. I did just that the very next day, and within two days I had an appointment to interview for the position of chemical operator. I did not even know what that was, but they really were hiring a quota of women with no prior experience. I was ecstatic! This could be my way out of the poor house. My broker and everyone in the office were thrilled for me because they knew of my dire situation.

In the two years I had lived in that town, there had never been an occasion to drive out that country road in the direction of the huge chemical plant. After passing one rice field after another, it only took me around fifteen minutes to get to the turn off road to the plant. I came to a gate where I had to check in. The place was all very secure. As the guards at the gate pointed out the main office building, I was overwhelmed by the enormity of it all. It was like a big city with tall metal towers and pipes running everywhere. I saw ladders going up the outside of the tall structures and nervously wondered if I would ever have to climb those. I could not let them know about my fear of heights. I had to have this job! During the initial interview I discovered that women operators were just beginning to become mandatory thanks to the feminist movement, but finding a woman with experience was rare.

Therefore, I was not expected to know anything about a chemical plant. That was a relief! I also found out from my female interrogator that women operators were not exactly welcomed by a small percentage of men in the units, and they could sometimes make the job tough on you. However, she commented that the majority of the male population were nice and helpful. Then I went on to be interviewed by two male shift foremen who did not seem at all bias against women. Although, one did ask me, "If you were accidentally sprayed all over with a chemical, would you have a problem stripping your clothes off to get under a safety shower in the unit?" I said, "No problem!" I thought to myself that I had stripped naked many times for no money, so taking them off for that kind of pay was a no brainer. Then the other foreman did ask me if I was afraid of heights. I had to think about how to answer that one. I was not sure if they would hire me if I said yes, and I did not want to lie, so I could not outright say no. After a few seconds of quick thinking I commented, "I believe anybody who says they are not afraid of heights is a fool." The man sat back in his chair with a puzzled look on his face, then finally said, "I guess you are right." Whew! I had made it past the interviews. After two more days, I received a phone call that I had been hired! That was an unbelievable moment! All of the emotions and struggles of the past year came flooding out of my eyes as I cried and cried stress relieving tears. I felt like I had won the lottery! In one week, I went from the lowest low to the highest of highs. Words could not express the feeling of relief that flowed over me. I was SO happy! My life went from desperation and poverty to earning a man's salary that was huge because of the shift work and because it was considered hazardous duty. And even with the tall structures, the shift work and the physical and mental challenges of trying to learn something so foreign to me, I just knew I could do it! I had to do it! Whatever the job was I had to learn it! The pay was incredible; more than I could ever have imagined I could earn. I could not say "Thank you" enough times to my broker for suggesting the job. After I quit real estate, he and his wife remained lifelong friends of mine. When I went to bed that night, I kept thinking what a difference this will make in our lives. I thought, "Boy, was I lucky to just so happen to be working at that particular real estate office, that just so happened to be selling land for the head of personnel at that plant, who I just so happened to know very well. What a coincidence!" Of course, I eventually found out there was no such thing as luck or coincidence, but for now those thoughts lulled me off to a much needed peaceful sleep.

In one week, I would be starting on the graveyard shift, twelve midnight until 8:00 a.m. I figured that would be no problem since I had always been a night person. Sleeping during the day was easy for me. I didn't even need dark curtains. But the biggest issue was lining up child care for Heather and how she would get to school and back. She was only seven at the time. After a few weeks of friends helping out, I finally found a single lady with three children of her own who could keep Heather overnight. She took her kids to the same school, so Heather blended right in. It was perfect. On midnights I could pick Heather up from school, have supper with her and help her with home-work or play a game. Then I still had time to get her bathed and ready for bed and drop her off at the sitter around 9:00 p.m. That would give me an hour or so to finish getting ready for work and get to the plant in plenty of time. On day shift, 8:00 a.m. until 4:00 p.m., I could take her to school on the way to work and pick her up from the sitter on the way home. That was the best shift because Heather could sleep in her own bed all night. The swing shift, 4:00 p.m. until midnight, was the roughest one for me and Heather. I would have to wake her up in the middle of the night after work and put her back to bed at our home. Then in a few hours I had to get us both up in time for breakfast and school, come back home to get a few more hours sleep, get back up to shower and dress for work and make it back to the plant before 4:00 p.m. Sometimes I would even have to squeeze in some errands before work. The sitter would pick Heather up from school with her kids. That was the only way to do it or I would not see Heather for five days. The shifts rotated every five days with what was called a *long change or long weekend* after graveyards. That lasted for a few days, and Heather and I always made the most of my time off. The schedule worked pretty good with the sitter unless there was a Call Out, or I had to work over an extra four hours. The jobs in the units always had to be covered 24/7, so if someone could not come to work you had to stay over half a shift and someone else had to come out early for the other four hours. I told them I could always stay over, but an early call out was not possible with having a sitter. The foremen were pretty understanding, and to make up for that sometimes I would take a scheduled early shift that I could plan for. The guys did not like it if you would not try to take your share of the load. The extra hours were really nice on the paycheck because they were time and a half and double time on holidays. That could add up fast considering we were paid a handsome hourly wage. I could not believe the amount of money I was earning. I was able to get caught up on all my bills fairly quickly. But even with that much money, we still had to budget. I was no different than the guys that raised a family on one paycheck. I had a child that was involved in several activities, a house to maintain and payments, a car to maintain and payments, clothes and groceries to buy and pets to take care of. I had no child support, so I was very thankful for that job. Heather and I were in a comfortable place now and were able to have some fun, but it still was not easy being a single parent. My life was on the clock around the clock.

My first few months at the plant, I was assigned to work at the Lab. All of us that were hired for the new unit had to be placed somewhere until everything was prepared for our orientation training. I drove a truck all around the plant twice a shift with dozens of stops to pick up process samples for the lab technicians to analyze. I also had to clean and dispose of cases of glass bottles and use hot steam to clean heavy steel cylinders they called *bombs* and then deliver clean ones back to the units. My first week at work was on the midnight shift. I figured that would be a breeze, but I had a few unexpected rough spots. The first night I didn't know that the Lab was the only unit that did not have a kitchen, and there was no place to get food on those hours, so I did not eat the whole night. The second night I could not get the pad lock to open on my locker, and the foreman had to use bolt cutters to get it off.

I just knew that he probably thought I was stupid and had forgotten the combination. Then on the way home the next morning, I fell asleep driving and woke up just in the nick of time to miss going into the deep ditch on the side of the road. There was no drowsy warning when I fell asleep. One second, I was wide awake, and the next second I was asleep! I was shaken to the core to think what could have happened. After that I brought an apple to eat on the way home. I called it my *stay awake* apple. Then on the last night of graveyards, after taking Heather to the sitter, I was so tired I sat down on my recliner just to relax for a minute, and I was out like a light. I awoke with a startled reaction and it was 11:45 p.m.! "Oh, no, I cannot be late!" I frantically thought in a panic. I grabbed everything I needed and rushed out the door thinking I could maybe speed and make it. Then the situation went from bad to worse when I turned on the car and remembered I was going to get gas on the way to work. The gage was completely on empty! I thought, "My foreman will just have to understand that sometimes things happen that cannot be helped." After all, in my fourteen plus years in the work force, I had been late a few times, and it was usually not a big deal. By the time I finally got to the Lab, I was almost half an hour late. I thought maybe I could just sneak in unnoticed while everyone was busy. But there was one huge detail about shift work that I did not yet quite comprehend. I did not realize or had even thought about when a plant runs 24/7, they must have 24/7 job coverage. Therefore, the person in your position on the prior shift cannot leave until you get there. I thought, "This is it! I am definitely going to get fired!" The man I relieved was really upset, and the foreman wanted an explanation. I told him I ran out of gas, but not about the falling asleep part. He sternly stared at me then wisely counseled, "Do you know that everyone in this lab tonight has a car that runs on gas and not a one of them were late?" I was never late again during all the years I worked on shift. In fact, I came to understand that if you were not there early, you were considered late. As I mentioned before, I thought working those hours would be a snap since I was a night person, but shift work took a while to get used to. Once I realized your shift was the priority in your life and everything else revolved around that, then all went smoothly. I enjoyed my brief time working with the lab because, other than the office building, it was the only place where there were more women than men. Usually, all of the units only had one or two women per shift. To some of the guys, that was too many.

Finally, the day came to bring all the new hires together in one room for our plant orientation classes. I was excited to meet the other new women who were as clueless as I was. There were only six of us and about forty men. Although I was beginning to like shift work and was just getting acclimated, it was nice that for six weeks we would all be on straight days, Monday through Friday, 8:00 a.m. to 4:00 p.m. Our first week started out with a tour of the entire plant which covered hundreds of acres of land and was very self-contained. Our first stop on day one was to have lunch in the cafeteria. The shift workers rarely used the facility because all the units had kitchens where they did their own cooking. During the week we toured the safety department where the fire trucks were kept and an enormous warehouse filled with every imaginable item needed to keep the pipes flowing with product. Next, we saw a huge chemical storage area called the tank farm, plus the waterway channel where big barges brought in the oil and were also loaded with finished product to ship out to customers. Then we visited every unit, learning about how each different product was made, what it was used for, and an overview of the dangers in each area. We were told to always pay attention to which way the wind was blowing *just in case*. The last day of that week we finally made it over to the gigantic area where they were building the unit we were all hired for. It was the size of two or three of the other units put together. That was the first time that I realized they had hired all of us a year before the new facility would be finished. There were many questions running around in my head, but I did not want to ask stupid ones, so mostly I tried to figure things out with a little information here and there.

The next few weeks were filled with classroom training utilizing the foremen from various units. Included was a lecture from the head of the safety department along with chemical engineers who tried to explain the plant's use of chemistry in layman terms. Sometimes that was either very funny or totally confusing. I actually found most of their teaching very interesting since I had always enjoyed chemistry in high school. The engineers explained the hydrocarbon compounds and how they reacted to heat and cold and pressure. Then they unveiled how our new unit would use that process to break the carbon rings apart to form different products. Most of the guys were bored because just about all of them were experienced processors. They were always cutting up and cracking jokes. On breaks they would invent games to play using whatever was laying around. They were like little boys in big man bodies, and they were fun. It was refreshing to be around decent guys who were not always trying to get in your pants. I found the majority of them were okay having women operators while only two or three had an attitude. You know since I had no brothers and had mainly worked with all females in the past, I discovered working with all men to be a welcomed change. Women can be so catty and back-stabbing which can make for a difficult work environment. The main topic the men were serious about was doing their job. Everything else was fair game for testing boundaries and having fun. If you gave me a choice whether to work crazy hours with a bunch of guys or to have normal hours with lots of women, I would pick the men hands down. It became quite an education that I really needed and am so thankful for. But it was definitely not easy being a greenhorn in a chemical plant. The most difficult day of orientation for me was when we had to do fire training. We had to wear fireman coats and waders and big rubber boots. With my size five feet even the smallest pair of boots was way too big. The fire suit was already heavy, but then we had to walk through a smoke house while wearing an oxygen tank and mask. It seemed to take forever to find the door to the outside. I kept repeating in my mind, "Do not panic, do not panic. The door is almost there!" I had to do the task. There was no other option. Then we had to learn how to employ a deluge water system and how to handle a real fire hose with real pressure shooting out volumes of water. It took a team of people to hold the fire hose steady so it would not whip around. You have seen a garden hose flop around when the water is turned on, well a fire hose nozzle could kill you if it was not securely held when the water pressure comes through the hose. Each one of us had to take a turn at holding the large nozzle while the rest of the team held the hose. The object was to maintain a circular spray of water coming from the nozzle and approach a real flaming pipe in order to reach a shut off valve and stop the fuel source. If you did not keep the nozzle at the proper waist high level and centered on the flame, then the fire could jump out and get you. Well, right off the bat there were two big obstacles with more to come. Waist high to the guys was about armpit high to my five foot two frame, and my huge boots were causing major problems. My turn on the nozzle was even harder than the smoke house because it was extremely heavy and difficult to keep raised high enough to fan the flame. To make matters worse we had to walk through a mud pit to get to the shut off valve. My oversized boots kept getting stuck in the mud, and I could not walk forward without my foot coming out of the boot. The guys on my team who were holding the hose kept hollering for me to hurry up. I had to try and drag my feet through the mud instead of taking steps, plus concentrate on not allowing the nozzle to drop below chest high. It took me longer than anyone else, but I did not quit, and by some miracle I got my team to the shut off valve without getting burned. That was by far the most difficult physical challenge I had ever done in my entire life.

Then at the end of the training and orientation, we were all divided out into one of the existing units, all on different shifts, and would just see each other in passing for the next year. The unit I was assigned to only had one other woman working on my shift, and she had been an operator for several years. I was very glad there would be at least one woman I could hopefully learn from. That particular unit was an old one that had been forced to accommodate for women, so they had put a toilet, a sink and some lockers in the janitor closet. The tiny room was barely big enough for both of us to turn around in. It was all a lot to take in, but I was up for the challenge. However, little did I know trouble was waiting for me just around the corner at that particular unit, on that particular shift. I had been told in class that if I had any questions or needed any help I should go directly to the shift foreman, and he would teach me. Well, unbeknownst to me, my foreman hated my guts and had already turned a handful of guys against me. What an environment to go into knowing nothing about my job or that he felt that way. I had never even met him before. He not only would not help me, but would not even talk to me. Fortunately, the other woman on shift with me became a good friend and my teacher. I would have never made it through that year without her. She was also able to enlighten me as to why I was being treated like an outcast. It seemed that back during orientation when we were being driven around the plant by the head of the safety department, I had asked a very innocent question. We had been taught in class that you never go near the furnaces without full protective gear on. Well, on that tour we happened to be driving by my future unit when my now foreman was on the day shift. And, I happened to notice a guy over by the furnaces without protective gear on. So, because of what we had just been taught, I innocently asked the head of safety why that man was not wearing protective gear. All he said was he should be and that was that. What I found out from my new friend was that the foreman and the guy by the furnaces both got in hot water with the head of safety. So wouldn't you know, I would be assigned to that exact unit and shift. Sometimes I wondered if they had done that on purpose just to see if I could hack it. I also learned that it was not unusual to go without protective gear in the units along with other so called *unnecessary rules* that were not normally followed. Everyone worked safely, but there were some regulations the guys felt were ridiculous and did more harm than good. Anyway, that one small question caused my initial introduction to that unit to be nothing short of miserable for quite a while.

I didn't know which of the guys had been disciplined until he retaliated one night on shift and even jeopardized the safety of my area and the whole unit just to get me in trouble. And, the craziest thing was that he was on our unit safety crew and a volunteer fireman in our town. It all started when I was to open a valve in the pipe rack to allow a trickle of hot steam to come through a very long section of pipe to warm it up. You had to open it just a little at a time which could take the whole eight hour shift before the valve would be wide open. If you did not open it gradually, too much hot steam would come through a cold pipe and would cause the pipe to shake violently throughout the entire pipe rack, creating a potentially dangerous situation. In order to reach the valve, I had to climb a very tall step ladder which really made me nervous. This was my first introduction to heights. The step ladder was at least eight feet tall. Well, the guy who had got in trouble offered to climb the ladder and crack open the valve for me. Not knowing who he was, gullible me was thrilled he was offering to help. If I had known any better, I would have realized the guys would not help out that way because they expected everyone to do their own job. So, he went up the ladder and turned the valve wide open. I didn't know he had done that until the whole pipeline started banging and shaking. The noise could be heard throughout the entire unit. The foreman ran out of the control house yelling at me, "What the blankety blank have you done?!" The guy that had set me up had disappeared. I grabbed the ladder and quickly climbed up and closed the valve until the shaking stopped, then barely opened it to allow a small amount of hot steam to escape. The foreman was still chewing me out in front of some of the guys when the real culprit showed back up. What nerve! But there was no way I could accuse him. Who would they believe? The newbie woman or a member of the safety crew? After a couple of months my horrible foreman was moved to a daytime project in another building and a new much nicer man took his place. I stayed clear of the troublemaker, and life on shift improved. As the other guys saw I was a hard worker and really trying to learn, they allowed me into their good graces. Then the job became enjoyable, and shift work became routine. That was until one summer night on graveyard shift. Fortunately, Heather was in west Texas visiting my mom at the time. It had rained steady all night causing us to spend all our time outside in rubber boots and a slicker suit, basically completely covered and miserably hot. We had noticed the pipe ditches were filling up with water, but none of us had any idea how much rain had fallen from midnight to 8:00 a.m. until people started calling in before shift change. One by one every person that called had a flooded house, flooded cars or a flooded road and could not get to work. Then came the report that the entire road from the town to the plant was under water as was our employee parking lot. No one could come in or leave. As calls kept coming in, we realized the entire town and all the surrounding area was flooded with as much as four to five feet of water in some places. I was very concerned about my house as it was considered to be in a flood zone. Everyone in the whole plant had to continue working in order to keep the units running. At that point, most of us had been up more than fifteen hours straight, and there was no food left over from the shift. The rain had let up a little, so later that afternoon some amazing ladies that lived across the road from the plant entrance had made dozens of sandwiches and had taken a boat to deliver them to the front gate. The delicious sandwiches were divided out to all the units and shared among the workers. That night the guards had been able to rob all the vending machines and divided the spoils. Now going on two days with no sleep and little food, a call had come in from the plant manager to all the unit foremen to try and get to the cafeteria where they could share all the food they could find in the refrigerators and freezers. We ate good after that. We even cooked steaks and baked potatoes. After no sleep for a third day somebody brought in a cot, and we all took turns getting a one hour nap. Going without sleep for all that time made you feel like a zombie. Dead inside, but still moving. Finally, by the morning of day four the water had gone down enough to bring in the relief workers. Water still covered the roads so they were riding on a flatbed trailer pulled by a big truck with tall tires. By noon, we had all made shift change and could officially leave. But since all of our cars were still flooded in, plus most of the road to town, we all had to ride on that flatbed trailer back to town where we were dumped in the middle of the main business district. I am sure we were quite a sight to see. I had already called a friend to pick me up and was able to get home. Miraculously, my house and my neighborhood had not even come close to flooding. But there were dozens of houses in other areas that were not in the flood zone that had four plus feet of water in them. Unfortunately, my friend Dorothy was one of them. And, none of the people in her subdivision had flood insurance because they never thought it was necessary. It was so sad to see her once beautiful neighborhood with piles of furniture and appliances in front of every house. Again, I just considered myself lucky. My shower and my bed were worth a million dollars. And fortunately, my shift was now on our long weekend, so I was able to sleep until I was completely rested. A couple of days later we were allowed to go get our cars. The water had not gone inside my car or the motor. Lucky again, I thought. I am sure glad God has grace for his ignorant kids and never stops taking care of us, much like we do with our own children. I was certainly very relieved that Heather was safe and sound with my mom in west Texas.

Sixteen

From the Pit to the Promise

The paycheck we received after the flooding incident was huge. All the hours we had worked because we could not leave were considered overtime. With all the money I was earning at the plant, I was able to buy a newer vehicle and to be in a financial position that allowed Heather to be part of many fun activities. I wanted to make sure she had a chance to try everything and enjoy being a kid. Throughout the years she participated in softball, dance class, twirling, drill team, tennis, basketball, orchestra and eleven years in Girl Scouts. I was involved in Heather's activities as much as being on shift work would allow. I helped coach her softball team for four years and volunteered at Girl Scouts as long as I did not have to go camping. Heather loved camping, but not me. I was so glad she could enjoy dozens of trips with her scout troop and other parents. I always said my idea of roughing it was staying in a cheap motel. Heather was in our local yearly parade several times either with her ball teams or twirling class. Beverly and I were devoted Moms, running down the street multiple times to get ahead of our girls in order to take pictures of them coming toward us. Although Heather was the daughter of a single mom, I was determined that she would not miss out on a normal childhood. I promised myself when she was born that I would do everything within my power to make sure her life was a happy one. As mother and daughter, we got along great, best friends. Of course, we were not perfect, but we were basically a compatible team who loved each other. There was also enough money to make many improvements to our house. I worked very hard to ensure that our home would not look run down like many places I had seen where single women lived. I spent three days by myself painting the exterior trim of my brick home, plus garage doors. I helped lay a 10 x 20 concrete patio, literally standing in rubber boots and spreading cement as they dumped it. One of the guys at work volunteered to labor all day to help me lay it and with no fringe benefits. He was just being nice. Then I had the patio covered and screened in. I had a really good chain link fence installed around the whole backyard to give our two dogs freedom to run around. Finally, I planted several trees, front and back, and always kept a manicured lawn. The interior was in equally nice condition, so our home was a very comfortable place that Heather could be proud to bring her friends to. So, from all appearances, my life was in perfect order and well kept. However, after a while I ran out of projects to occupy my mind, and life became ordinary and idled in maintenance mode. And what is the old saying, "An idle mind is the devil's workshop." Soon, my old obsessions found their way back into my life. If only my mind and emotions could have stayed in as good of shape as the rest of my world. I could control how I took care of Heather, the house, and even my job, but I had no control over the fears and hopelessness that beat me into submitting to my addiction.

My financial windfall had enabled me to finally have some adult fun, which was not necessarily a good thing. When I was flat broke and working all those jobs, I still had a sexual encounter every now and then with this one certain man that was married. But at the time, my obsession for love had seemed to have taken a back seat to a different kind of desperation, the emotional turmoil of surviving without money. Now I had enough money to pay a sitter, often, so I could go to clubs or parties. My pledge to not have one-night stands anymore had gone by the wayside. Working shift work gave me many opportunities for an afternoon delight while Heather was at school. Before long I was right

back to my old promiscuous life style and increasingly disastrous emotional highs and lows. For the next five years or so I was back to leading
two lives again. This time, one of a hard working involved single parent
and the other of a flirtatious, immoral, and depraved unpaid prostitute.
For a while, I allowed this married man I knew from real estate to
continue coming over during the day. He was always so excited to see
me and he had dimples. His constant smile made me feel good and
the sex was enjoyable, too. He was handy to satisfy my resurfaced need
to be loved. But after a while, I began to meet more and more single
guys at the clubs, and I didn't have time for him anymore. At first, I
spent every Friday or Saturday night I was off at the Parents Without
Partners dances. When Heather and I first went to PWP it was to have
outings for the kids, but now she didn't need that because her schedule
was very full where we lived. At one of the kid's events, I had met a
woman named Michelle, and we became instant close friends. So, she
and I would always meet up and sit together at the dances. We both
loved to dance and since we were good dancers, we had the attention
of a lot of men. Michelle was not as interested in hooking up with the
guys as I was. She had one man she saw every now and then. I actually
dated some of the men I met at the dances and some were just over-
nighters. One man I dated named Michael was older than I, but a very
good dancer. When I could I would often stay at his place. We had a lot
of fun for a while, then his job transferred him to another state. I was
fine with that; he was just for dancing and sex. My love addiction was a
strange bedfellow. Most of the time if someone left, I would go into an
absolute tailspin, but on a rare occasion I would barely have a reaction.
I guess it depended on how *hooked* I was on them. Then I started dancing quite often with Patrick. He also had dimples and was short like
I liked. He never dated anyone from PWP, but occasionally he would
come to my house for sex. That was my ticket to being one of his dance
partners because he was one of the best dancers there. Rumor was that
he was fairly well off financially from flipping houses and doing the
work himself, and he was tight fisted with his money. So, what Patrick
did for me one day was an incredible surprise. He told me he wanted to

spend all day Saturday at my house, which was a complete shock. Then he showed up in his work clothes with his work truck loaded with plywood, 2 x 4's and a table saw. He proudly announced he was going to make hurricane covers for my windows. I had never even thought about needing something like that. I had lived in my nice brick home about two years, but had never considered the chance of a hurricane hitting my house. I was several miles from the Gulf of Mexico and totally uneducated about storms. He said I needed them; he had leftover wood to use up, and it was all free. So, Patrick spent the entire day measuring, cutting and marking boards for all my windows. I could not believe it! I made him lunch, and that evening before he left, he didn't even ask to have sex. I thought how lucky I was to have someone who wanted to spend all that time and effort to help me protect my house for free! And, he did not even want anything in return. Through the years I used those boards four times, once for a full-blown hurricane. If it had not been for Patrick's generosity, I probably would not have been prepared. God certainly works in mysterious ways.

I went through several men from Parents Without Partners, losing a part of myself after each encounter. My mental and emotional state of mind was dipping lower and lower. I must have started being too open about my fears and depression because one guy I was with looked at me like I was crazy and told me I needed to go to church. That seemed to be a strange comment from someone who was hopping beds, too. But I guess I took his advice to heart because I decided I really should be taking Heather to church, not that I needed it or anything. So, we started going to a local church every Sunday. Also, maybe that was why I started going out with this guy from PWP named Gregory. He wore a big cross and talked about God all the time. On one of our dates, he even took me to this cute little white wooden church that was located in an older section of the town where I lived. There was a singing group performing there that Gregory wanted to hear. All I remember was that it was not like the church that Heather and I attended. Everyone was singing and clapping their hands; they all seemed so happy. I thought maybe I had finally found a nice guy because he liked to go to church. But, dating Gregory was emotionally confusing because he would be preaching at me one minute and having sex with me the next. One evening out of the clear blue he called me on the phone and began telling me what a sinful person I was because I had sex with all those men, and that he could not have somebody like that in his life. I thought, "What a hypocrite!" His slate was not clean by a long shot. By the time we hung up I was completely beaten down by his words. I did not have any self-esteem anyway, so I crumbled and cried and cried and cried. Immediately, I became extremely depressed. But then, I got mad and thought the nerve of him! The madder I got, the more I heard words forming in my mind again for a poem. Another emotional train wreck had caused words to once more rapidly pour into my head. This is what I heard.

ME

I'm sorry I'm just me for all the world to see.
But somehow I just know, there's someplace else to go.
My words, the world may say, seem not to fit the play.
But, it's not in my heart to try to act a part.

Though some I chance to meet won't stay; they call Retreat.
I still can't seem to change, and I don't want the blame
For being what I'm not just to satisfy the lot.

God in heaven did create for me my perfect mate.
And when his eyes meet mine, the good in me will shine.
My faults will plant no seeds to mar his book of needs.
For only good will grow as side by side we know

To be me and apologize would be living a disguise.
So, our love will never stray, and with pride I can say
I'm happy to be me for all the world to see.

Writing that poem got me through the verbal beating, and before you knew it, I was out looking again. It did not matter how badly I was treated by a man, I had to find my next supplier as soon as possible. I stopped going as often to the PWP dances and started spending more time at various clubs. I had met a new party friend named Christina who went to my church. She and I were like-minded when it came to having sex with whoever became available. Sometimes both of us would even go home with roommates. Separate bedrooms, of course. I was never ever going to have any of that kinky foursome stuff again. Also, neither of us minded being left to go home alone if only one of us got hooked up. Christina and I became close friends and were always out at the clubs together. One night I met this sweet man named Richard. He was such a gentleman, had a very pleasant personality and was a good dancer. He was also very sexy and affectionate and married. He lived in another state and came to town periodically to head up construction crews in the area. He told me up front that he was a happily married family man, but he always wanted companionship when he was away from home for a long time. He said if I would like to be with him every time he came to town, he would always treat me right. I asked why he did that if he was so happily married, and he said he did not want to go that long without sex. But he didn't want to just pick up somebody new every time. He was looking for one woman to be with when he came to town, and that was all that should be expected. He was so charming and honest; I could not resist. The thought of being his only special girl appealed to my obsession to be needed. So, I ended up seeing Richard off and on for a couple of years. He always took me to nice restaurants and then dancing. We always made love at his place. But of course, I still went out with other guys when he was gone. One of those men was a friend of my co-worker's boyfriend. They wanted me to go on a blind date with him. I said I would, so she and I met up with the boys at a club. Garrett was a lot older than I, but a real cut up who made me laugh. He invited me and Heather to go out in the Gulf on his boat. We had such a good time. That evening we stopped at a marina and ate supper, and Heather loved the whole day. He wanted to see me all the time and had money to take me to nice places. One day Garrett invited me over to his house for dinner and asked me to bring my toothbrush. My feeling loved meter went to the top because I knew I was spending the night. Whenever Heather had a sleepover or an all-night sitter, I would stay at his house. He treated me very well. We had been going out quite a while, and my expectations were high until one evening Garrett asked me to stop by his house on an odd night. He had been drinking which was not unusual because he was a borderline high-functioning alcoholic. He started berating me with crazy talk about me being unsophisticated. That I had bad manners because one night I had used a toothpick in public. Unbelievable! He was not exactly Prince Charming. He was just an old, balding blue-collar foreman at a pipe factory! Boy, the devil always knew how to hit me below the belt by attacking my self-worth, which was practically non-existent. Garrett ended our relationship that night, and I never saw it coming. I went into my usual shock and panic. I cried all the way home, completely devastated and plunging into deep depression. I could not fathom why so many guys were beating me up with condemnations. The spirits of fear and rejection were still working overtime in my life, and now condemnation had joined the party again. For the umpteenth time, I had lost my supplier for my addiction. The woman who had introduced us called me the next day. She had heard about the breakup from her boyfriend. When I told her what Garrett had said to me, she could not believe it either. Then she told me that he had met another woman, but there was no excuse for him treating me the way he did. I felt sorry for the other woman getting a man like Garrett, but I still wallowed in rejection. After a couple of days of wallowing, along came another poem.

A SAD POEM

Plastic people all around; some are up and some are down.

You can't tell by what they say just where you stand day by day.

I'm the one that's meant for you, but we're not to say, "I do."

Baby, you're the one for me. Give me time and we will see.

I'm for real and that's no lie. If you don't push, we'll get by.

To you only I'll be true. I just want to live with you.

I love you, I will not sin. That phone call was just a friend.

I'm a true one-woman man. Don't tie me down to a plan.

They say this, but then do that. Hard to tell just where it's at.

So confusing, can't believe. What you get's not what you see.

It's no wonder we can't trust with selfish lies choking us.

It's too sad; it's got to end. Still no tears? Read it again.

You would think after all those terrible breakups I would do something different, but instead, I just kept putting myself out there to be trampled on. Unknowingly, that was a chronic pattern for people trapped by love addiction. And that was exactly how it felt, like an addiction. I could not survive without my fix of sexual contact. I even started doing what I said I would never do, flirting at work. Except for a couple of guys, all the men in the unit were married, but that did not stop some of them from flirting back. The sensual looks and smiles made us feel excited that someone was interested. One person I was doing some heavy flirting with was my foreman in the new unit where we now worked. One night on shift I had to call him on my radio to look at a potential problem with a pump. We were alone in an isolated section of my work area and were standing very close together, sometimes touching. Temptation and lust were so rampant we did not have to say a word to get the message. We continued talking about the pump as we undressed each other with our eyes. It was a potentially overpowering sensation and dangerous territory. There was a zero-tolerance policy at the plant about physical contact between sexes at work. In the past, men and women had been fired on the spot for fraternizing on the job. Oh, how we yearned to grab each other in a passionate kiss, but neither one of us wanted to do anything to jeopardize our job. At least we both had enough natural fear and sense to have restraint, but I know we really enjoyed the moment. We had actually planned to get together outside of work, but his wife became seriously ill. I was very disappointed. Unbelievably, he still wanted to come over to my house. But even with my depraved mind, I still had a glimmer of decency and respect for his very sick wife. I told him no and that ended that. Another time I was kind of flirting with this younger guy from the construction crew. I knew he was married, but he was very good looking and built. I thought he had potential for some good loving. He responded, so I invited him over to my house to play pool. We had drinks, shot pool, and things were heating up nicely. But then, just in idle conversation, he happened to mention that his wife taught twirling. I asked her name; she was Heather's twirling teacher! I thought, "No way am I having sex with Heather's teacher's husband! And she was really cute and young. Why was he wanting me?" Well, I put the brakes on that situation real quick. He kept trying, but I nicely escorted him to the door. I tell you; it is true that some men's brains really are in their pants.

By now, I had completely stopped going to Parents Without Partners dances and just hung out with Christina at the clubs. There was no temptation out there that I would not bow to. I was going deeper and deeper into oblivion. I would talk to anybody that would listen to me about all my crazy thoughts and fears. I was searching for anything that might ease my torment. I was so hoping that if I could talk to enough people that surely one of them would have an answer to my dilemma. I would call people in the middle of the night that had been nice enough to listen to me. I gave no thought to inconveniencing them. I had to have somebody to talk to! I was totally selfish with my desperation. I really did not even want sex anymore, but I still had to have it. I could not stop! I needed that fix. After sex I felt cheap and often experienced nausea. Someone suggested I talk to this woman counselor, but all it turned out to be was some ridiculous self-hypnosis techniques. I even went to talk to my pastor, but he was no help. He never even prayed with me or opened the Bible. He just suggested I read two popular self-help books, *I'm OK, You're OK* and *Your Erroneous Zones*. The books offered some superficial help, but I was getting worse by the minute. I was constantly telling people, "If only there was just one word I could say and all this garbage would just disappear." But even through all this torment and despair, I was still doing my best to be a good mother and a good employee and kept our home in good condition. Keeping up appearances, as in any addiction, was the order of the day. But you can never tell what is really going on inside a person's mind or spirit. The fact was well hidden that there was no common sense left in me. My feet were standing in quick sand, and there was absolutely no means of escape. How I wished someone would read between the lines of what I was saying and hear my cry of desperation and help me!

Then one night at a disco club, I met this smooth-talking Cajun named Julian. He had a line and a lure and reeled me in with every word. I was hooked. We went out to the parking lot to see his shiny new black Camaro. Of course, we got in and of course, we began to make out. We did everything around that *four on the floor* gear shift except have intercourse. He was very sexy and knew exactly what a woman wanted. After going back into the club, I told Christina I had a ride home. We often traded off doing that, so it was no big deal. Julian lived near the club, so we went to his apartment. He told me he was once a model and a male stripper, and believe me he had all the right moves. It was a night to remember. When he took me home, he said he would call me and he did. We met up several times at the club for a dance date and would go to his place afterwards. Having sex with Julian was absolutely intoxicating. It was like the most passionate sex scene in a movie. Soon, he was like a strong drug. When you are an addict and reach a high like that, you have got to have more. One Friday night I went out to eat and clubbing with a girlfriend from work. We went to the disco where Julian usually hung out, but he was not there. I thought, "Where is he? Julian is always here." I felt a surge of desperation and panic. I was expecting to see him! I needed to see him! Normally, I did not drink much at all, but my friend did. She kept buying us both one after another. Well, the more I had to drink, the more depressed I became that Julian was not there. Before long, my depression turned into an obsession to be with him. I needed my fix! My friend said she would take me to his place. But I whined in fear, "What if he isn't there, or he is with someone else, or he just does not want me!" She said she would go to the door and ask him if I could stay the night. "You would do that for me?" I cried. "But, if he says No, just tell me he wasn't there." I would not have been able to take being rejected. So, I stayed in the car, and soon she returned and said it was okay to spend the night. She was an amazing friend! I was elated, hope renewed! Cloud nine was on its way! Julian was waiting for me at the door and immediately put his arms around me and just kept hugging me until I stopped crying and apologizing. I felt so secure and safe lying in bed with him. I felt as if it was a breakthrough in our relationship because he had let me in with no questions asked. When I woke up the next morning, I was so happy.

Julian was already up and getting dressed to go out. I started talking about maybe we could spend the day together or even the whole weekend. Heather was on a scout trip. Julian was just looking at me with that cute Cajun grin of his. Then the phone rang. During the short conversation Julian told the other person that he would stop at the grocery store on the way there and wanted to know what the kids would like to eat. Then he hung up with an, "Okay, I'll see you soon." "See who soon?" I thought. As I tried to push back panic in my voice, I asked him who that was. Still grinning, he answered, "Just a lady I see occasionally." Shocked, I asked, "Are they your kids?" He laughed and said, "Oh, no, no." He never as much as took me out to eat, but he was buying groceries for this woman and her kids! And spending the day with them! Then he said, "Come on and get dressed now. We need to leave, so I can take you home." My spirit was completely broken. I wanted to spend the weekend with him. I felt so incredibly rejected. The trip back to my house was in complete silence. He did not even get out of the car. I was just dropped off. I sat on my couch and cried and cried, the depression was overwhelming. I cried, "I just cannot take this anymore!" My head was spinning with torment. I kept a loaded pistol by my bed. I took it out and sat on my bed with the gun in my hand. Every negative word, every hopeless situation I had ever experienced battered my mind. A full-length movie from my childhood to my now depraved existence played out every detail of my pitiful life. All I could see was a cesspool of filth and degradation. All of my thoughts focused on what a horrible person I was and how much I hated myself. I kept hearing a voice in my head telling me how worthless I was and how nobody wanted me or ever would. Down, down, down I was going into obscurity, into the pit. Then I heard that vicious voice say, "Go ahead, pull the trigger, and it will all be over, and you will finally have peace. Your life is a hopeless mess. You have nothing to live for!" Suddenly, those words, "You have nothing to live for" caused a spark in the darkness. "Heather! Heather!" I shouted out loud! I yelled, "I do have something to live for! I have Heather! I can't leave her alone! I can't do that to her!" I cried and cried and the spell was broken! The devil almost had me in the pit of hell for eternity, but the love I had for my daughter brought me back to my senses. "Oh my God! What day is this?" I wondered. My battle with the prince of darkness had lasted for hours! A whole day and night had passed like a flash of light. It was Sunday morning! I had to go get Heather that afternoon. I showered and got something to eat and was looking so forward to holding Heather in my arms. I quickly drove to the scout house, and when I saw her, I had to really fight to hold back a waterfall of tears. I just hugged her with all my might. No one had any idea what I had just been through. As I held her tightly, deep inside I promised Heather and myself that I would never allow thoughts of suicide to overwhelm me again.

After my close encounter with my own demise, I somehow felt stronger. I was thankful I had defied the odds, and no two-bit guy would ever drag me down like that again. I felt an unusual surge of confidence, like I was no longer vulnerable. I called my friend Christina to see when we could go out again. But this time, I was not interested in flirting or getting picked up; I just wanted to dance. Christina could tell I was different, but even she did not know about the gun. I was not going to tell anyone. She drove us to a new country western club near the airport. I knew I looked good when I walked in wearing my new jeans and my nice cowboy boots. All I wanted to do was find a good dancer, have a fun night, and go back home alone. We had not been at our table long when this man came over and asked if he could sit down. I was not particularly attracted to him, and he did not look the type that could do a two-step. I surely did not want to be stuck where guys would not ask me to dance because he was sitting there. I bordered on rude when for some strange reason I coldly said, "If you want to." He had a terrific smile as he sat down, almost as if I had said something funny. Most of the time I was not even looking at him as he tried to talk to me. But he kept trying, and grinning as if something was humorous. Finally, still grinning, he said, "Am I cramping your style?" I turned and looked him straight in the eye and smartly replied, "I do not have a style to cramp." He just laughed and asked, "Do you want to dance?" For some crazy reason I said yes. He was different, intriguing, and somewhat genuine. And what do you know, this guy could dance all the country dances and was good at it! I was starting to become a little more impressed with him, and interested. Not only could he dance, but he was very easy to talk to, had a great sense of humor and was a gentleman. By the end of the night, I had a feeling, a sensation, an epiphany. I did not know exactly what to call it. But I sincerely felt as if I had known this man named Dawson my entire life. There was an aura of comfort or familiarity, even completion. As if we were one person. It's very hard to explain, but I had never experienced anything like that with anyone, ever. Not even William or Gabriel. I was having a difficult time coming up with words in my mind to describe what I was feeling. There was no love at first sight, and he did not really turn me on or anything like that. It was much deeper and peaceful. When Dawson offered to take me home, because he lived in the same town I did, it felt so normal that I should be with him. I remember driving off with him after telling Christina goodbye; it was as if I had done that a hundred times before. In the car, riding back home, our conversation and the general atmosphere was so natural, almost like we were married. I know that sounds very strange and crazy, but again I cannot seem to find an appropriate description to explain exactly what I was experiencing. If there was such a thing as soulmates, then that would have been the best way to understand what was happening. I believed he felt it, too. When he walked me to the door, the moment felt so special, so pure. We did not even kiss goodnight, but he wrote down my phone number. As I tried to go to sleep my mind kept reliving our amazing evening. I thought about stories I had heard over the years from people telling how they felt when they met their soulmates. What I went through that night was similar. All I knew as I dozed off was there had been something strangely new and special about the evening's encounter. Could Dawson be my soulmate?

On Monday Dawson called me at work, which was actually a surprise because I had only given him my home number. I did tell him where I worked, so I was impressed that he had tracked me down. He asked to go to dinner that night. Of course, I said yes. At dinner he shared with me an unbelievable opportunity he had been offered, but he would have to leave the next week and be gone a month. He wanted to see me as much as he could before he left. The night we met Dawson had told me he worked at the airport with planes and crews and stuff. But he must have totally down played his importance considering the incredible journey he had been asked to be a part of. Amazingly, his collaborative adventure went down in the aviation history books. Dawson had been chosen to be a member of the chase plane crew for a flight around the world. I did not really comprehend at that time what a monumental feat Dawson was involved in. When he told me about going, he was so matter-of-fact and did not really make a big deal out of it. It was years later that I discovered the details of the trip and was amazed. Since I barely knew anything about the journey, I was not at all apprehensive about him being gone so long or his safety. I just knew he and I would be together. We had another nice dinner date a couple of nights before he was leaving, and when he took me home, we stood at the door and talked a minute. Then he said, "You know, here I am about to fly around the world, and I don't even know if you can kiss or hold hands." He grinned, I smiled and pulled him towards me and planted a passionate kiss on his lips. After coming up for air I asked, "Do you want to come in?" He spent the night, and it felt as if he belonged there. Since he was leaving the next day, he asked if he could come back in a few hours and stay the night before he left for the trip. I had not allowed anyone to stay over while Heather was there, but it all felt so natural that Dawson was in the house. It was as if he already lived there. Heather met him and immediately liked him, so we had a fun family evening. He even did some of his laundry. He had to leave very early the next morning. In the few days since I met Dawson, he had made quite an impact on my life. Although he was leaving, I did not have the usual fears or anxieties about him not coming back. I had peace of mind. Later that day I found he had left some of his things in my dryer. That small gesture made me so happy. I thought, "He's really coming back!"

As time passed by, I tried to imagine where in the world, literally, Dawson might be. I did miss him, but not in a sad way. I was counting the days until I would see his smiling face. Then early one morning around 3:00 my phone rang. Dawson was calling from India! I was so excited he was thinking about me! He told me all the countries they had been through and that he missed me. I could not believe it. He called me from India in the midst of this historic trip to tell me he missed me. He said he probably would not have another chance to call again, but as soon as they were back in the states he would call. This was in the days before cell phones when you actually had to have patience and wait for a place to find a phone to use. I was so elated by his call there was no more sleep for me. I just laid there picturing him doing all that he had told me about and dreaming about being together again. A couple of weeks later Dawson called to tell me they had landed back in Dallas. In a few hours he would be back home at his apartment, but he really needed sleep. He asked me to come over there the next day and wake him up. It was a dream come true! He must definitely feel the same way I did! When we finally got back together, he seemed as excited as I was. We picked up Heather to go out to eat, and she was also glad to see him. The world was a happy place! The next day he showed up at my door with a large plastic container full of cans of Dinty Moore Beef Stew that were left over from the trip. Dawson was always full of surprises. We all three enjoyed each other's company so much that he started staying at my house full time. I would not have let him move in with us if I had not really believed that this relationship was serious. Our time together was perfect. We all got along so well. Heather and I would go with him to visit his mom. We both really liked her. She loved to play a board game she called *Marbles*, and we would often join in. One time Dawson and I went to Las Vegas for three days, and Heather stayed with his mom. They had a great time playing games, and Dawson and I had fantastic fun in Vegas. He brought me a rose when he picked me up to head for the airport. I told him I would like to share in the expenses and he said $100.00 would be enough. He covered everything else including a show on the strip. I was playing a quarter slot machine that paid out in silver dollars, and before I knew it, I had filled a tray with $100.00. I immediately took the tray over to Dawson and said,

"Here's the $100.00 I owe you." He just laughed and probably fed them back into his slot machine. How I would love to have that tray of silver dollars today. They were in abundance everywhere in Las Vegas in those days. His mom told me later that he had said it was the best time he had ever had in Vegas. You know that made me feel really special. Everything we did together was terrific, and we never had an argument. Heather and I continued to go to church every Sunday, but Dawson never offered to go with us. I didn't care one way or another, so we did not discuss it. One night Dawson came home late from work. I was already in bed, and he sat at the foot of the bed with a worried look on his face. Then he said, "I just cannot go with you all." I was completely puzzled, "Go where?" He said, "To church." I was like where did that come from? He repeated, "I just cannot go with you and Heather to church." "Who asked you to?" I questioned. "It does not matter to me what you do," I added. He just left it at that and got ready for bed. He never brought it up again. From what I know now that I did not know then was, he was feeling convicted. However, he did go with us for our Christmas service. Then he invited me to a big New Year's Eve party at a Houston hotel. We both dressed up fancy, and Heather stayed at his mom's. There was to be a nice sit-down dinner with drinks and dancing to a live orchestra. I thought, "Finally, I will have a lover to kiss at midnight!" There was just one problem. Dawson got lost in Houston and could not find the place. We drove around for over an hour looking and looking. It was all so strange, like it was hidden from us. There was no place to ask directions because everything was closed, and there was no such thing as GPS. I felt so sorry for him. He did not get mad or flustered and eventually managed to find the right road. We arrived at the ballroom an hour before midnight. The food was long gone, but there were snacks on the tables and drinks at the bar, so we made the best of the rest of the evening. The important thing was I got my midnight kiss, and all was well with the new year. The band played on after twelve so we were able to enjoy the dancing. Dawson felt terrible about what had happened, but I tried to assure him that I thought it turned out to be a wonderful evening.

After the holidays we all settled into life as a family. Although it was never mentioned, I believed we were both falling in love. But it was a different kind of love than I had ever known, like it was just meant to be. For several months everything was perfect, but then the baggage from both our pasts began to creep in. Still no arguing, but more like insecurities. He had been married several times along with multiple relationships, and with my history we both had our demons trying to confuse us and ruin our happiness. Our problems really started when Dawson's job moved him from the airport near where we lived to the enormous international airport which was over an hour away. He left in the morning before sunrise while I was still asleep and came home late and tired. I don't think I fully appreciated the effort he was making. After a few weeks of trying to keep that schedule Dawson announced he was getting an apartment by the big airport. His plan was to come home on Friday night and leave for work on Monday morning. Then I got upset, which I should not have. He got the apartment, and for several more weeks we tried the weekend arrangement. It was tough. Neither of us had the emotional foundation to make that situation work. Every weekend we could feel our perfect world disappearing more and more. Knowing Dawson was getting tired of even driving home for the weekend, I suggested that sometimes I would come stay with him. He liked that idea, so I would leave Heather with his mom and go over there on Friday night and come back on Sunday. He had his apartment fixed up really nice, almost too nice. It looked too permanent. That made me nervous. We always tried to have fun weekends, but things seemed tense. I would catch him just looking at me with kind of a sad stare. One night at his place I was at the bathroom sink brushing my teeth, and he came up behind me and put his arms around my waist and laid his head on my back. He looked as if he was in deep thought. I always tried to respond to his love and let him know how special he was to me. However, I had no idea how conflicted he was that night. We made love, and I left the next day thinking everything was fine. The following weekend he came home; nothing seemed unusual. I let him know how much I missed him and wished he could get back to the other airport. I did his laundry with mine. We cooked out and watched TV. It was a normal abnormal weekend. When he was leaving Monday morning, he woke me up, hugged me, and kissed me goodbye. That was different, but I thought it was really sweet, and I went back to sleep. Later, when I got up to take a shower and get ready for work, I went to the walk-in closet to get my clothes and got punched in the stomach! Dawson had taken all of his clothes! A panic greater than all the panics I'd ever had consumed my body! I was trembling from head to toe, "Oh my God, NO! God no!" Then I remembered we had left clothes in the dryer; he would have to come back for those. I rushed to the garage and dug through the dryer only to find he had taken all of those, too! More panic!! Worse panic!! I was out of my mind with panic! All I could think was I have to talk to him! I have to find him! I frantically called his apartment, but there was no answer. He did not have an answering machine, and I didn't know his work number. I had to go to his apartment! I could not breathe. I thought, "I cannot go to work! I have to drive over there!" I called my boss and left a message that I was taking a vacation day. I tried to pull myself together enough to wake up Heather and get her to school. I told her she would have to eat breakfast in the cafeteria. It was so hard to maintain my emotions in order to keep her from knowing what had happened. As soon as I possibly could, I headed for his apartment on the other side of Houston. I wanted to beat the morning traffic and hopefully Dawson would still be at his apartment. I rationalized that he was probably in the shower when I called. I was freaking out with fear and grief. I made it over there in record time and drove around the parking lot looking for his car. It was not there, but I still went and frantically knocked on his door. He had to be there! I had no idea where he worked at the airport or how to get his office phone number. The airport complex was so spread out there was no possible way to find him. I was beside myself with fear and panic! I sat in his parking lot for the longest time, hoping Dawson would come back. I finally left and drove the freeway back and forth between his apartment and the airport hoping to somehow see his car. I did that like a crazy person for over an hour. Desperation destroyed all reason because a rational person would know that his car could not be spotted on a crowded multi-lane freeway while going seventy miles an hour. Then I went back to his apartment and sat in my car hoping he might come home for lunch. I sat there crying for a couple of hours. I could not bring myself to leave. I might miss him! I didn't want any food, but I was so thirsty I finally left and went to a nearby motel restaurant-bar to get something. They had a pay phone I immediately used to call his apartment every five minutes. I was a mess. My head was hurting, my stomach was aching, and my eyes were red from crying. I must have looked like I needed a drink because the only other person in the place asked if he could buy me one. I told him I really did not want to talk to anyone. I used the phone a few more times then left to drive around some more. I went to the airport and drove around there for an hour. Then I went back to my lunatic freeway search. I had to keep looking to ease my desperation. Hours had passed and it would soon be time for Dawson to get off work, so I drove back to the apartment and parked where there was no way I would miss seeing him drive up. I rehearsed in my mind how the conversation would go when I saw him. I frantically waited almost two hours until it was starting to get dark, but he never came. Finally, I thought, "Oh my God, Heather should be home by now, and she probably already called me at work and I was not there. I needed to call her, so I had to leave the parking lot. I went back to the motel pay phone to check on her and told her I would be home in a couple of hours. She was twelve now and was good at being home alone. I tried Dawson's number one more time, but still no answer. Feeling as if I was going to just miss him by seconds, I reluctantly drove back home. But before going to my house, I went to see his mother in hopes that he might be there. He was not, but she welcomed me in. I asked if she had talked to Dawson today; she had not. I told her what had happened and asked if she knew why or if he had talked to her about me. She said that she always tried to stay out of his business, and they never talked about things like that. She tried to be comforting and said Heather and I were always welcomed there. I finally went home, tired and emotionally drained. I tried to put on a good face for Heather. I did not want to tell her yet because I knew she really liked Dawson. I thought I would wait until the weekend when he did not come back. I thought maybe I would be more able to handle it then without breaking down as much. After Heather went to bed, I kept calling his number to no avail. I called over and over all week long with no answer. I thought maybe he moved or went out of town. By the weekend I was an emotional catastrophe. I still broke down when I told Heather which caused her to cry, too. I felt so sad that I had caused her to experience hurt. I had truly believed that Dawson and I would be together forever.

This breakup was very different than all the others. The effect it had on me was almost unexplainable. I felt as if my very soul had been ripped out of my body, and there was a big hole there. It was like an important part of me had been amputated. My depression was not just in my mind, it was in my heart and in my body and it was unbearable. I knew I truly loved Dawson. He really was my soulmate. And, I sincerely believed that he had felt it, too. It was obvious now that he had been struggling with that decision for a while. Unfortunately, the road we had both taken to get to each other had muddied the waters so badly our relationship did not have a chance. Not only was my life a mess, Dawson had been married five times. Three to the mother of his children, one common law marriage that ended in a court battle and one other divorce I did not know much about. Now, I had lost all hope in ever finding love again. There could never be another person I would love as much as Dawson. That special soulmate feeling of oneness was a unique kind of love that could not be repeated. I didn't feel down on myself like all the other times, just incredibly and overwhelmingly empty. I just gave up on having any future that mattered, but not to the point of suicide again. I always kept my promises. Every day I felt lower and lower. Not only more and more depressed, but very sad, unbelievably sad. I was on an emotional skid row and living in the gutter. Barely standing on the edge of the abyss, just one more step and I would be in the pit. I was just going through the motions of work and being a mother. My insides were dead. I had absolutely no interest in going out anywhere. What was the point? There would never be another Dawson. It was weird though, guys I had known before began calling me, wanting to get together for sex. It was so interesting how the devil works. I had not heard a word from any of them in almost a year, and there was no way they could have known I was alone again. I told them to stop calling. But, the agents of the prince of darkness did not stop there. One day, out of the clear blue, my old Cajun sex buddy, Julian, showed up at my house! He had never ever just stopped by my house like that! Remember, he was the one I begged my friend to take me to his apartment. The one that became the tipping point and caused me to hold a gun in my hand. It had been over a year since that happened. He came to see me during the day and for some reason Heather was not home. He wanted to come in and have sex. He had never been inside my house before, or for that matter, he never even wanted to whenever he brought me home. In the past, I would have been elated that he wanted me, but this time I was just not interested. He said, "Let's go for a ride then." So, I did. Why in the world did I say yes? It did not feel as if I was the person in the car. I felt numb, like I was in a trance. After driving around for a short while he said, "Why don't we go to a motel for old times' sake?" I certainly did not want to do that, and a loud voice in my head kept saying, "Don't go! Don't do it!" My inner conflict was a raging wild fire! Then Julian pulled up to a small local motel and went inside and got a room. I guess he took my silence as an affirmative. I was there, but not there, as he led me to the room. When inside he began to kiss me, and I willingly had sex with him. But afterwards, I felt sick to my stomach. I could not help feeling as if I was cheating on Dawson. Then Julian took me home and actually walked me to the door this time. I thought to myself, "What have I done?" I did not want anyone but Dawson. After that encounter I started getting even more depressed. The devil was working overtime. Guys were coming out of the woodwork, calling me at all hours. Some of them had never called me before. We just met up at the clubs. I didn't even know they had my phone number. It was unreal. There were definitely evil forces at work trying to drag me back into my old lifestyle. My time with Dawson had been so wonderful all I wanted was to be left alone with my memories. Then one night a very strange thing happened. This guy I used to hook up with called me wanting to have phone sex. He was another one I had not heard from in over a year. I said no way, but he kept talking. I kept silent. I should have just hung up on him, but I didn't. I hated myself because I was always so accommodating. The guy finished jacking himself off without me saying a word, but I had listened. Immediately, as soon as I hung up the phone, I heard an audible voice, not in my head, but from somewhere in my bedroom. It sounded as if it was coming from an actual person, but no one was there. The voice said, "What if you're doing this when Jesus comes back?" For some strange reason I was not afraid. Maybe that was because of the many unusual occurrences I had experienced in my life since childhood. I did not freak out, but I did not move as I repeated the words in my mind, "What if you're doing this when Jesus comes back?" I knew exactly what *this* meant, living this lifestyle of screwing around with all these men. Then I thought to myself, "I didn't even know Jesus was coming back!" To me Jesus was just a baby in the manger at Christmas. How would He be coming back? What seemed interesting was even though I claimed to be an agnostic and not sure who God was, I knew without a doubt that the voice I heard was sent from God. Nothing else happened, but from that moment on I could not get those words out of my mind. They were on constant replay as I went through my daily grind. There had been a lot of strange happenings in my life, but this one took the cake. I thought back on the angel praying by my bed, the snap inside my head that ushered in fear, being snatched from my bed when the walls were closing in, words coming out of my mouth that saved me from a rape, guessing a Deja vu seconds before it happened, the crazy Ouija board stuff, the old man at square dancing and the poems that flooded my mind from out of nowhere. Now I hear an actual voice? The sound of the voice was not condemning, but more like trying to get me to think about the possibility of that actually happening. And I did think about it, constantly. But I did not understand what it meant. I was afraid to tell anyone I was hearing voices, a voice. People would think I was crazy. Not knowing what to do I just went on with my life of missing Dawson more and more.

Even with the voice and all that had happened, I was not actively seeking after God or Jesus or any religion. But I was constantly crying out for help from SOMEBODY! My friend Christina had been invited to go hear some speaker at a hotel conference room and she drug me along. He turned out to be a preacher. I sat and listened, but truly did not hear a word he was saying. Satan literally had my ears covered, so I would not hear the Gospel. The man that was speaking could have been talking about the weather for all I knew. All I heard was, "Blah, blah, blah." Then Christina wanted to go to a club. I told her I was not interested in going dancing or meeting guys. She said we could just go hear a couple who did a comedy routine and then go home. I certainly needed a laugh or two, so we went. The comedians were hilarious with crude humor, sexual innuendos, and some off-color language. It was good to laugh for a moment, but that feeling was not lasting. I finally decided I needed to talk to a counselor, so I went to the Counseling Center in town. I had not tried to call Dawson again for fear of more rejection, but one day I just could not stand it any longer. I needed to hear his voice. So, I used the counseling as an excuse, and I called and he actually answered. I melted into the phone. It was so wonderful to talk to him. I was completely rational and told him I was going to counseling. I asked if he could help by calling the counselor and telling her any information that might help her help me. He was very nice and said he would. I don't know if he ever did, but I did not care about that. My mission had been accomplished. I got to have a brief moment in time with the man I loved. Well, I had been to a couple of counseling sessions when the day arrived that would completely change my life forever. The session started out the same as all the others, but then the counselor said, "I want to try something different. Close your eyes, and I want you to imagine being in a red room. Now continue keeping your eyes closed, and picture an escalator going up. Go over to it and ride up, and when you step off you are in an orange room. You see another escalator. Ride it up, and get off into a yellow room. Do you see all this clearly?" "Yes," I answered with my eyes still tightly closed. The counselor continued, "Now ride up again and this room will be green." Then with one more escalator ride I got off and entered a beautiful blue room. This room was very relaxing and serene. "Do you feel the peacefulness?" she inquired. Again, never opening my eyes, I calmly answered, "I guess so." Then she said, "Now, I want you to picture a door in the room, and when you open the door, I want you to walk out on to a scene that you consider your most peaceful place." She was quiet for a minute as I navigated through my mind to find that special scenario. I was not really a beach person, but I loved the sound of the ocean waves as they gently splashed upon the shore, especially at night. So, when I opened the door in the blue room, I pictured a full moon hovering over an empty beach at night. The moonlight was shining on the water, so I could see the beautiful white capped waves peacefully finding their way to the shoreline. That vivid scene was like a vision in my mind. It was so real I felt as if I was watching a movie. The longer I stared at the serene nightscape, the more I seemed to actually be standing on the beach. Then the counselor quietly asked, "Do you have a peaceful place?" My eyes remained shut as I whispered, "Yesss." I felt really calm. "Now," she said, "I want you to picture someone walking towards you that you can trust." Screech!! She just ruined my happy place. I still had my eyes closed watching my ocean movie, but thinking, "Who in the world am I going to picture walking towards me because I do not trust anyone." While I am thinking that and trying to come up with somebody, I noticed that on the right side of my beach scene something began to move in the darkness. I thought, "What in the world is going on? I'm not thinking of something moving." I was looking down the beach, with my eyes closed, to try and see what was in the darkness. I could not quite make it out, so I was really staring at the movement. Then, in the shadows, I saw a figure beginning to walk down the beach towards me. It seemed to be a person; I saw legs. "Who is that and how did they get in my vision?" I was literally leaning forward in my chair and staring into my mind to see who it was. I was not making this happen. Something else had control of what I was seeing. The shadow, which resembled a man, continued walking in the darkness along the beach, getting closer and closer to me. Then he turned and his appearance changed as the moonlight shone on his face. He walked straight up to me, his face inches from my face. It was Jesus!! I saw Him clearly. His loving eyes stared into mine. His countenance was so tender as He showed a slight smile. As I stared into His eyes, the most tremendous unconditional love poured out of them like a raging waterfall. I could feel that love like it was a tangible entity. Every part of His face exuded love. It just kept flowing and flowing into the depths of my soul, filling every part of my being. I had never experienced that kind of manifestation of love before, or since, from anyone else. I just wanted to stay in that moment and soak up more and more of that love, so I did not open my eyes. But then, like a bolt of lightning, I was shocked back into the counseling room when she asked, "Do you have someone?" I was not going to allow this unwanted interruption to cause my eyes to open. I just wanted to stay with Jesus. As I tried desperately to keep my eyes closed, the counselor asked again. So, with Him still staring at me, I slowly answered in an almost puzzled, how can this be tone of voice and said, "Yes. It's Jesus." My counselor sat very still and quiet, but eventually said, "Oh, that's nice." She finally made me open my eyes. After that I really don't remember much about the session. I guess it was over when Jesus came into the picture, and His impact on my life was yet to come.

After that moment with Jesus, I felt as if I was living in a different realm of reality. It's very difficult to explain how things changed. My eyes saw the world in a totally different way. For instance, that same night, after I had seen Jesus, my friend Christina had already planned for us to go to our usual country western club. I had already told her I did not want to go because that was where I had met Dawson, and I still missed him something awful. Now, after seeing Jesus, I really did not want to go! But she insisted, and I did not dare tell her about Jesus walking up to me. That was just too unbelievable. Christina was anticipating a fun night when she picked me up and nothing was unusual until we walked into the club. As I looked around this time everything looked different. Even though I was in the room it was as if I was standing outside looking in. I slowly sat down at a table and began to watch the people drinking, flirting, being seductive, and it was like nothing I had ever seen before. The scene looked totally lustful, repulsive, filthy, and sad. I rubbed my eyes, not understanding how this was happening. I thought to myself, "Why are all these people doing such terrible things? Can't they see what I'm seeing?" Christina was off somewhere having fun as we both usually did, but I could only sit in unexplainable awe of what was playing out before my eyes. Eventually, she came over to the table with a couple of guys. She said, "Come on, we are going to go to their condo. They live in a gorgeous place on the lake." I had to go this time; I had no way home. We arrived at a truly beautiful place on the water. The guys mixed some drinks for us at their fully stocked bar. Christina and her fellow went to his bedroom, and me and the guy that was supposed to be mine were left sitting on the couch. Normally, that would be my cue to make sure I made my way to my guy's bedroom. I had been quiet all evening, so I am sure he was not surprised when I gave him the cold shoulder. Strangely, I really did not want to be there. I felt so out of place. That was new for me! But some guys take that as a challenge, so he continued to try to get cozy and suggested a boat ride on the lake. You could tell by the furnishings and their cars that these guys were well off. Christina always had an eye for the rich ones. So, my fellow and I went down to the dock where he had a nice pleasure boat and a row boat. He chose the row boat. Maybe he thought it would be more romantic. He slowly paddled us along the shore of the calm lake. It was a beautiful night with a bright moon shining on the water. All I could think about was when I saw Jesus by the water in the moonlight. When we walked back to the condo he put his arm around my waist, but I didn't respond. When we got back inside, he took my hand and led me over to his buddy's bedroom and opened the door. There was Christina and that guy in bed just laughing and screwing. She was sitting on top of him having a good old time. My guy probably thought seeing them would turn me on. But, as I stood in the doorway staring at my naked friend, all I felt was sadness for her. I turned away and went back to the couch and sat down. Now considering my guy could have got really mad, he instead was being very patient. When it finally became obvious to him that I was not going to follow Christina's path, my exasperated host went and made a phone call. I heard him asking someone to get out of bed and come over. Then he came back and sat down in a chair by the couch and said a friend of his would be there in a few minutes. He said, "I never go to bed alone." We just sat there in silence. In about fifteen minutes he escorted this really cute, rather young girl to another chair by the couch. There we were, me on the couch and him and the girl at each end of the couch in chairs, facing each other. Really, you cannot make this stuff up! I just sat there thinking why did this sweet looking young woman get out of bed at 3:00 a.m. to come over to this guy's apartment? Was he paying her? She certainly did not look the part for that. I wondered what she was thinking about all this. Believe it or not, the three of us just sat there making small talk for what seemed like an eternity. It was an extremely weird situation. Finally, Christina and her boy toy came out of the bedroom and both of them looked puzzled by the unusual scene. She, of course, had no idea how my evening had been spent. Christina looked curiously at the girl and mouthed to me, "Who's that?" I just said, "Come on let's go," and we left. What a crazy night! On the way home I told Christina about my evening with the guy. The only thing she reacted to was why didn't I want to have sex with him. I just said I was not in the mood. I still wasn't too sure if I should tell her about Jesus and the unexplainable change I had seen at the club. If I did not understand it, how in the world would anyone else be able to.

By Monday I thought all the strangeness of Friday night was over. My weekend activities with Heather had been pretty normal. At work there was this nice-looking guy named Edward that I had tried to flirt with many times in the past, before Dawson. I had wanted very much to go out with him, but now I still missed Dawson more every day. I was not interested in any other man. Well for some reason, out of nowhere, Edward began talking to me about religious stuff. Even though I had seen Jesus, I was not too keen on hearing what Edward had to say. But he persisted, and I began to be drawn in by his cuteness and his dimpled smile. So, for a while, I didn't care what he talked about as long as he talked to me. It was a nice distraction from my longing for Dawson. But Edward kept inviting me to his church. I told him repeatedly that I already had a church where I went with my daughter. He attended some little store front place they called a church, so I was not too sure if they were some kind of weird cult. In the past I was burned by that guy at Parents Without Partners who acted all religious, but was really a hypocrite, so I was not too sure about Edward and his church thing. Almost every day he would come by my office and tell me something about the Bible. It went in one ear and out the other, but I enjoyed the attention. One day he suggested that if I did not want to go to his church, I might enjoy going to a home group on Friday night. Well, Friday was usually my party night, so I did not think that would work. However, I had not been back to the club since that strange evening. Then I had a bright idea and teasingly said, "I will go to your home group with you if you will go to a club with me." It was a challenge I was sure this Bible thumper would not take, and he would finally stop asking me. But surprisingly, he took me up on the offer! I had gone several times to see that crude comedy couple because they were so funny; I would practically roll on the floor laughing. So, I thought that would be the perfect place to take Edward. He picked me up that Saturday night and drove us to the club. When the waitress came to take our drink order, Edward asked for milk. Yes, milk! And they actually had some! I thought with a snicker, "How cute, the religious guy ordered milk." Then the show began with one of the same comical routines I had seen before. But this time, nothing was funny. All their jokes sounded obscene, filthy and embarrassing. I kept apologizing to Edward, "I don't know what's wrong. They used to be so funny. I am sorry the show was so bad!" I could not understand why the same show I had seen before could look so different to me now. But Edward knew why. The Jesus in him had brought light into the darkness and the sinfulness of the show had been revealed. I still kept apologizing on the way home, but he did not mind because now I had to uphold my end of the deal. The next Friday night Edward picked me up again, and we went to his church home group. There were only ten or so people there and they seemed normal, not weird. In fact, everyone was very friendly and so happy, not fakey, but genuinely happy. We ate a delicious pot luck meal, and then a guy pulled out a guitar and everyone clapped their hands and sang. I had never heard those songs at my church. They were exciting songs about Jesus. The lyrics were so uplifting and filled me with a sense of hope. Then we all played some fun card games. They all prayed and soon the evening was over. I did not want to leave the wonderful atmosphere. On the way home Edward asked how I liked it. I told him it was the best Friday night I'd had in my entire life. I was actually smiling. Then he asked me again to come visit their church. This time I told him I would try to go Sunday night, but Heather and I would still go to our church on Sunday morning. When I got home and told Heather about all the fun I had, she seemed interested. So, Sunday I went to the evening service at Edward's little store front church. I left Heather at home because I wanted to check it out first. These people had some unusual ideas about how to have church. I was not real sure about everyone lifting their hands, dancing around, and especially speaking in a strange language. The music was wonderful and the preaching was so inspiring, all about Jesus. All I knew was I felt happier when I left there. I liked that they talked so much about Jesus. I never heard about Jesus in the church I went to. I knew there had to be something special about Him, because my life sure started changing after I saw Him face to face. I even thought these people at Edward's church would probably not think I was crazy if I told them about the voice I heard and about seeing Jesus. The next Sunday evening I took Heather with me to see what she thought about it. She was mature for her age and I valued her opinion. She really liked it, too. I was beginning to understand why Edward had been so persistent about me going there because I felt my life was getting better after just two times. Then the following Sunday morning Heather and I still went to our usual church. Now it all seemed so cold and boring and dead. There was no real worship or even a message of hope. The sermon was just traditional positive thinking stuff, and the pastor never opened the Bible. The preaching offered no real answers to my problems. I wondered why I had never noticed that before. I began to realize that Jesus was the reason that things were changing. I remembered when I would tell my friends, "If only there was just one word I could say, and all this garbage would disappear." The one word was Jesus! The following Sunday was Mother's Day, so Heather and I skipped our usual morning service and went to the mall to eat and shop awhile. But all day, I found myself anxious to get to that new church for evening service. I really enjoyed the incredible praise and worship. I didn't know songs like that existed. I mainly just listened to the words and did not sing much. The lyrics brought tears to my eyes. That night's message went straight through my soul and spirit like a sword. I started crying and could not stop. The pastor gave the call for salvation to give your life totally over to Jesus. I was sobbing uncontrollably. I dropped to my knees, a crumpled-up sinner crying out, "Help me please!" Someone sat on the floor with me while others laid their hands on my head and shoulders. I prayed for Jesus to forgive me for my life of sin and confessed I needed Him to be my one and only Savior. I begged Jesus to help me. I could not stop crying, but the tears felt so cleansing, as if all the filthy gunk inside of me was being washed away. I wanted so much to get rid of all of it. I had no idea how long I was on the floor crying, but the whole time everyone else was just praying and praising and worshipping Jesus. They told me that when a sinner repents and comes to Jesus the angels in heaven rejoice! Finally, when I was able to get up, Heather came running over and hugged me. The pastor's wife said she had explained to her what was happening. I said laughing, "So, now explain to me what just happened!" Heather asked me if she should ask Jesus to be her Savior. We told her it had to be her decision, so two weeks later Heather was also born again. My born again experience was very radical, and I was extremely glad it all happened just the way it did. I was changed in an instant and never looked back. Temptation, backsliding or even wavering in my faith never happened for the rest of my life because Satan had lost completely and forever. There is a Bible passage that conveys that those who have much to be forgiven for will love much, and I still love Jesus more every day. I certainly had a bunch to be forgiven for, but my terrible life was what eventually lead me to Jesus. And to think, He stepped out of Heaven to show His face to a filthy, totally depraved sinner, so I could experience true unconditional love.

Needless to say, Heather and I never went back to our old church. My friends were amazed by my sudden change, which really was the end product of a long process of being drawn to Jesus. I could see that now. Jesus had been working on me my entire life, slowly bringing me to the net, so I would not let go of the hook. The scales fell off my eyes, and I was able to see a whole different world I never knew existed. I told people it was like I had spent my entire life looking through a peep hole in the door and now the door was flung wide open, and I could see the big picture. I was like a sponge soaking up all the knowledge I could from the Bible and from Christian television. I wanted to learn everything I had never been taught about the Bible, about God and Jesus and the Holy Spirit. Another single woman named Doreen that I had befriended from my new church patiently spent hours with me as I drilled her with questions. Most importantly I learned that those three evil agents that the devil had sent to torment me my whole life were no longer able to touch me. Now I had access to the promises of God that are in scripture. And His promises are always Yes and Amen (II Corinthians 1:20). I spoke God's Word to the spirit of Condemnation: There is therefore now no condemnation to those who are in Christ Jesus, who walk not after the flesh, but after the Spirit (Romans 8:1), to the spirit of Fear: For God has not given us the spirit of fear, but of power, and of love, and of a sound mind (II Timothy1:7), and to the spirit of Rejection: And the Lord, He is the One who goes before you. He will be with you; He will not leave you nor forsake you (Deuteronomy 31:8). Praise God my old life had totally disappeared. One day in the grocery store I ran into one of my old party friends. She wondered where I had been. I explained to her how my life had changed since I saw Jesus, and she announced in a loud voice, "My God, you've been born again!" I said, "Yesss!" I was surprised she knew about such things because she did not go to church. A guy from my past called me one night and I explained how I was born again. He said, "I tried that one time, but it didn't stick." I felt sad for him and had more questions for Doreen. I even called William, my first husband, and asked him to forgive me for any suffering I had caused him. I felt such a peaceful release after that. Then, seven months after receiving Jesus, the most unusual thing happened. It was New Year's Eve, and Heather and I had been grocery shopping for snacks to eat while watching the Times Square ball drop. We were unloading bags from my car in the garage when a car pulled up into my driveway. Unbelievably, the person that got out of the car was Dawson! Talk about a shock! I immediately walked over to him and hugged him. Heather came back out and when she saw him, she also ran and hugged him. We invited him to come in, and he and I sat at the kitchen table to visit. That was where my sanity left me. I was still a baby Christian and had no wisdom about telling people about my experience with Jesus. I unloaded about how Jesus had changed my life and that he needed to do that, too. In my exuberance, I said more than I should have about being born again. Dawson listened patiently, but finally said he had a party to go to. I have regretted that overbearing moment my entire life. I could only pray that somehow God would use my immaturity in Christ to bring Dawson to Jesus. He must have genuinely cared for us or he would not have stopped by. God only knows what might have happened if I had been more understanding. But like I always say, "Everything happens for a reason." Hopefully, someday I will see Dawson in Heaven.

About eight months after receiving Jesus and being baptized by the Holy Spirit I felt I was not learning enough at that little church. I was hungry for a deeper meaning of the Scriptures and there was so much more out there to discover. One Sunday when we were getting ready for church, I told Heather I felt we needed to go to that large church off the highway. She mentioned, "You mean the one you used to make fun of?" That was an *Ouch* moment. Back in the day I joined in with the guys at work and cracked jokes about that misunderstood Spirit-filled church. Also, one of the Scout troop mothers went there and she was always saying, "Praise the Lord" about everything. At the time I thought, "Give it a rest lady!" Now I was praising the Lord right along with her. God's grace is amazing. Incredibly, that was also the same church hypocrite Gregory had taken me to when they were in the small white church. But now, they had tripled in size and had built a new sanctuary. As we walked up to their door that Sunday, Heather asked me if I was sure about this. When I put my hand on the door handle, I felt the power of God, and I answered, "I have never been so sure about anything in my life." It was certainly the right decision because during the over twelve years we went there before moving out of state, it was like going to a Bible college. We listened to preachers, teachers, and evangelists from around the world. Heather and I filled our week with Sunday classes and services, Tuesday prayer meeting and Friday home group. Heather was very involved with the youth group which gave her great support for an awesome high school experience. She also has never wavered in her walk with Jesus, even through college where she met a Christian man. I experienced every aspect of the church I could fit into my schedule. I was involved in prison ministry, street witnessing, and youth ministry. Who would have ever thought, when I went to that little white church with Gregory, that one day I would be raising my hands high and worshipping Jesus at that same church. Eventually, their second building became too small when they tripled in size again and they built another larger church building. That was where Heather and her Christian man had their beautiful wedding. When all is said and done, I would not have changed a thing about my journey to Jesus. Because, all the devastating events in my life are what brought me to Him and are the reasons I love Him so much. And He always loved me, even when I was deep in the muck and the mire of sin. Now, Jesus has been Lord of my life for thirty-nine years and counting. Jesus is my protector, my provider, my comforter and above all, my one and only true soulmate.

I said at the beginning of this book that "The Un-Paid Prostitute" is not some kind of self-help book. That's because none of us can really help ourselves. There were so many times in my life that I could not help myself no matter how hard I tried. Without Jesus there are no true remedies to any situations we face, only Band-Aids. It took me many decades of torment to finally understand that a personal relationship with Jesus was the only solution to all my problems. And thankfully, during my rebellious struggles to get to that point God patiently helped me and protected me so I would not die in my sin and live eternally in Hell. I am sure there were hundreds or thousands of times His warring and guardian angels hovered over me throughout my life. Looking back at just a few of those moments, His protection was very obvious. That night, as a teenager, when God kept me from being raped, or the night I was driving stoned and drunk. I could have died or killed someone. And, meeting a total stranger in another town for a weekend was so dangerous. Even when I sat with a gun in my lap, Jesus was right there with me. This one is difficult to admit, but I continually praise Him for protecting my body from some incurable disease I could have acquired from any one of the dozens of men I had relations with. But I will not be condemned or judged for my awful sins because Jesus took them all to the Cross for me and covered them with His Blood. And the good news is, Jesus died for everyone. I am no one special. He loves us all equally. If you are living a life void of Jesus like I was, you don't have to continue down that path. Maybe your life was not as bad as mine or maybe it was a whole lot worse, Jesus has a better future planned for you. It does not matter how good or bad we are, we all still need a Savior. You may say, "Well, I have never seen Jesus like you did." Please just believe He is always there by your side even if you have not physically seen Him. Jesus will reveal Himself to you in a way that He knows is best for your situation. Only believe He died just for you and was raised from the dead, so you can live with Him for eternity. He has an abundance of love and mercy for whatever sins are in your life. If you confess those sins and ask Him to forgive you for doing them, the Blood of Jesus will completely cover them all. Then connect with a church that teaches about Jesus by using scriptures from the Bible. Just faithfully believe these words as you pray this simple prayer:

Lord Jesus, I need You. Thank You for not giving up on me.
I confess with my mouth and believe in my heart
that You died for me and rose from the dead,
so I can be with You for eternity.
Forgive me for all my sins.
I confess You are my Lord and Savior.
Help me to gain knowledge for a firm foundation,
so I may be a witness of Your mercy and Your love.
Holy Spirit, I ask You to fill me with power
to defeat Satan and his lies.
I pray in Jesus Name,
Amen

Ephesians 6:12; For we wrestle not against flesh and blood, but against principalities, against powers, against the rulers of the darkness of this world, against spiritual wickedness in high places.

- *The King James Version of the Bible*